SUTHERLAND & CHALK

FOOTBALL FANTASY

WIN, LOSE OR DRAW – YOU PLAY THE GAME

Wizard Books

Published in the UK in 2004
by Wizard Books, an imprint of Icon Books Ltd.,
The Old Dairy, Brook Road, Thriplow,
Cambridge SG8 7RG
email: wizard@iconbooks.co.uk
www.iconbooks.co.uk/wizard

Sold in the UK, Europe, South Africa
and Asia by Faber and Faber Ltd.,
3 Queen Square, London WC1N 3AU
or their agents

Distributed in the UK, Europe, South Africa
and Asia by TBS Ltd., Frating Distribution Centre,
Colchester Road, Frating Green, Colchester CO7 7DW

Published in Australia in 2004
by Allen & Unwin Pty. Ltd.,
PO Box 8500, 83 Alexander Street,
Crows Nest, NSW 2065

Distributed in Canada by
Penguin Books Canada,
10 Alcorn Avenue, Suite 300,
Toronto, Ontario M4V 3B2

ISBN 1 84046 596 4

Typesetting and design by Nicholas Halliday
info@hallidaybooks.com

Printed and bound in the UK by Clays of Bungay

FOOTBALL FANTASY

WIN, LOSE OR DRAW – YOU PLAY THE GAME

Wizard is proud to present the first, and only, interactive sports books in the world. Fun, easy to play, innovative and exciting – designed for one or two players.

Football Fantasy is a stunning new series of football gamebooks in which YOU decide the outcome of the match. YOU choose the tactics, whether to attack or defend, find your opponent's weaknesses and dominate the game.

YOU can play the game solo, or with another player. Create your own leagues, cups and competitions. This revolutionary new series puts YOU on the pitch. YOU see what a footballer would see and make decisions he would make. View the pitch through over 240 different illustrations and see the results of over 8,500 possible options!

Simple to play and challenging to master, every game is different. Learn the tricks and tactics of the game and lead your team to victory!

CONTENTS

GETTING STARTED

You control eleven players: a goalie, defenders, midfielders and strikers. If you have the ball, you will have the choice of six attacking options and if you don't have the ball you will need to choose from six defensive options. Just like a real game of football, it's all about keeping control of the ball and getting it into a position where you can have a shot on the opponent's goal.

We'll have a look at the various options offered to you and what they do, but if you are desperate to start right now, here's all you need to know.

First things first: swap books with your opponent, because in *Football Fantasy* you always see the opponent's players, just like in a real game of football. On each page, you will see one of the opponent's players; he will either have the ball at his feet or he'll be facing you trying to get the ball. If you have the ball, you will have six attacking options, including running with the ball, making passes or taking shots on goal. If you don't have the ball, you will need to guess what you think the player with the ball will do with it; will he go left or right, will he pass, will he shoot? If you guess right, then you can take the ball from him, if you guess wrong, then he will slip past you.

First flip a coin or decide who is going to kick off. The player kicking off starts on page 1 of the game and the player who is facing the kick-off starts at page 2 of the

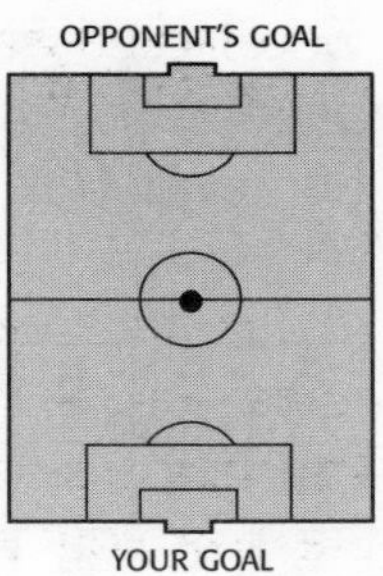

game. The drawing will always show you what your player can see, either an opponent with the ball or an opponent without the ball, trying to get it from you. The dot on the map of the pitch shows you that the ball is on the centre spot (*shown here*). As you make moves you will always know where the ball is by looking at this map.

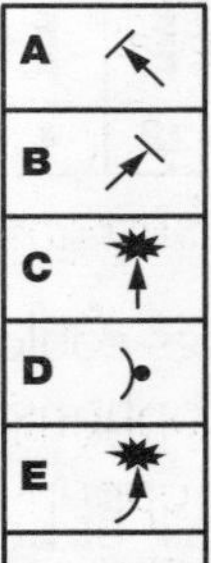

Both players have a set of six options; the player kicking off can pass the ball or run with the ball in various directions. The player who is facing the kick-off needs to choose one of his six options that include tackles and blocks. If he chooses correctly, then there's a chance he might intercept the ball and gain control of it.

Each of the options has a letter marked A–F. When both are ready to make their choices the player with the ball calls out his letter first and then immediately after the player without the ball calls out his letter. This ensures that the defending player can't change his mind after hearing the attacking player's choice. Both players then look at the grid at the bottom of the page to see what page they need to turn to. If the player kicking off wants to make a short pass forward, he would call out B; if the player without the ball wants to tackle, then he calls out C. Both players look at BC on their grid to see where the ball has gone and who has it now. Remember that the pages that each player will turn to will always be different! In this case, the player who kicked off has lost the ball because he is now on page 2. The player who didn't have the ball will see from his own book that he has taken it, and is on page 1 of his book.

A A	A B	A C	A D	A E	A F	B A	B B	B C	B D	B E	B F
28	28	1	28	35	28	18	18	2	1	28	18
C A	C B	C C	C D	C E	C F	D A	D B	D C	D D	D E	D F
14	2	14	2	28	14	20	2	29	20	28	20
E A	E B	E C	E D	E E	E F	F A	F B	F C	F D	F E	F F
38	24	20	2	28	24	10	4	20	2	28	4

Once you're into the flow of the game, five things could happen each time you call out your options:

1. The player with the ball may still have the ball, or he may have passed it to another of his players. This means that in the next turn the player who had the ball will still be the attacker and will call out first. It's always obvious who has the ball. If you see a picture with a player who has the ball then it means that you are the defender and will have defensive choices. If you see a player without the ball, then it means that you are the attacker and will have attacking choices on the page.

2. The player with the ball may have lost the ball and the defender may have successfully taken possession of it. This means that the player that had the ball will be the defender next turn and will call out his letter second.

3. The ball may have gone out of play. The new page will show you who is to take the throw-in.

4. The defender may have fouled the attacker and may have given away a free kick or perhaps a penalty. The player who has the free kick or penalty will have new options on what to do with the ball.

5. Finally, the ball may now be in the back of the net if the attacking player has scored a goal. This means that the next turn will take you to the kick-off once again.

How Long is a Game?

We recommend that you play 15 minutes for each half, thereby giving you a game of half an hour. You could play two halves of 45 minutes, but don't be surprised if the game ends 9–7!

As an alternative you could always end the game when one of the sides manages to score three goals, i.e. the first to three is the winner.

Golden Goals and Penalty Shoot-Outs

Everyone hates losing a game this way, but many cup competitions have golden (and silver) goal rules. Here's how it works. If you are playing the golden goal rule, then the next team to score in extra time wins the game. Extra time should be about five minutes per half. If you are playing the silver goal rule, then if a team scores and is still ahead when the first half of extra time ends, they have won and the game ends. If the other team has equalised in the first half of extra time, then the game goes into the second half of extra time.

If all this fails to produce a winner, then it's down to the dreaded penalty shoot-out. Flip a coin; the winner can choose to either take the first penalty or force the other player to step up to the penalty spot first.

If you are taking a penalty, turn to page 61 of your opponent's game. This will give you your shooting options.

If you are the goalkeeper attempting to save a penalty, then turn to page 212 of your opponent's game. You will see the opponent's striker about to take the kick.

Remember, if you don't get the ball in the back of the net with your first strike of the ball, then you have missed – there are no second chances! Both players take 5 penalties and the player that scores the most goals wins the game. If the score is still even after the 5 penalties have been taken, then it is a sudden death penalty shoot-out. The first player to miss, assuming that the other player has scored, is the loser.

HOW TO PLAY SOLO

You might not have a live player to play against; maybe you just can't wait to get into the action! It doesn't matter; you can play *Football Fantasy* on your own and still have a great game.

Firstly, decide whether or not you are going to kick off and either turn to page 1, if you are kicking off, or page 2 if you are not. Find the Random Letter Generator on page 300 (you might want to photocopy this or download and print a copy of this from *www.footballfantasy gamebooks.com*).

You will see that the letters A–F are printed on the grid. When you have made your choice, close your eyes and use a pencil or a pen to 'point' at the grid. The letter closest to your pencil tip is the letter chosen by the other player. Don't forget that if you are the attacker, your letter comes first when you look at the grid at the bottom of the game page, and it comes second if you are the defender.

Solo play is a great way of getting used to the moves and you can never predict how the 'dummy' player is going to play the game. You can also play Advanced *Football Fantasy* Solo; see page 30 on how to play.

TYPES OF FOOTBALLER

Let's look at the different types of players you will find in your team.

The Goalkeeper

The goalkeeper mainly operates in his own penalty area, but he can also take free kicks for the team in certain places. Goalkeepers have a number of different skills; they can dive right or left and jump to deal with high balls or shots. They can also block to the right, or the left, to deal with shots along the ground. Some goalkeepers will be able to rush out and try to grab the ball from the foot of a striker. Some can also body check or slide in for a tackle and try to take the ball; these can be dangerous choices to make as you may give away a penalty.

Defenders

There are two different types of defender: the centre backs and the right and left backs. The centre backs tend to be very defensively-minded and don't stray into the opposition's half too often. Their skills include tackling, sliding tackles and blocks to the right and left. They can also track back, trying to keep pace with the attacker in the hope that they can stay between the attacker and the goal. Some defenders will be able to close down the attacker by getting in close to him and stopping him from making a pass; others will be able to body check the attacker. This can be a dangerous move as it may give away a free kick or even a penalty. Sliding tackles and ordinary tackles might also do this in some cases. Defenders who have the ball can also make forward moves and passes. They can run with the ball, run back with the ball and make short, medium and long passes. Right and left backs are useful players; they operate on the wings and can make telling passes into the opposition's box. They tend to be faster than central defenders, better at getting forward, but not quite as good in defence. All defenders can take free kicks as well as giving them away.

Midfielders

Midfield players who operate in the middle of the pitch are called central midfielders, and those who work on the wings are called right and left midfielders. The central midfielders have a mixed set of abilities. They are fast and good at getting forward; sometimes they will have the chance for a shot on goal. The central midfielders can help break up the opposition attacks and help you develop your own attacks. Midfielders tend to have the broadest range of skills, including passes, the ability to run with the ball, and take shots, make tackles and track back. The right and left midfielders tend to cover the flanks and work alongside the right and left backs. Right and left midfielders are typically fast players, but not great tacklers; they are better suited for attack than defence. Right and left midfielders are the players that take the corners and some of the free kicks in the opposition's area.

Strikers

A striker's job is to outwit and get around the defenders to score goals. They are fast and tricky, able to shoot, run with the ball, make incisive passes and take the penalties. Strikers can't be relied on to get the ball from defenders. Strikers operate in the opposition's penalty area and in the middle of the pitch around the centre spot. They are also the players who kick off at the beginning of the game, in the second half or after the opposition have scored a goal.

LEARN THE SKILLS

There are many moves in *Football Fantasy*. The basic game allows your players to do almost anything, either in attack or defence. In the Advanced Game, you will need to look at the team sheet because not all of your players will be able to make all of the moves. Just like real players, they will be great at some of the moves, not so good at others. As a rough guide, don't rely on your strikers to stop the other team's attacks or your defenders to head in goals.

Strikers tend to be fast and are good at slotting the ball into the net. Midfielders are typically good passers of the ball and often score spectacular goals from outside the box. Defenders have to cope with everything the opposition throws at them; they are there to break up attacks and pass the ball on to the midfielders and the strikers. One of your most important players is your goalkeeper. At times he will need to take risks, but he is the only one that can help you keep a clean sheet.

The moves are broken down into four different types: offensive (attacker), defensive (defender), free kicks and penalties, and throw-ins. Each of the moves has an icon; full descriptions of each are featured later when we talk about moves and counter-moves.

The icons next to each player on your team sheet, in Advanced *Football Fantasy*, will tell you exactly what that player can do, with or without the ball. Any player taking a throw-in can do any of the six available types of throw-in.

When you are offered a series of different moves on a game page, you will only be allowed to choose moves that your player is allowed to do on your team sheet. If you are playing the basic game, then you will be able to choose any of the six options offered.

ATTACKING MOVES WHEN YOU HAVE THE BALL

Run forward with the ball – this means the player who already has the ball makes a forward run, keeping the ball and not passing it to another player. Typically, defenders will try to get the ball by using a tackle or a body check.

or

Run left with the ball – this is similar to run forward with the ball, except the player heads off left, keeping the ball. Blocking to the right is the defender's ideal choice. The direction the arrow is facing will tell you whether the run is horizontal or diagonal.

or

Run right with the ball – again, similar to run forward with the ball, except this time the player heads off to the right, keeping the ball with him. Blocking to the left is the defender's ideal choice. The direction the arrow is facing will tell you whether the run is horizontal or diagonal.

Run back with the ball – this is the opposite of run forward with the ball; the player retreats with the ball in the hope of being able to move forward or make a pass next turn. Sliding tackles are one of the ways the opposition can get the ball if this move is made. Sometimes, you will be able to run back to your left or your right and not just straight back. The direction the arrow is facing will tell you the direction of the run.

Short pass forward – this means you are passing the ball to another of your players ahead of you.

Short pass right – this is a move used to outwit the defenders; the problem is that these passes are often a little obvious as a choice. Defenders will block the pass by choosing block left and a goalkeeper may grab the ball by choosing rush out. The direction the arrow is facing will tell you whether the pass is horizontal or diagonal.

or

Short pass left – the same as short pass right, but in the other direction. Defenders will intercept by choosing block right and goalkeepers can take the ball by choosing rush out. The direction the arrow is facing will tell you whether the pass is horizontal or diagonal.

or

Shot forward – this is a straight shot on goal that can be either a high shot or a low shot. Goalkeepers can deal with shot forward by a jump to catch the ball before it crosses the line. At short ranges, goalkeepers handle this by rushing out to take the ball off your player's foot before he shoots.

Shot right – this is a shot on goal to the right-hand side of the goal and can be either a high or a low shot. Goalkeepers deal with this by diving to the left at longer ranges and blocking left at closer ranges.

Shot left – this is the alternative to either shot forward or shot right; it can be used in the same situations as the other two. Shots to the left can be either high or low. Goalkeepers deal with longer-range shot left by diving to the right, or with a short-range shot by block right.

Back pass – a back pass can be made in a number of different places, particularly if your player is boxed in and has no chance of getting past the opposition. This passes the ball back to another player who is following the player with the ball. That player may have the skills to get past the defenders, or may have more space. A sliding tackle can sometimes deal with back passes, but there is always a chance the back pass won't reach the player you are aiming at. The direction the arrow is facing will tell you whether the pass is straight back, or back left or right.

Centre – this is a ball played to the centre of the pitch. The direction of the pass depends on where the player is on the pitch. This is often a tactical move to make, as you can re-build an attack from the middle.

Long pass – the icon will tell you in which direction the attacker is making the long pass. Defenders can ruin this move by trying to head the ball as it flies through the air. If they make contact, the ball could go anywhere. A compass sign with an arrow shows you the direction of your long pass.

Medium pass – again, the icon will tell you what options you have to make a medium pass. These are not as far as a long pass, so your options will be limited to a handful of your players. Defenders can intercept your pass if they guess which way you are going to pass. If you pass left and they block right, they will grab the ball from you. If they have chosen the chest the ball option, this may also have an effect on where the ball is heading. A compass sign with an arrow shows you the direction of your medium pass.

Pass into the box – this is a pass which aims to get the ball into the opposition's penalty area. The pass is designed to place it near a striker who can shoot on goal next turn. Defenders can deal with it in different ways depending on how far from the penalty area the pass is made. At long distances, a header may stop the ball or send it flying somewhere else. At shorter distances, the defender may block left or right depending on the direction the ball will take. Sometimes, the ball may fly off and hit a defender, and then the goalkeeper may grab it. Goalkeepers may often jump up to snatch the ball before it lands near one of your players.

DEFENDING MOVES WHEN YOU DON'T HAVE THE BALL

Tackle – the most useful and basic move. Your player attempts to get in close to the opposition's player and take the ball from him. Attackers will get away if they pass before you get the tackle in, run to the left or right with the ball, or pass it back to another player.

Sliding tackle – the extreme version of the tackle. This is always a risk. If you don't judge the right time to use this, then the ball could end up anywhere!

Block left – this is the ideal move if you think the opposition is going to go to his right; it should deal with passes, runs, and shots in that direction. If he goes the other way, your player will be stranded and left for dead.

Block right – this covers the opposite side to block left. It deals with the opposition doing most things to his left. Again, if he chooses the other direction, then all is lost and he, the ball or both will slip past you.

Body check – this is an aggressive move, as it means your player is going to attempt to barge the opposition off the ball. Body checks will work in some cases if your defender faces a player trying to run with the ball. It is a tricky and dangerous choice, but it is usually the only thing that might work if you are faced by a fast attacker trying to run around you.

Chest – this move is useful if you think the attacker is going to make a medium pass. Your player tries to get his body in the way of the ball and chest it down to his feet. Sometimes the pass isn't a medium one, but you still have the chance to block the ball, although it could go anywhere.

Track back – this means falling back and hoping that you can outpace the attacker. It keeps you in the zone around the ball, harassing the opposition and not giving him any space. He'll leave you for dead if he makes a long pass or shoots.

Header – this is an attempt to intercept the ball by jumping up and either nodding the ball down to your feet or to another one of your players. Heading the ball is only useful if you think that the opposition is going to try to kick a high ball.

Close down – this move means getting in really close to the opponent and limiting his space to move. This is an ideal choice if you think that your opponent is about to make a pass, as it gives you the chance to take the ball before the pass is completed. If the opposition chooses to run with the ball, he will leave you standing.

GOALKEEPER MOVES

Block – this move is used by the brave goal-keeper who wants to stand his ground. The goal-keeper remains rooted to the spot, and attempts to block the forward shot move.

Dive left – this is the goalkeeper's ideal choice to deal with an attacker's shot right. The goal-keeper assumes that the attacker is going to shoot high enough to need a dive. Obviously, if the ball is hit with a shot left or shot forward, or if there is no shot at all, then the goalkeeper will be left on the ground with mud on his face.

Dive right – this means that the goalkeeper is assuming that the attacker will be using a shot left move and that the ball will be heading towards the goal on his right. If the ball is hit in the opposite direction, there is every chance the attacker will score.

Sliding tackle – just like a defender, a goalkeeper can attempt to knock away the ball from the feet of an attacker with a sliding tackle. The problem is that goalkeepers are not normally as good at this move as a defender, so the risk is that they might give away a penalty. A sliding tackle is one of the alternatives to take if you think you might not be able to save a shot.

Block left – this is used by a goalkeeper to beat away low shots from close range. The move assumes that the ball won't gain much height as it leaves a striker's boot bound for the goal. Block left deals with shot right at close range, but little else.

Block right – this means that the goalkeeper is attempting to stop a shot left from a striker at close range. If the striker is far enough out then the ball may well sail over the sprawling body of the goalkeeper.

Body check – this move means that the goalkeeper jumps up and barges the striker out of the way in an attempt to grab the ball. It is an option that the goalkeeper may choose when the ball comes into the penalty area either from a corner or a free kick. Most referees will give the goalkeeper the benefit of the doubt if he collides with a striker in the penalty area.

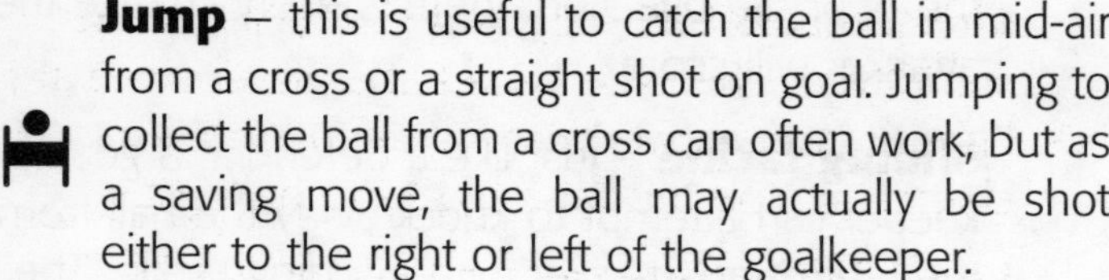

Jump – this is useful to catch the ball in mid-air from a cross or a straight shot on goal. Jumping to collect the ball from a cross can often work, but as a saving move, the ball may actually be shot either to the right or left of the goalkeeper.

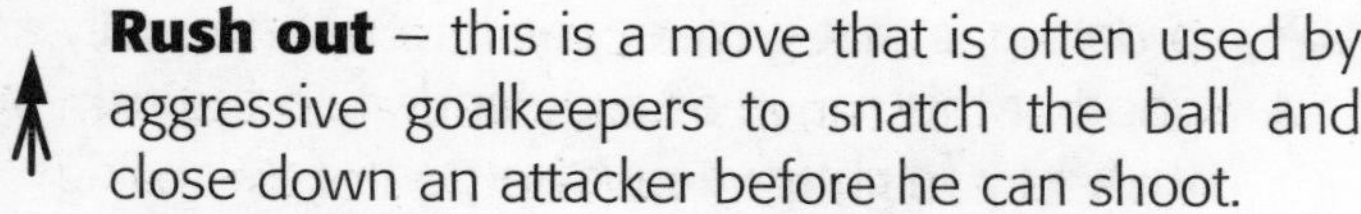

Rush out – this is a move that is often used by aggressive goalkeepers to snatch the ball and close down an attacker before he can shoot.

Rush out right – this is similar to rush out except your goalkeeper charges out to his right to try to snatch the ball.

Rush out left – this is the same as rush out right, but this time your goalkeeper heads out to his left.

THROW-IN MOVES

Some of your players will take responsibility for throwing the ball back in if it has crossed the touchline. You won't find the throw-in moves on the team sheets because everyone can use any of the following throws:

Short throw forward – this is a throw aimed at a player close-by and straight ahead. A defender can try to stop this with a chest move.

Short throw right – again, this is a short throw, but aimed toward the thrower's right. A defender can stop this if he blocks to his left.

Short throw left – the last alternative of the short throw, this time aimed at a player close at hand to the thrower's left. A defender has a chance to stop this if he blocks to his right.

Long throw forward – a long throw with good height aimed at a player some distance from the thrower, but fairly dead ahead of him. A defender will try to get in the way of this by attempting to head the ball down.

Long throw right – a long throw off to the thrower's right aimed at a player some distance away. A defender might use a header to stop this, but the ball could end up almost anywhere!

Long throw left – the final long throw option which means the ball is sent high into the air towards a player some distance to the thrower's left. A header is also useful in dealing with this, but there is no guarantee that the defender will end up with the ball.

FREE KICKS

Free kicks are awarded to a team that has just suffered a foul from the opposition. If the ball is within range of the goal, then the free kick may be a shot on goal. In most cases, the side taking the free kick will take the opportunity of whipping the ball into the box or as far up field as possible. Many of the normal defensive moves are not allowed when free kicks are taken, but blocks and headers can intercept or change the direction of the ball. Remember, you can't tackle someone who is taking a free kick, so be prepared for the ball to be booted some distance away.

PENALTIES

Penalties take place either as a result of a foul by a defender or the goalkeeper in their own penalty area, or at the end of a cup game when the scores are level. The penalty taker can either shoot high or low, forward, left or right. The goalkeeper can choose whether to dive or to block, forward, left or right. Remember, the goalkeeper always has to pick the opposite direction to get in the way of the ball. If you think the penalty taker is going to shoot to the right, you will need to go to your left. The advantage is always with the penalty taker and as a goalie you need to try to double-guess what he might do. The result of a penalty is either a goal, a goal kick (because the goalie caught it), or a corner (because the goalie got a hand to it and tipped it over the bar or around the post).

CORNERS

Corners happen when one of the defenders or the goalkeeper puts the ball out of play behind their own goal. The attacker will try to get the ball into the box or will make a shorter pass and build his attack. If you think the ball might be heading straight into the penalty area (with a pass into the box move), then the goalie should try a jump to get out there and grab the ball before one of the strikers traps it and takes a shot. Sometimes, you won't be able to stop the attacker from making a short pass, because you will be controlling what your goalkeeper is doing.

DIRECTING THE BALL

Don't forget that sometimes you will see two different options to do the same thing when you have the ball. For example, you may be able to run to the right twice. This means that your player can run diagonally forward with the ball or run right with the ball without actually going forward at all (horizontal).

The same thing goes for longer passes such as long or medium passes; you will be able to direct the ball into a particular area ahead of you, either straight ahead, to the right or to the left.

When you have the same choice more than once, look at the way that the symbol is angled and it will give you an idea where the ball should be heading when you kick it.

That's it; the only way to master the game and score the goals is to play. Just keep the ball moving and don't be too obvious about what you are going to do! Remember, football is not just about skills, it's about being cunning too; always keep the opponent guessing what you'll do next.

ADVANCED *FOOTBALL FANTASY*

On your team sheet on page 292, you'll see the moves that each of the players can do. You might want to photocopy or copy out the moves that your players can do so they are in front of you when you play. Don't forget that throw-in moves are the exception; every player can use any of the six throw-in moves.

Don't cheat! You can only use the moves we've given the players on the team sheet, so make the best of what they can do. This means that when you look at your six choices on a page, you will only be able to pick from those that match your player on the team sheet. This makes for a much tougher game and you'll have to think more carefully before you make a decision. Agree with the other player that both of you only have 10 seconds to make up your mind about the move you are going to make: it adds to the pressure and the excitement of the game!

Players that aren't that great at tackling, such as strikers, will often give away free kicks, because they will only have the choice of extreme tackles, like a sliding tackle. Midfielders tend to be good all-round players, not bad at tackling, quite fast and always looking for a chance to get the ball into the box. Defenders can be fast, great tacklers, but have to be careful when they are facing nippy strikers who try to get around them. Your goalkeeper may well have some weaknesses: maybe he doesn't like charging out and grabbing the ball; perhaps he can't deal with crosses.

The more you play Advanced *Football Fantasy*, the more you'll get to know your own players' strengths and weaknesses. The more you play your friend's team, the more likely he'll know them too!

If you are running a league or a cup competition with friends, you could agree that every few weeks you can choose a couple of players from your team and add one more skill to them. Some players improve during the season. If you really want to make it realistic, you should let the others in the league or cup decide which of your players is the worst player and knock one of their skills off your team sheet! Some real players actually get worse as the season goes on.

In Advanced *Football Fantasy* you play the games exactly the same as the normal game. The only real difference is that you don't have so many options some of the time!

ADVANCED *FOOTBALL FANTASY* SOLO

We've included your team's reserve squad in this book on page 296. You should use this as your team sheet to play against your first team. Use only the skills on the reserve team sheet, but still use the Random Letter Generator to pick the first team's letters.

Advanced *Football Fantasy* Solo is a great way of learning how to deal with limited choices, as your reserve team will not be as good as a first team. If you really want to get advanced, you will need to look at the first team sheet as well, and if you have picked a letter for a move that a first team player can't do, then you need to choose again. The quickest way of doing this is to pick the next letter on the right and use this letter instead.

You can, of course, use the first team sheet from another book in the series to play against any of the other teams. Instead of using your reserve team squad, you use the first team of the other book.

WHAT HAPPENS IF YOU LOSE YOUR PAGE?

Try to remember who had the ball and roughly where the ball was on the pitch. Here are the pages to use to start the game again.

If you had the ball

If the ball was in the middle of your half – Turn to p. 187 and have your opponent turn to p. 235

If the ball was on the left side of your half – Turn to p. 152 and have your opponent turn to p. 238

If the ball was on the right side of your half – Turn to p. 128 and have your opponent turn to p. 165

If the ball was in the middle of your opponent's half – Turn to p. 195 and have your opponent turn to p. 196

If the ball was on the left side of your opponent's half – Turn to p. 38 and have your opponent turn to p. 214

If the ball was on the right side of your opponent's half – Turn to p. 166 and have your opponent turn to p. 44

If your opponent had the ball

If the ball was in the middle of your half – Turn to p. 196 and have your opponent turn to p. 195

If the ball was on the left side of your half – Turn to p. 44 and have your opponent turn to p. 166

If the ball was on the right side of your half – Turn to p. 214 and have your opponent turn to p. 38

If the ball was in the middle of your opponent's half – Turn to p. 235 and have your opponent turn to p. 187

If the ball was on the left side of your opponent's half – Turn to p. 165 and have your opponent turn to p. 128

If the ball was on the right side of your opponent's half – Turn to p. 238 and have your opponent turn to p. 152

TYNE ATHLETIC

Tyne Athletic was founded in 1898 as an amateur team for local shipyard workers. For the first 40 years the team played on the old recreation grounds beside the gasworks. After the war the whole of the centre of Tyne was redeveloped and the club relocated to the outskirts of the city. Here they have remained, and after a new stand was built in 1982 they renamed their stadium The Shute Stadium.

Tyne won their first British Super League Championship title in 1961. They went on to win it again in 1980, 1986 and more recently in 1995 and 1999. Their first two British Football Organisation Cup wins came in 1955 and 1956. There was a lean period for the club as far as the cup was concerned and they did not secure it again until 1980. The cup was returned to Tyne once again in 1994 and 2000.

Tyne's first successful European run took place in 1987, when they secured the European Champions' Shield. They have been unable to qualify for the competition again until this season.

The 1970s were disappointing years for the club and there were rumours that it would close, particularly when major problems were found in the north stand, which temporarily closed the stadium. When Frank Shute bought the club for £100 in 1978 he immediately set about redeveloping the stadium and trying to attract the flair players for which Tyne Athletic have become famous in recent years. Shute sold his interests in two shipyards, a brewery and a chain of newsagents and has ploughed literally millions of pounds into the club.

Progress has been slow but steady and as early as 1994 Tyne could boast five different nationalities and eight proven internationals. The current squad has no fewer than three Frenchmen in it, as well as the remarkable Brazilian Laurencio. Possibly the single disappointment is the fact that Dave Chell is the only Tyne Football Academy player to have broken into the first side over the last couple of seasons.

Tyne's Anglo-French strike force of Hall, Deschamps and Le Clerc has now been together for two seasons. Last season between them they netted a staggering 68 goals in all competitions. Le Clerc is considered to be one of the most prolific strikers in Europe and Sir Barry has successfully fended off bids in excess of £30m from both Ebro FC and AC Tiber for him. There have been problems with the players as a result of the signing of Laurencio, whose wages are rumoured to be in excess of £70,000 a week. With most of the rest of the squad on less than £30,000 a week this has caused friction. Frank Shute has had to dig deep into his pockets during the wage reviews in the past few months.

The wage problems have not affected the team's performance on the pitch and they finished a creditable third last season. They now have a solid defence, an elegant and talented midfield and a rampaging forward line that has never failed to score at least two goals in a game in the past six months.

This season is now in your hands. Can you take the club and players to even greater achievements? Can you put them at the top? Will you be with them in Europe again next season?

SIR BARRY TODD – THE MANAGER

Todd was an inspirational England midfielder in the 1960s and 1970s who won over 100 England caps. He just missed the 1966 World Cup win through injury.

He began his career with Tyne back in the late 1950s and left them after their league win in 1961. His transfer to Trent Albion was, at the time, a British record. Todd went on to play for Bridgewater and Mersey City, and spent three years in Italy with Inter Arno.

Todd retired from professional football at the age of 38 and plied his trade as a coach and manager in the lower divisions. When Frank Plane was sacked by Tyne in 1992, Todd was at the top of the fans' list as a successor. The club's board appointed Todd and in just two years, after what many believed was a ruthless reorganisation, he led the team to win their first honour for 14 years in the 1994 BFO cup.

Todd has been persistently linked with the England manager's job and on at least three occasions he has been approached by Spanish, Italian and German teams. Now, as a major shareholder in Tyne and in possession of a new six-year contract, it seems unlikely that Todd will ever leave the club he loves.

Todd led his new-look side to win the championship in 1995 and again in 1999. He received his knighthood in the 2000 New Year's Honours List, for his lifetime contribution to football.

MATTHEW SCADDING

Born: Bridport, Dorset
6 January 1976

Nationality: English

Height: 6′ 1″

Weight: 12.8

Caps: 2

Position: Goalkeeper

Scadding, a former Dee Town, Trent Albion and Medway United keeper, made an uneasy start with Tyne last season after a £3.5m transfer from Medway. He recovered, being recalled to the England squad for friendlies against Peru and Uruguay. A great shot stopper, last season he managed an eight-hour clean sheet sequence in the league. He has lapses of concentration that have produced some howlers over the years; this has probably restricted his England career.

PIERRE PASQUALLE

Born: Marseilles, France
14 August 1977

Nationality: French

Height: 6′ 1″

Weight: 12.7

Caps: 10

Position: Right back

Now in his second British football season, Pasqualle's all-round game makes him one of the best top division defenders. A tenacious player, with boundless energy, he is also capable of scoring vital goals from set pieces. After an unsteady start at the beginning of his first season, Pasqualle settled in and last season featured in every league game. Pasqualle plays for France in his preferred position of centre back.

LAURENCIO

Born: Boa Vista, Brazil
20 September 1977

Nationality: Brazilian

Height: 6′ 0″

Weight: 11.13

Caps: 9

Position: Central defender

Laurencio was a member of Brazil's World Cup winning side. He transfered from Brazilian side Paranaiba to the US team Rapidan FC for $34m, a US transfer record. Unable to settle in the US, he opted for a free transfer to Tyne rather than renew his contract after two years. A precise and elegant player and a rare left-footer, he has signed for Tyne for three years on a record-breaking wage.

DAVE CHELL

Born: Stoke on Trent
3 July 1982

Nationality: English

Height: 6′ 2″

Weight: 11.12

Caps: 7 (under 21)

Position: Central defender

This young defender was a first team regular until last February when injuries meant he played only four times in the second half of the season. Rising from the Tyne Football Academy, he spent his first season-and-a-half on loan to Kennett Albion, the 2nd Division side. Chell was tipped for an England squad call-up before his injuries last season. He is a Trent Albion supporter but when Trent's youth team coach refused him at fifteen Tyne snapped him up.

BRETT GREEN

Born: Melbourne, Australia
6 August 1982

Nationality: Australian

Height: 6′ 2″

Weight: 11.2

Caps: 16 (Youth and Under 23)

Position: Left back

Last season was frustrating for Green; after forcing his way back into the first team he suffered a painful shin fracture. Out between October and February, he came back in March, playing for the Australian Under 23's against Portugal. Green's game features neat touches, boundless energy and a desire to get forward. Le Clerc and Deschamps gratefully receive his trademark crosses into the box. Green enjoys sailboarding and has dubbed Whitby 'Bondi Beach'.

HELMUT BREMEN

Born: Düsseldorf, Germany
7 March 1978

Nationality: German

Height: 6′ 3″

Weight: 12.2

Caps: 49

Position: Central midfielder (Captain)

This quietly spoken midfielder is an automatic choice for the Tyne first team. Although understated and not recognised, the team is weaker without him. Bremen rarely scores, but managed two goals last season against Calder City and Thames United. He plays behind the front three, in a holding role, protecting the defence. After playing for several European teams, including Rhine, AC Tiber, Waal and Jucar, this is his third season with Tyne following a Bosman transfer from Jucar.

TERRY HINER

Born: Birmingham
24 April 1980

Nationality: English

Height: 6′ 1″

Weight: 11.6

Caps: 0

Position: Left midfielder

Now in his second year with Tyne Athletic, Hiner was spotted playing non-league football for Fazeley United. He spent his first season on loan to Stour Rovers, but was recalled for the last four games to replace Tyne's longstanding midfielder, Bradley May. Despite speculation that Tyne were going to sign Caldon's Welsh midfielder, Duane Doggett, Hiner proved himself in pre-season friendlies. He and Aaron Hall have a friendship and pitch understanding that adds to Tyne's attack.

ROSS HEWITT

Born: King's Lynn, Norfolk
9 June 1978

Nationality: English

Height: 5′ 10″

Weight: 11.10

Caps: 2

Position: Right midfielder

Hewitt, a product of Wensum Wanderers' youth system, was released three years ago because of financial difficulties. Snapped up by Tyne as a replacement for the veteran player Jamie Forbes, Hewitt's first season proved him a pacey and competitive right-sided player, earning him an England call-up. He played well against the Republic of Ireland and made a vital interception in the Denmark game, leading to England's fourth goal.

AARON HALL

Born: Walthamstow, London
11 August 1979

Nationality: English

Height: 5′ 8″

Weight: 11.11

Caps: 1 (under 21)

Position: Left winger

A rare left-sided player, with an impressive range of skills, Hall has yet to break into the England first team, despite being called to the squad four times. Bought four years ago from Cray Town for £750,000, the Tyne board turned down a bid by Avon United, valuing him at £4.8m. In an EC Shield away tie against Dynamo Dneipnr, he scored twice in the 6–1 rout. Hall regularly scores, and ended last season with a tally of fourteen goals.

FABIEN DESCHAMPS

Born: Bordeaux, France
10 October 1981

Nationality: French

Height: 5′ 11″

Weight: 11.7

Caps: 5

Position: Right winger

Bordeaux-born, his Cameroonian parents tried to persuade Deschamps to play for their native country, but he opted for France. This paid off as he scored three goals for France in the last World Cup. Signing for FC Seine, he became a first team regular at seventeen. Transferring to Tyne eighteen months ago he is now an established fans' favourite, netting eighteen goals last season. His pace, lack of injury and energy make him a media darling.

HENRI LE CLERC

Born: Paris, France
3 February 1977

Nationality: French

Height: 6′ 1″

Weight: 12.6

Caps: 54

Position: Striker

One of the best strikers in Europe, he interchanges positions with Hall and Deschamps. Lethal as a centre forward, Le Clerc makes long runs deep into the opposing half. Talented, intelligent and ambitious, with an electric pace he weaves his way around defenders making a direct goal attack or a telling pass to a winger. Voted European Player of the Year, last season he scored 36 goals for Tyne and is an automatic choice for France.

TAFC

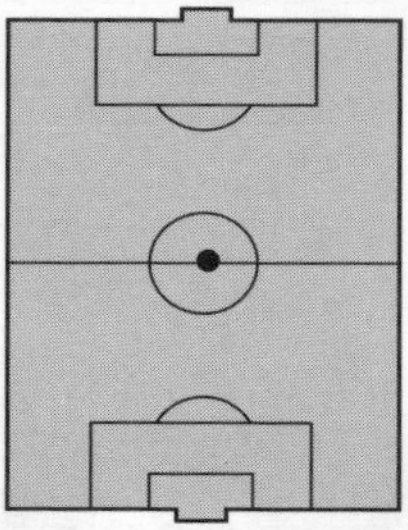

Henri Le Clerc 1

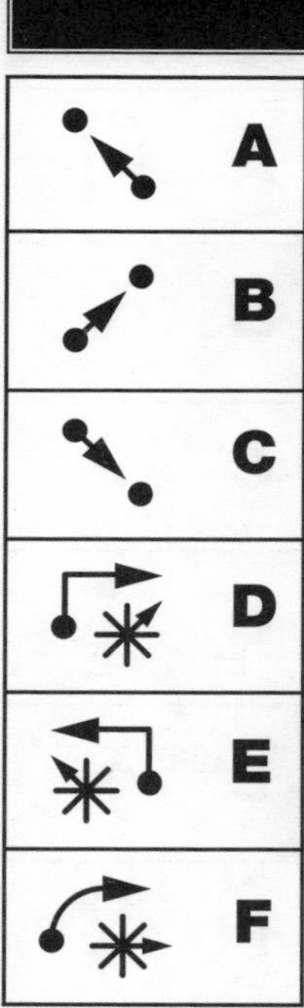

A A	A B	A C	A D	A E	A F	B A	B B	B C	B D	B E	B F
66	66	161	66	66	19	33	118	33	33	33	87

C A	C B	C C	C D	C E	C F	D A	D B	D C	D D	D E	D F
87	87	87	87	87	93	65	133	65	65	155	65

E A	E B	E C	E D	E E	E F	F A	F B	F C	F D	F E	F F
123	123	226	123	161	123	17	11	17	17	17	17

2 Henri Le Clerc

A A	A B	A C	A D	A E	A F	B A	B B	B C	B D	B E	B F
93	93	87	93	93	155	164	145	164	164	164	161

C A	C B	C C	C D	C E	C F	D A	D B	D C	D D	D E	D F
161	161	161	161	161	66	104	226	104	104	19	104

E A	E B	E C	E D	E E	E F	F A	F B	F C	F D	F E	F F
25	25	133	25	87	25	97	129	97	97	97	97

A

B

C

D

E

F

A A	A B	A C	A D	A E	A F	B A	B B	B C	B D	B E	B F
29	29	128	111	29	29	7	3	111	128	7	3

C A	C B	C C	C D	C E	C F	D A	D B	D C	D D	D E	D F
51	51	111	69	51	51	24	32	24	7	24	24

E A	E B	E C	E D	E E	E F	F A	F B	F C	F D	F E	F F
17	17	17	128	86	17	101	69	69	3	69	69

Fabien Deschamps

A

B

C

D

E

F

A A	A B	A C	A D	A E	A F	B A	B B	B C	B D	B E	B F
24	24	24	4	109	4	30	30	30	30	186	186

C A	C B	C C	C D	C E	C F	D A	D B	D C	D D	D E	D F
20	109	20	20	4	20	109	4	40	40	40	186

E A	E B	E C	E D	E E	E F	F A	F B	F C	F D	F E	F F
125	109	115	145	186	186	133	109	76	32	186	186

A A	A B	A C	A D	A E	A F	B A	B B	B C	B D	B E	B F
39	105	13	5	65	5	39	65	65	65	65	5

C A	C B	C C	C D	C E	C F	D A	D B	D C	D D	D E	D F
17	166	17	17	166	17	80	237	39	5	237	5

E A	E B	E C	E D	E E	E F	F A	F B	F C	F D	F E	F F
63	166	63	166	39	5	65	166	62	62	166	62

6 Dave Chell

A A	A B	A C	A D	A E	A F	B A	B B	B C	B D	B E	B F
38	226	14	123	123	123	38	179	14	23	6	23

C A	C B	C C	C D	C E	C F	D A	D B	D C	D D	D E	D F
6	26	22	22	6	14	124	14	14	124	6	124

E A	E B	E C	E D	E E	E F	F A	F B	F C	F D	F E	F F
62	38	38	48	62	62	8	38	38	160	8	8

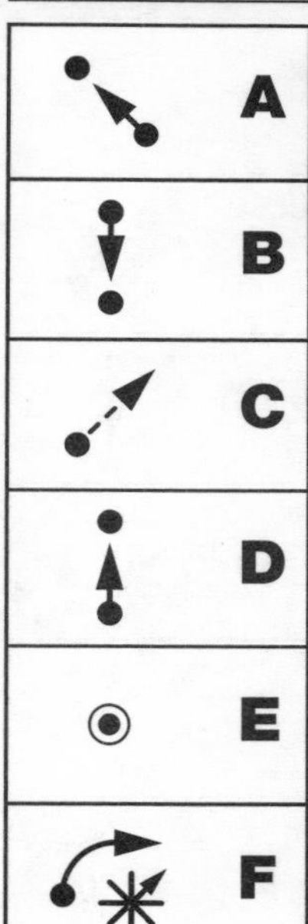

A A	A B	A C	A D	A E	A F	B A	B B	B C	B D	B E	B F
4	76	4	4	4	186	128	172	172	172	172	128

C A	C B	C C	C D	C E	C F	D A	D B	D C	D D	D E	D F
128	3	7	76	76	76	7	24	32	24	7	76

E A	E B	E C	E D	E E	E F	F A	F B	F C	F D	F E	F F
20	4	20	20	20	20	17	17	17	86	17	17

8 Terry Hiner

A

B

C

D

E

F

A A	A B	A C	A D	A E	A F	B A	B B	B C	B D	B E	B F
56	56	56	117	35	56	62	35	62	95	62	62

C A	C B	C C	C D	C E	C F	D A	D B	D C	D D	D E	D F
208	202	49	232	208	35	96	62	218	232	96	35

E A	E B	E C	E D	E E	E F	F A	F B	F C	F D	F E	F F
232	13	13	232	13	13	232	63	63	117	117	63

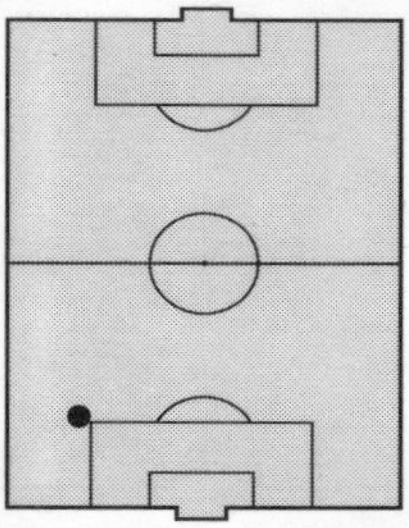

Fabien Deschamps 

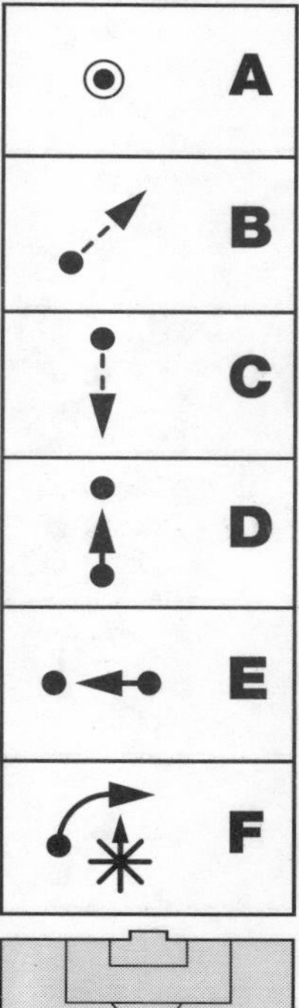

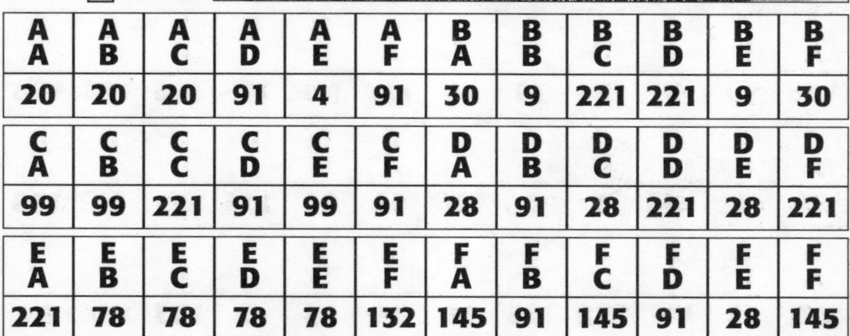

A A	A B	A C	A D	A E	A F	B A	B B	B C	B D	B E	B F
20	20	20	91	4	91	30	9	221	221	9	30

C A	C B	C C	C D	C E	C F	D A	D B	D C	D D	D E	D F
99	99	221	91	99	91	28	91	28	221	28	221

E A	E B	E C	E D	E E	E F	F A	F B	F C	F D	F E	F F
221	78	78	78	78	132	145	91	145	91	28	145

10 Aaron Hall

A A	A B	A C	A D	A E	A F	B A	B B	B C	B D	B E	B F
156	10	3	128	70	69	128	116	116	116	116	128

C A	C B	C C	C D	C E	C F	D A	D B	D C	D D	D E	D F
57	3	156	3	3	156	45	29	156	29	29	128

E A	E B	E C	E D	E E	E F	F A	F B	F C	F D	F E	F F
51	51	111	128	156	51	24	24	3	128	29	24

A A	A B	A C	A D	A E	A F	B A	B B	B C	B D	B E	B F
133	133	146	25	133	133	33	25	133	25	33	33

C A	C B	C C	C D	C E	C F	D A	D B	D C	D D	D E	D F
17	25	51	17	17	25	25	65	187	65	187	65

E A	E B	E C	E D	E E	E F	F A	F B	F C	F D	F E	F F
187	24	32	24	24	24	23	23	23	23	25	23

12 Aaron Hall

A A	A B	A C	A D	A E	A F	B A	B B	B C	B D	B E	B F
40	40	40	187	40	40	59	129	104	83	59	59

C A	C B	C C	C D	C E	C F	D A	D B	D C	D D	D E	D F
145	145	145	52	145	104	104	129	123	187	104	123

E A	E B	E C	E D	E E	E F	F A	F B	F C	F D	F E	F F
18	226	18	145	18	104	62	62	62	62	187	164

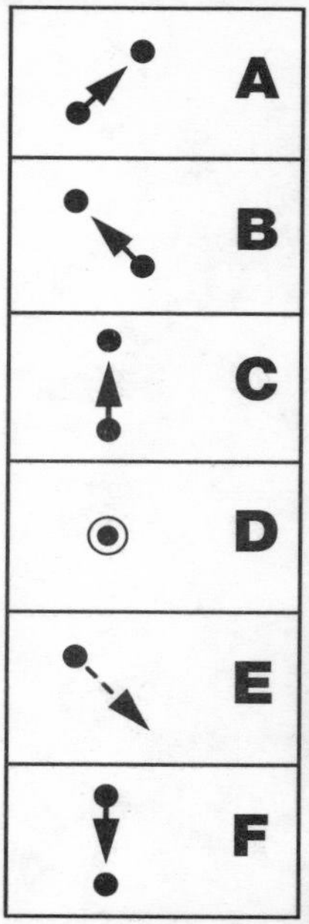

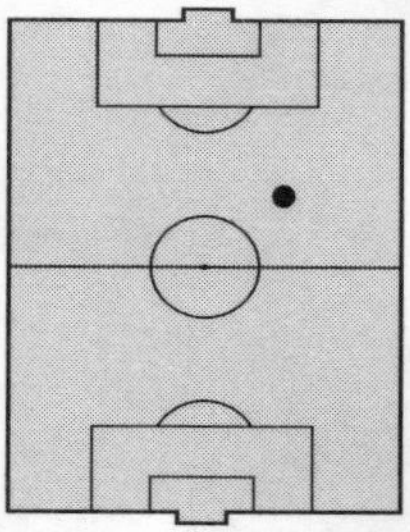

Laurencio 13

↗	A
↖	B
↑	C
◉	D
↘ (dashed)	E
↓	F

A A	A B	A C	A D	A E	A F	B A	B B	B C	B D	B E	B F
63	63	63	64	5	64	64	23	23	23	48	64

C A	C B	C C	C D	C E	C F	D A	D B	D C	D D	D E	D F
8	166	33	23	118	64	62	62	223	62	166	62

E A	E B	E C	E D	E E	E F	F A	F B	F C	F D	F E	F F
65	166	64	65	241	65	33	166	166	33	195	33

14 Dave Chell

A A	A B	A C	A D	A E	A F	B A	B B	B C	B D	B E	B F
226	226	235	160	6	226	179	179	235	95	6	179

C A	C B	C C	C D	C E	C F	D A	D B	D C	D D	D E	D F
6	42	235	127	42	42	6	129	235	42	129	129

E A	E B	E C	E D	E E	E F	F A	F B	F C	F D	F E	F F
134	134	235	124	134	235	160	48	160	235	15	160

Helmut Bremen 15

A A	A B	A C	A D	A E	A F	B A	B B	B C	B D	B E	B F
18	66	18	160	18	18	160	195	160	33	33	160

C A	C B	C C	C D	C E	C F	D A	D B	D C	D D	D E	D F
13	195	8	8	64	8	124	195	124	18	14	124

E A	E B	E C	E D	E E	E F	F A	F B	F C	F D	F E	F F
48	160	179	48	48	15	66	195	66	66	66	66

16 Henri Le Clerc

A A	A B	A C	A D	A E	A F	B A	B B	B C	B D	B E	B F
8	8	13	149	195	8	155	33	155	33	149	16

C A	C B	C C	C D	C E	C F	D A	D B	D C	D D	D E	D F
66	155	66	66	167	16	16	15	15	15	87	16

E A	E B	E C	E D	E E	E F	F A	F B	F C	F D	F E	F F
48	48	48	19	195	48	195	87	87	87	93	87

Aaron Hall 17

A A	A B	A C	A D	A E	A F	B A	B B	B C	B D	B E	B F
23	23	65	166	23	166	51	51	51	86	51	166

C A	C B	C C	C D	C E	C F	D A	D B	D C	D D	D E	D F
17	65	241	11	65	25	241	237	237	121	17	241

E A	E B	E C	E D	E E	E F	F A	F B	F C	F D	F E	F F
17	5	5	51	55	241	8	241	105	166	8	166

18 Helmut Bremen

A A	A B	A C	A D	A E	A F	B A	B B	B C	B D	B E	B F
195	48	48	15	226	66	195	6	6	226	6	145

C A	C B	C C	C D	C E	C F	D A	D B	D C	D D	D E	D F
123	123	226	129	123	104	15	15	15	160	226	161

E A	E B	E C	E D	E E	E F	F A	F B	F C	F D	F E	F F
195	6	124	195	124	195	195	160	8	195	48	195

Henri Le Clerc 19

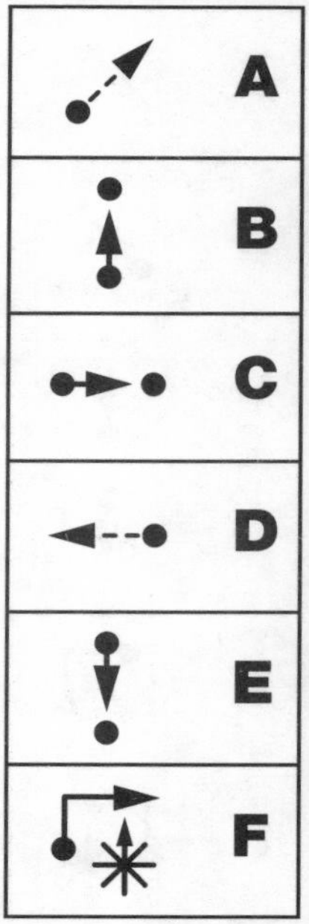

A

B

C

D

E

F

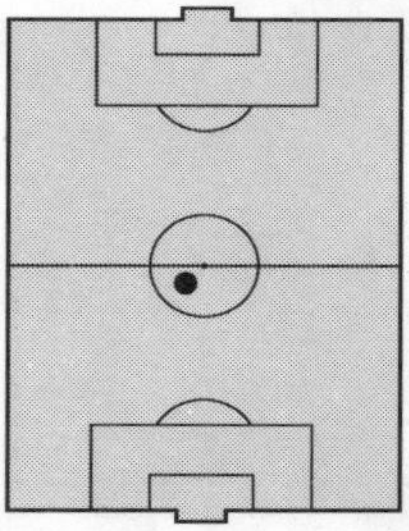

A A	A B	A C	A D	A E	A F	B A	B B	B C	B D	B E	B F
16	16	187	167	19	19	66	66	52	19	66	187

C A	C B	C C	C D	C E	C F	D A	D B	D C	D D	D E	D F
87	87	146	187	167	187	167	145	187	167	145	187

E A	E B	E C	E D	E E	E F	F A	F B	F C	F D	F E	F F
52	52	146	187	52	52	48	146	187	48	48	48

20 Helmut Bremen

A A	A B	A C	A D	A E	A F	B A	B B	B C	B D	B E	B F
187	145	125	20	125	145	133	125	133	133	20	125

C A	C B	C C	C D	C E	C F	D A	D B	D C	D D	D E	D F
187	52	20	52	20	125	4	4	187	4	20	4

E A	E B	E C	E D	E E	E F	F A	F B	F C	F D	F E	F F
59	59	187	164	59	59	17	149	187	17	17	17

Ross Hewitt 21

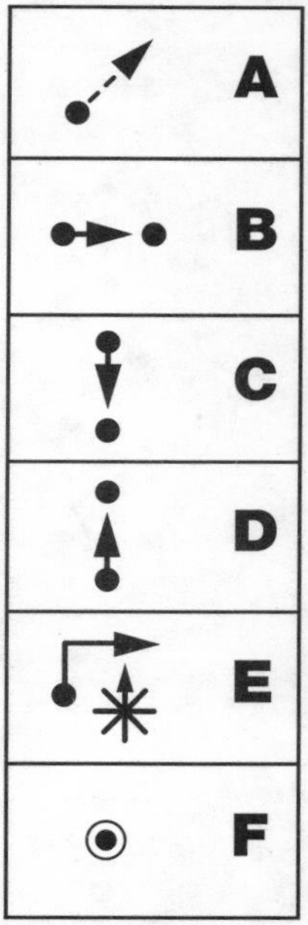

A

B

C

D

E

F

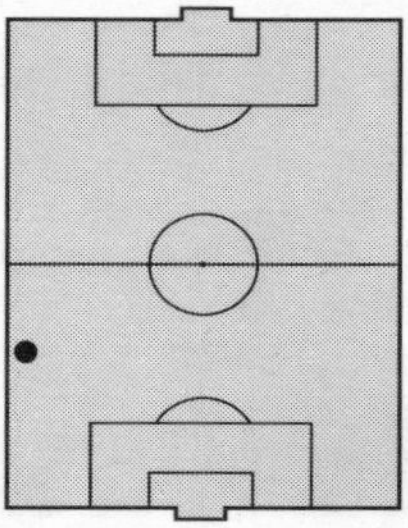

A A	A B	A C	A D	A E	A F	B A	B B	B C	B D	B E	B F
41	108	21	41	152	83	151	90	41	21	90	90

C A	C B	C C	C D	C E	C F	D A	D B	D C	D D	D E	D F
152	82	82	82	82	82	41	158	53	21	152	41

E A	E B	E C	E D	E E	E F	F A	F B	F C	F D	F E	F F
22	22	22	22	152	41	6	6	108	6	152	90

22 Dave Chell

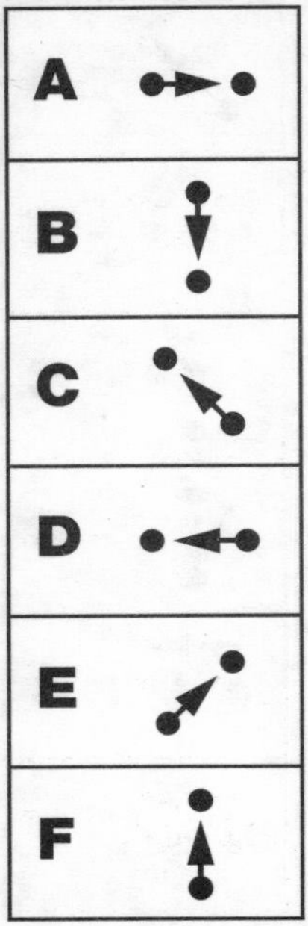

A

B

C

D

E

F

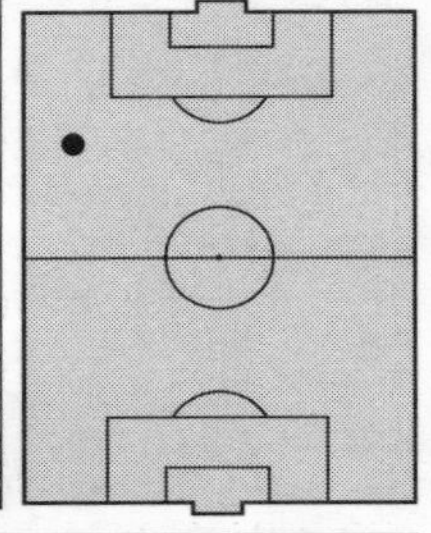

A A	A B	A C	A D	A E	A F	B A	B B	B C	B D	B E	B F
127	6	124	124	124	38	26	42	26	26	26	38

C A	C B	C C	C D	C E	C F	D A	D B	D C	D D	D E	D F
225	67	225	127	225	38	67	81	67	127	67	38

E A	E B	E C	E D	E E	E F	F A	F B	F C	F D	F E	F F
127	124	37	37	37	38	216	38	216	216	216	127

Dave Chell 23

A A	A B	A C	A D	A E	A F	B A	B B	B C	B D	B E	B F
8	8	8	95	95	13	124	95	124	124	95	6

C A	C B	C C	C D	C E	C F	D A	D B	D C	D D	D E	D F
48	48	48	48	223	179	62	62	62	62	95	23

E A	E B	E C	E D	E E	E F	F A	F B	F C	F D	F E	F F
6	23	95	6	38	223	95	34	34	64	34	223

24 Fabien Deschamps

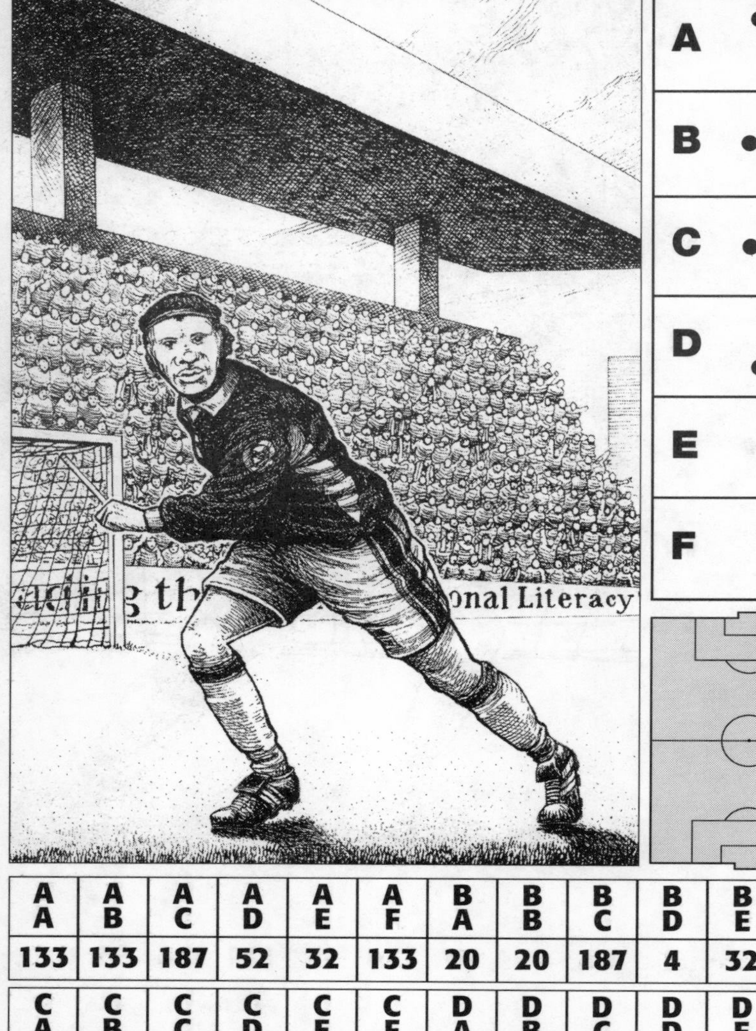

A A	A B	A C	A D	A E	A F	B A	B B	B C	B D	B E	B F
133	133	187	52	32	133	20	20	187	4	32	20

C A	C B	C C	C D	C E	C F	D A	D B	D C	D D	D E	D F
32	51	187	3	51	51	32	11	187	51	11	11

E A	E B	E C	E D	E E	E F	F A	F B	F C	F D	F E	F F
7	7	187	76	7	187	52	125	52	187	146	52

A

B

C

D

E

F

A A	A B	A C	A D	A E	A F	B A	B B	B C	B D	B E	B F
105	105	65	105	11	105	149	149	33	149	149	11

C A	C B	C C	C D	C E	C F	D A	D B	D C	D D	D E	D F
76	11	76	76	76	76	92	24	92	92	92	4

E A	E B	E C	E D	E E	E F	F A	F B	F C	F D	F E	F F
86	86	17	11	51	86	214	32	65	32	24	32

26 Pierre Pasqualle

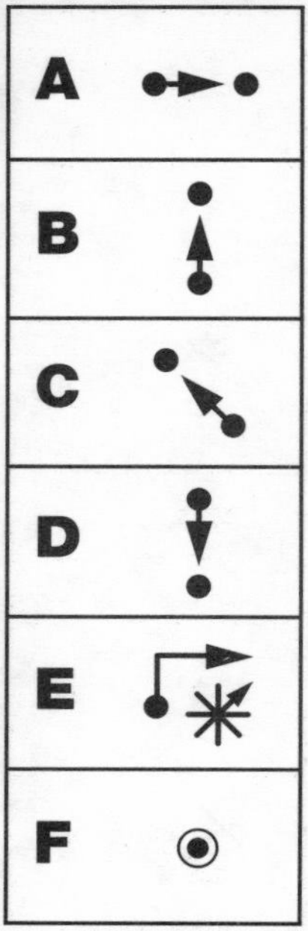

A	
B	
C	
D	
E	
F	

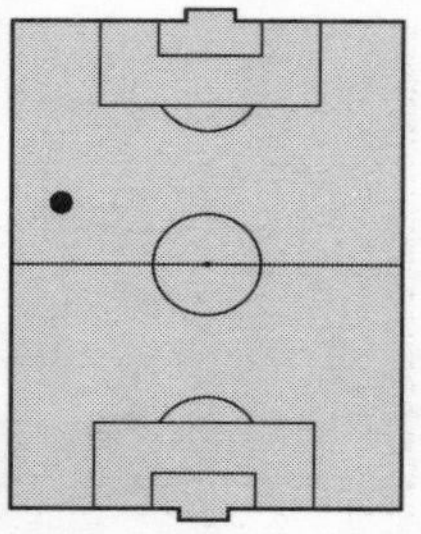

A A	A B	A C	A D	A E	A F	B A	B B	B C	B D	B E	B F
38	42	123	123	26	164	42	22	38	22	26	42

C A	C B	C C	C D	C E	C F	D A	D B	D C	D D	D E	D F
38	67	67	42	26	81	38	59	59	59	59	97

E A	E B	E C	E D	E E	E F	F A	F B	F C	F D	F E	F F
124	14	124	124	38	124	23	129	23	23	38	23

A A	A B	A C	A D	A E	A F	B A	B B	B C	B D	B E	B F
199	199	199	231	177	199	160	15	160	240	160	16

C A	C B	C C	C D	C E	C F	D A	D B	D C	D D	D E	D F
34	8	35	240	63	49	68	62	96	240	110	202

E A	E B	E C	E D	E E	E F	F A	F B	F C	F D	F E	F F
105	65	105	240	13	11	96	124	37	240	134	62

28 Henri Le Clerc

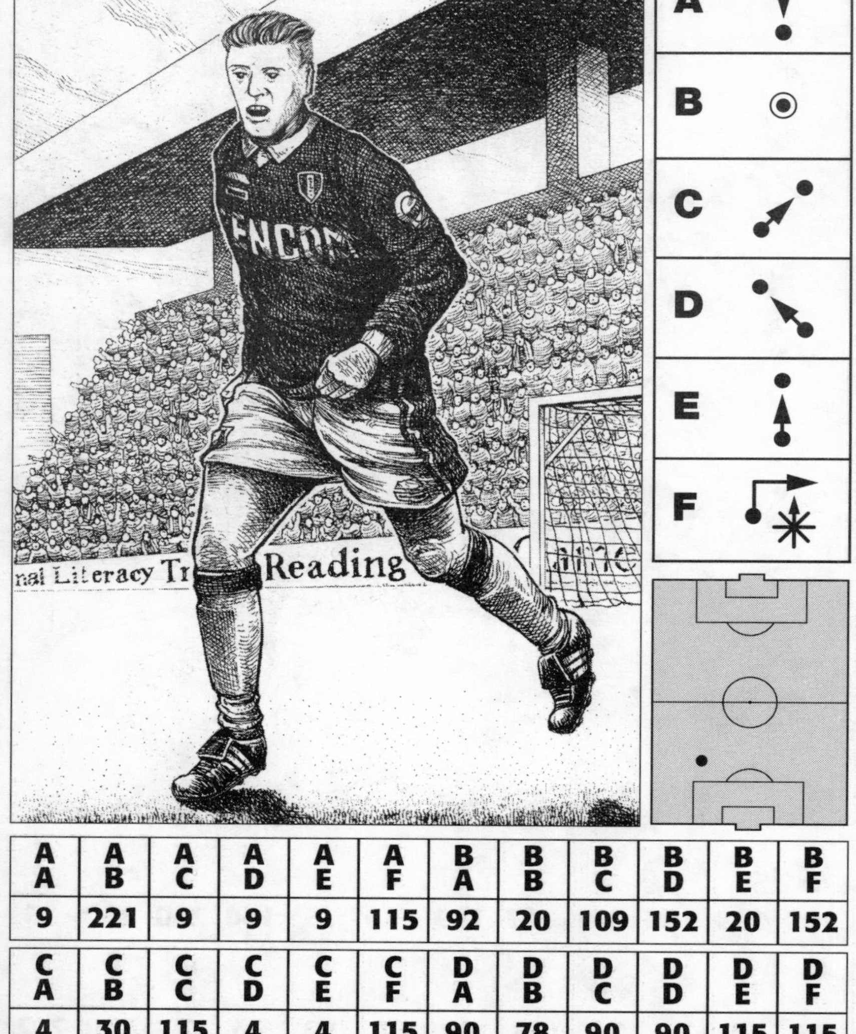

A A	A B	A C	A D	A E	A F	B A	B B	B C	B D	B E	B F
9	221	9	9	9	115	92	20	109	152	20	152

C A	C B	C C	C D	C E	C F	D A	D B	D C	D D	D E	D F
4	30	115	4	4	115	90	78	90	90	115	115

E A	E B	E C	E D	E E	E F	F A	F B	F C	F D	F E	F F
40	115	40	152	40	115	174	152	145	145	145	152

Brett Green 29

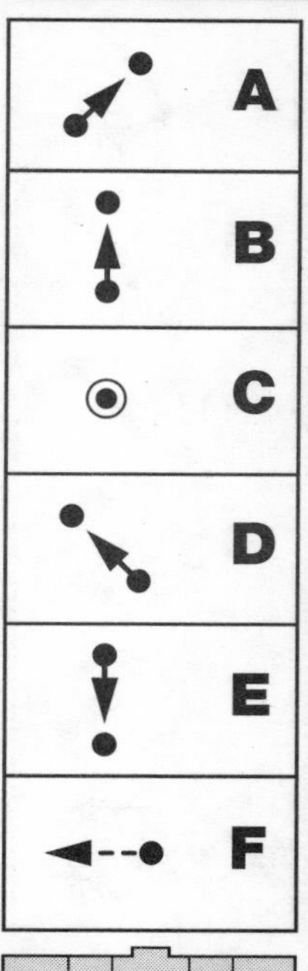

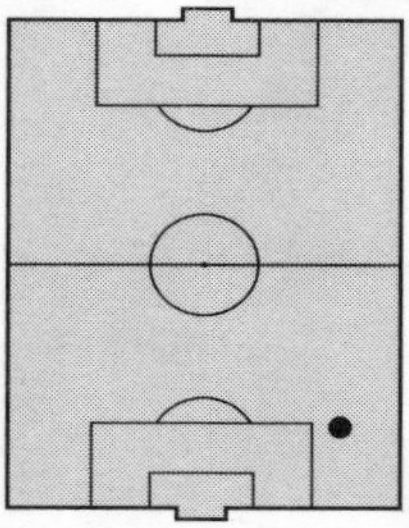

A A	A B	A C	A D	A E	A F	B A	B B	B C	B D	B E	B F
10	128	10	57	70	10	57	57	3	3	29	3

C A	C B	C C	C D	C E	C F	D A	D B	D C	D D	D E	D F
20	20	76	20	128	109	29	128	57	7	201	7

E A	E B	E C	E D	E E	E F	F A	F B	F C	F D	F E	F F
45	128	45	45	171	45	57	201	29	172	128	172

30 Fabien Deschamps

A A	A B	A C	A D	A E	A F	B A	B B	B C	B D	B E	B F
52	92	52	186	52	52	7	7	92	76	186	172

C A	C B	C C	C D	C E	C F	D A	D B	D C	D D	D E	D F
192	192	192	92	186	197	4	4	4	92	92	203

E A	E B	E C	E D	E E	E F	F A	F B	F C	F D	F E	F F
92	28	28	115	186	9	20	109	20	186	186	186

A A	A B	A C	A D	A E	A F	B A	B B	B C	B D	B E	B F
11	11	32	11	11	25	12	12	174	12	12	104

C A	C B	C C	C D	C E	C F	D A	D B	D C	D D	D E	D F
201	24	7	29	209	32	221	203	28	40	209	174

E A	E B	E C	E D	E E	E F	F A	F B	F C	F D	F E	F F
52	52	125	52	52	146	172	172	172	60	139	172

32 Fabien Deschamps

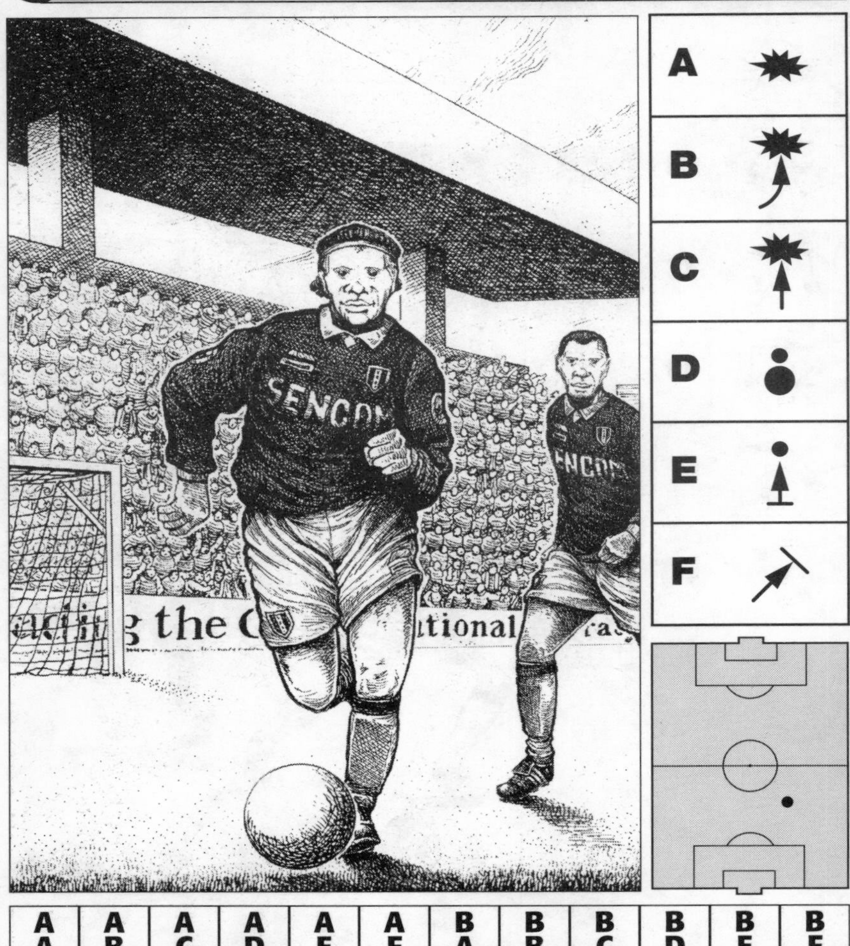

A A	A B	A C	A D	A E	A F	B A	B B	B C	B D	B E	B F
214	133	24	25	25	25	214	20	24	109	32	109

C A	C B	C C	C D	C E	C F	D A	D B	D C	D D	D E	D F
32	86	111	111	32	24	76	24	24	76	32	76

E A	E B	E C	E D	E E	E F	F A	F B	F C	F D	F E	F F
92	214	214	125	92	92	115	214	214	52	115	115

Henri Le Clerc 33

●▸●	A
◂--●	B
● ↘ ●	C
● ↑ ●	D
◉	E
● ↓ ●	F

A A	A B	A C	A D	A E	A F	B A	B B	B C	B D	B E	B F
65	118	65	17	33	118	33	195	15	195	118	15

C A	C B	C C	C D	C E	C F	D A	D B	D C	D D	D E	D F
118	118	48	179	33	48	13	118	13	149	33	13

E A	E B	E C	E D	E E	E F	F A	F B	F C	F D	F E	F F
160	62	179	62	62	62	133	195	133	195	133	133

34 Laurencio

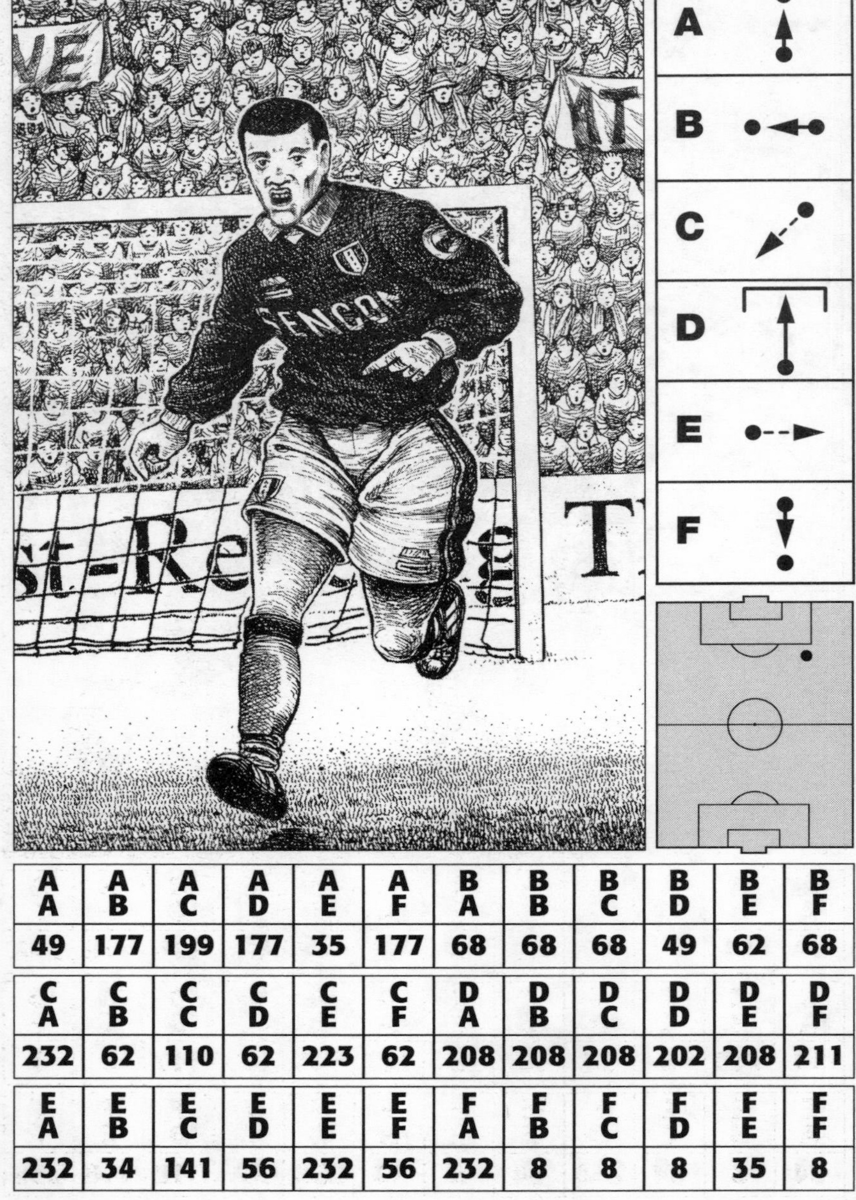

A A	A B	A C	A D	A E	A F	B A	B B	B C	B D	B E	B F
49	177	199	177	35	177	68	68	68	49	62	68

C A	C B	C C	C D	C E	C F	D A	D B	D C	D D	D E	D F
232	62	110	62	223	62	208	208	208	202	208	211

E A	E B	E C	E D	E E	E F	F A	F B	F C	F D	F E	F F
232	34	141	56	232	56	232	8	8	8	35	8

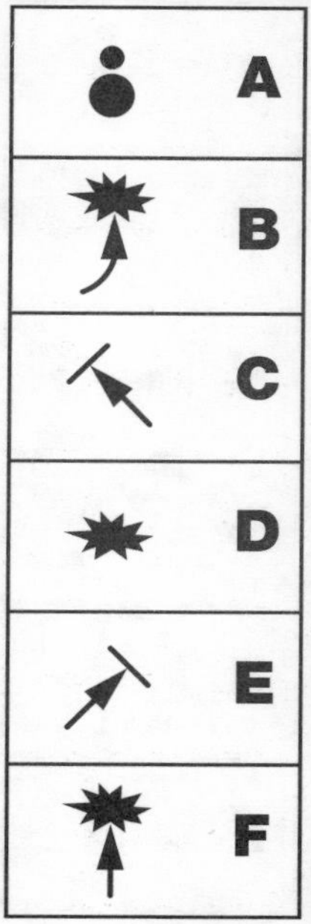

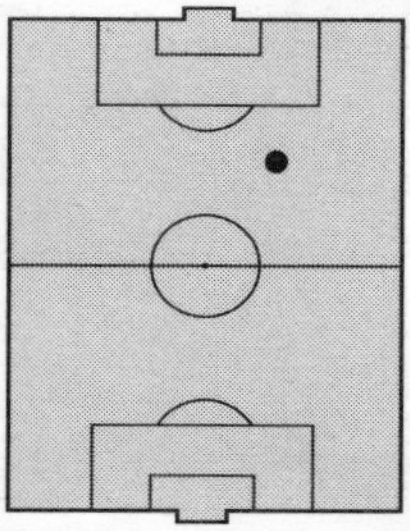

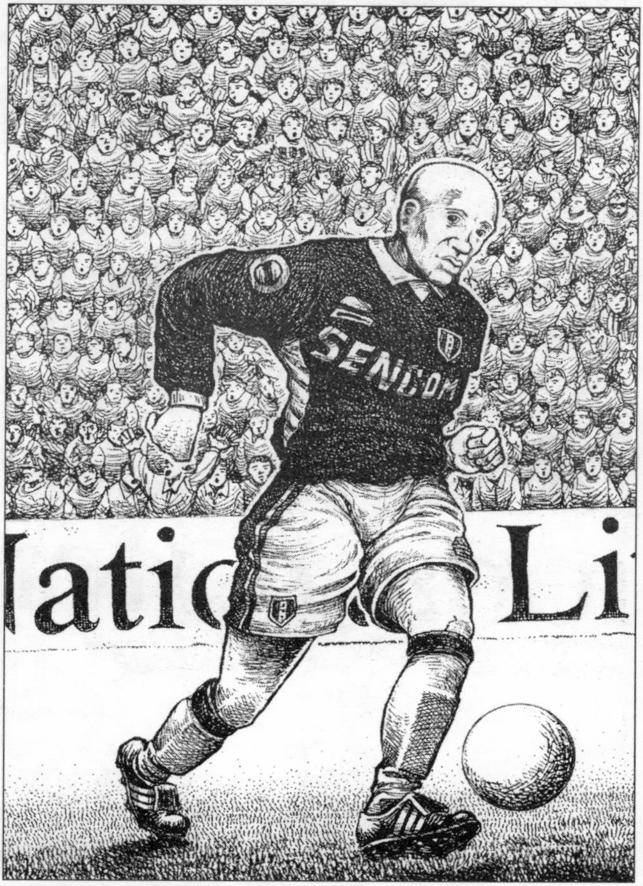

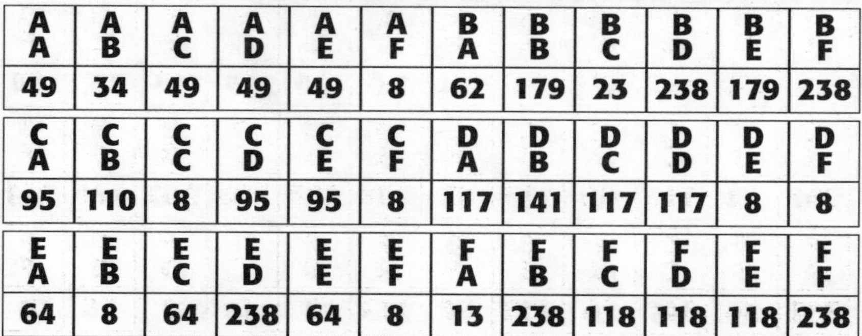

A A	A B	A C	A D	A E	A F	B A	B B	B C	B D	B E	B F
49	34	49	49	49	8	62	179	23	238	179	238

C A	C B	C C	C D	C E	C F	D A	D B	D C	D D	D E	D F
95	110	8	95	95	8	117	141	117	117	8	8

E A	E B	E C	E D	E E	E F	F A	F B	F C	F D	F E	F F
64	8	64	238	64	8	13	238	118	118	118	238

36 Dave Chell

A A	A B	A C	A D	A E	A F	B A	B B	B C	B D	B E	B F
193	193	193	84	193	154	72	180	215	154	73	154

C A	C B	C C	C D	C E	C F	D A	D B	D C	D D	D E	D F
180	181	73	50	36	181	73	50	50	106	50	206

E A	E B	E C	E D	E E	E F	F A	F B	F C	F D	F E	F F
43	43	106	43	43	43	62	62	218	62	62	62

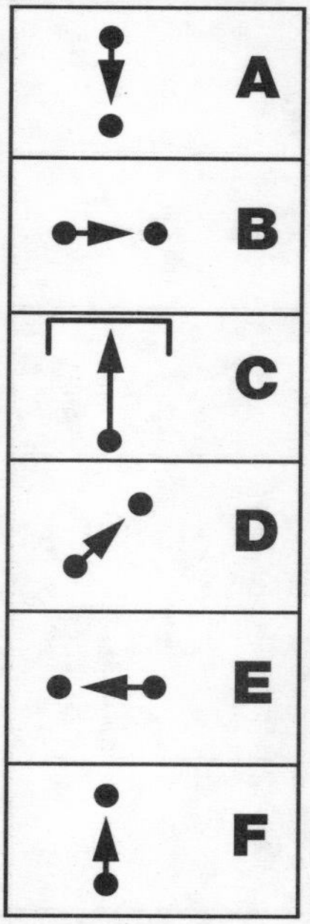

A

B

C

D

E

F

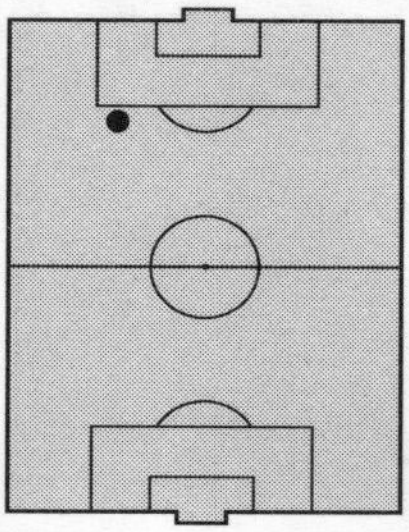

A A	A B	A C	A D	A E	A F	B A	B B	B C	B D	B E	B F
124	124	134	124	154	84	96	96	62	84	96	154

C A	C B	C C	C D	C E	C F	D A	D B	D C	D D	D E	D F
218	208	154	106	154	208	50	50	96	84	50	154

E A	E B	E C	E D	E E	E F	F A	F B	F C	F D	F E	F F
216	84	224	216	216	154	193	193	134	193	154	84

38 Dave Chell / Free Kick

A A	A B	A C	A D	A E	A F	B A	B B	B C	B D	B E	B F
23	134	124	124	124	134	81	67	159	67	67	67

C A	C B	C C	C D	C E	C F	D A	D B	D C	D D	D E	D F
71	225	234	225	225	234	62	124	62	110	134	62

E A	E B	E C	E D	E E	E F	F A	F B	F C	F D	F E	F F
208	124	208	211	134	208	127	22	22	22	22	127

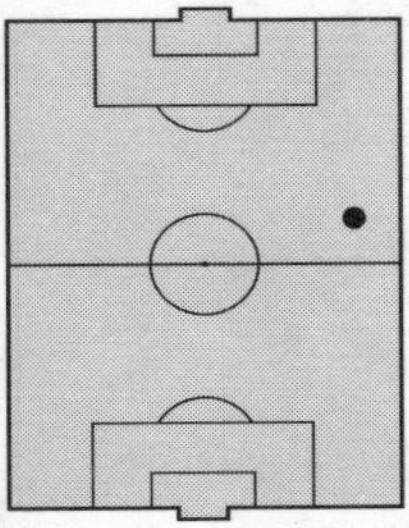

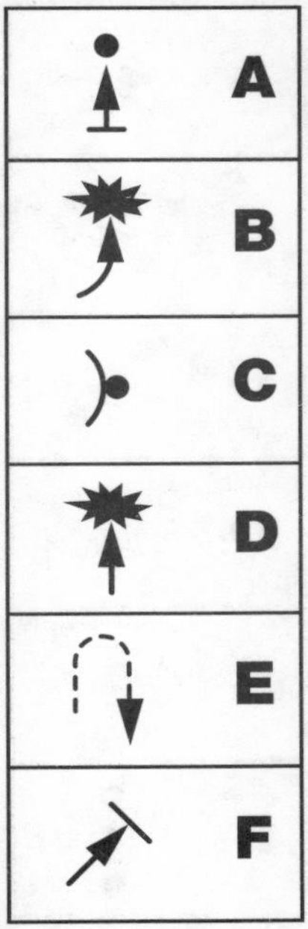

Brett Green 39

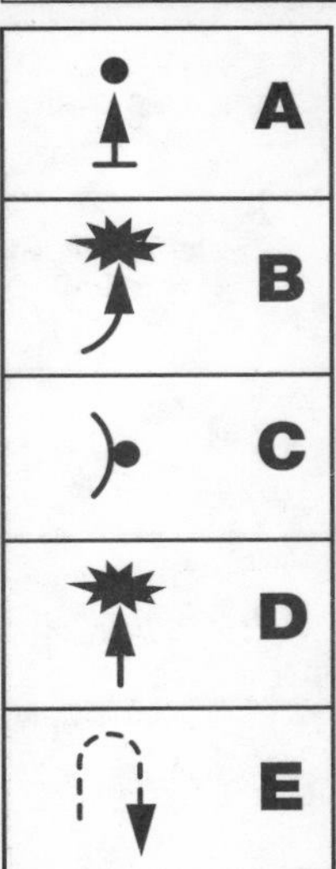

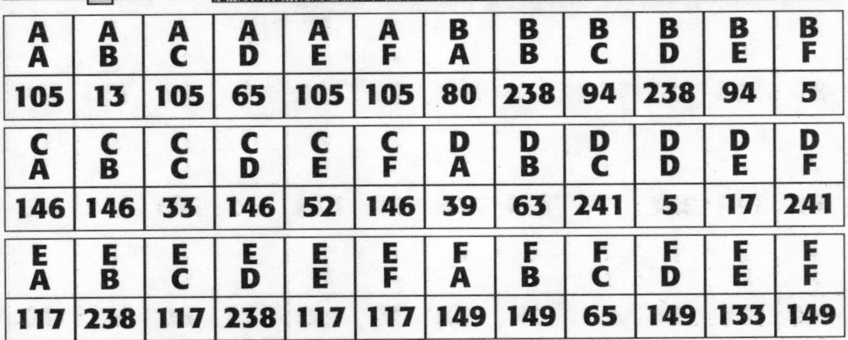

AA	AB	AC	AD	AE	AF	BA	BB	BC	BD	BE	BF
105	13	105	65	105	105	80	238	94	238	94	5

CA	CB	CC	CD	CE	CF	DA	DB	DC	DD	DE	DF
146	146	33	146	52	146	39	63	241	5	17	241

EA	EB	EC	ED	EE	EF	FA	FB	FC	FD	FE	FF
117	238	117	238	117	117	149	149	65	149	133	149

40 Aaron Hall

A A	A B	A C	A D	A E	A F	B A	B B	B C	B D	B E	B F
90	174	152	40	174	90	20	152	4	20	174	174

C A	C B	C C	C D	C E	C F	D A	D B	D C	D D	D E	D F
83	152	90	174	174	83	40	174	115	145	152	145

E A	E B	E C	E D	E E	E F	F A	F B	F C	F D	F E	F F
167	15	15	15	15	146	28	152	115	28	152	28

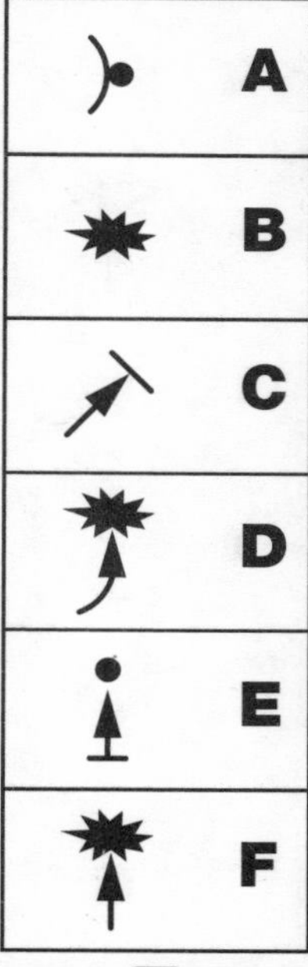

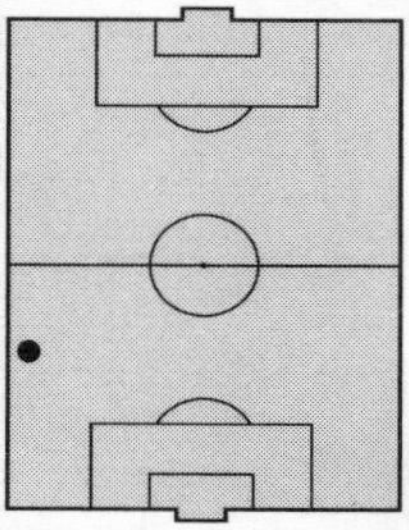

A A	A B	A C	A D	A E	A F	B A	B B	B C	B D	B E	B F
158	158	158	53	158	21	151	44	21	83	41	151

C A	C B	C C	C D	C E	C F	D A	D B	D C	D D	D E	D F
108	44	108	44	108	83	150	41	150	21	41	21

E A	E B	E C	E D	E E	E F	F A	F B	F C	F D	F E	F F
90	100	78	100	100	100	40	115	28	115	115	115

42 Pierre Pasqualle

A A	A B	A C	A D	A E	A F	B A	B B	B C	B D	B E	B F
42	165	165	26	159	159	127	165	127	127	127	127

C A	C B	C C	C D	C E	C F	D A	D B	D C	D D	D E	D F
97	26	165	42	97	97	26	26	165	42	158	158

E A	E B	E C	E D	E E	E F	F A	F B	F C	F D	F E	F F
125	125	125	125	145	123	129	26	165	42	26	129

Matthew Scadding

A
B
C
D
E
F

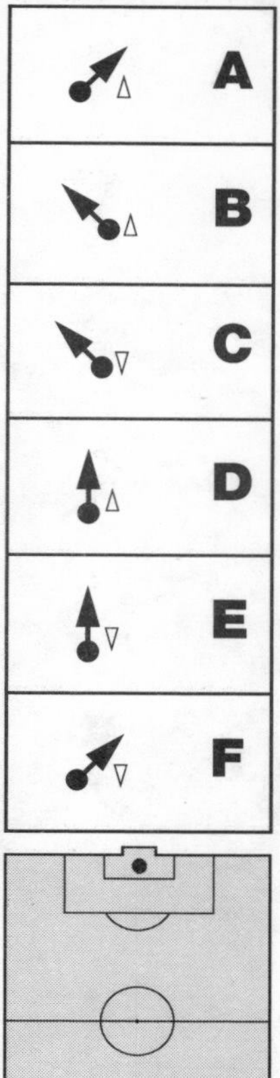

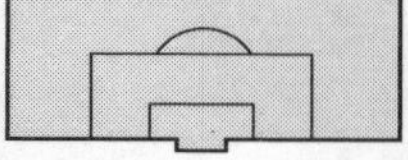

A A	A B	A C	A D	A E	A F	B A	B B	B C	B D	B E	B F
227	135	227	148	135	135	180	148	135	135	180	135

C A	C B	C C	C D	C E	C F	D A	D B	D C	D D	D E	D F
135	194	135	135	148	180	148	135	180	227	135	227

E A	E B	E C	E D	E E	E F	F A	F B	F C	F D	F E	F F
135	227	135	135	227	148	135	135	148	227	135	227

44 Pierre Pasqualle / Free Kick

A A	A B	A C	A D	A E	A F	B A	B B	B C	B D	B E	B F
28	184	30	184	144	184	115	115	90	115	115	40

C A	C B	C C	C D	C E	C F	D A	D B	D C	D D	D E	D F
28	90	192	221	9	183	4	92	28	92	30	213

E A	E B	E C	E D	E E	E F	F A	F B	F C	F D	F E	F F
100	100	100	100	100	90	40	109	20	109	4	125

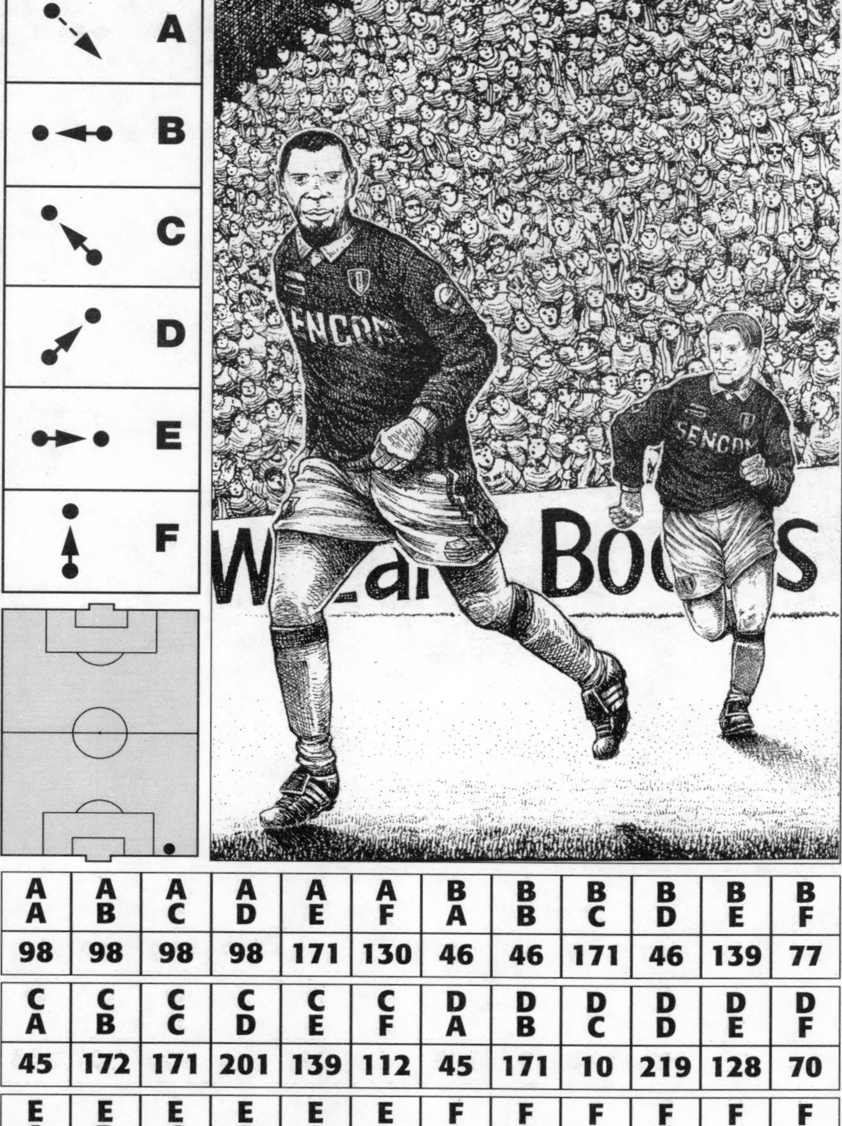

A A	A B	A C	A D	A E	A F	B A	B B	B C	B D	B E	B F
98	98	98	98	171	130	46	46	171	46	139	77

C A	C B	C C	C D	C E	C F	D A	D B	D C	D D	D E	D F
45	172	171	201	139	112	45	171	10	219	128	70

E A	E B	E C	E D	E E	E F	F A	F B	F C	F D	F E	F F
116	171	116	116	128	70	171	29	29	111	171	130

46 Henri Le Clerc

A A	A B	A C	A D	A E	A F	B A	B B	B C	B D	B E	B F
45	46	112	130	45	45	201	112	172	139	112	172

C A	C B	C C	C D	C E	C F	D A	D B	D C	D D	D E	D F
57	112	139	139	112	29	163	163	163	139	139	163

E A	E B	E C	E D	E E	E F	F A	F B	F C	F D	F E	F F
3	3	29	3	3	3	20	20	20	20	20	201

Ross Hewitt 47

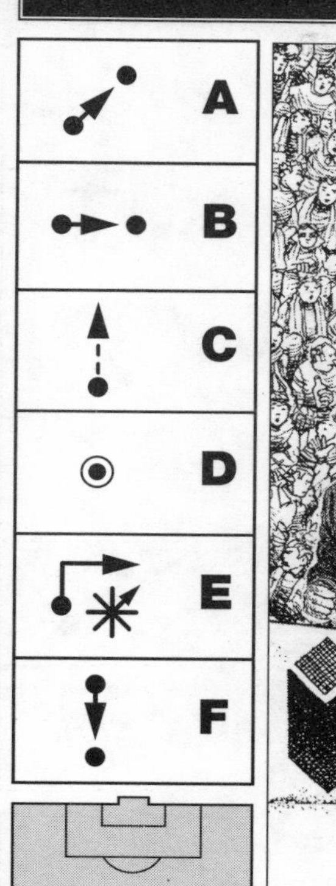

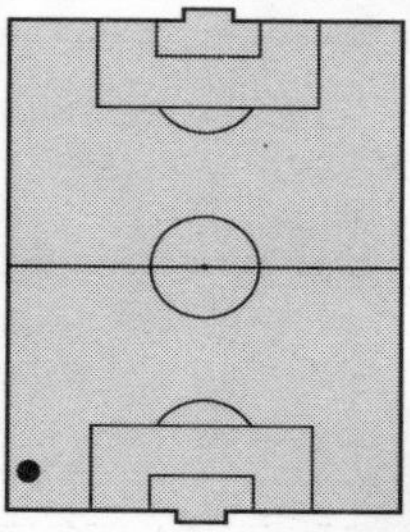

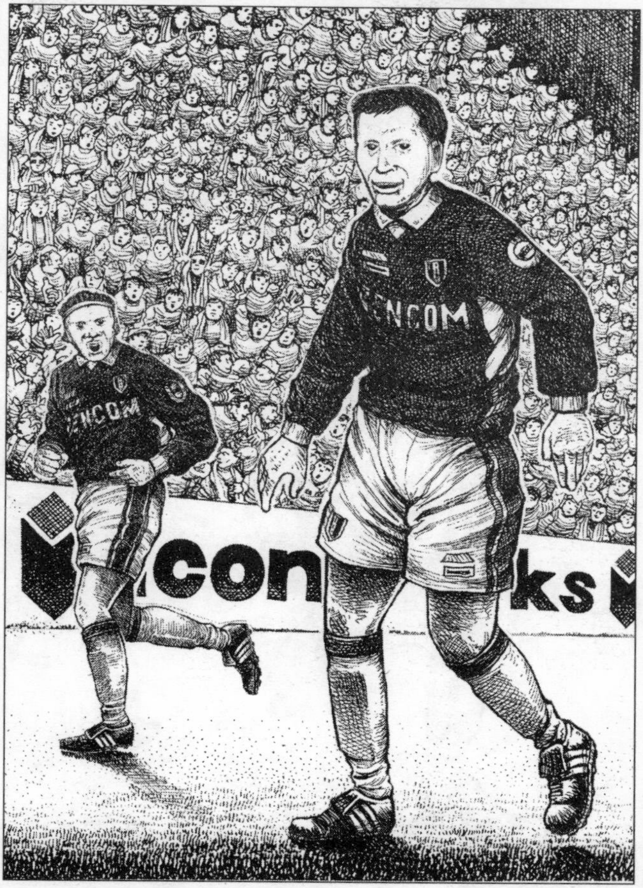

A A	A B	A C	A D	A E	A F	B A	B B	B C	B D	B E	B F
78	120	78	100	47	175	132	120	132	113	47	103

C A	C B	C C	C D	C E	C F	D A	D B	D C	D D	D E	D F
120	82	82	120	150	137	20	115	221	20	20	20

E A	E B	E C	E D	E E	E F	F A	F B	F C	F D	F E	F F
28	100	113	28	28	28	114	114	114	176	114	138

48 Henri Le Clerc

A

B

C

D

E

F

A A	A B	A C	A D	A E	A F	B A	B B	B C	B D	B E	B F
195	15	195	15	15	15	62	62	179	62	62	95

C A	C B	C C	C D	C E	C F	D A	D B	D C	D D	D E	D F
33	179	64	48	13	13	160	23	95	195	23	179

E A	E B	E C	E D	E E	E F	F A	F B	F C	F D	F E	F F
226	6	14	48	179	6	124	124	124	124	14	14

A A	A B	A C	A D	A E	A F	B A	B B	B C	B D	B E	B F
179	179	179	169	95	169	110	49	34	34	49	110

C A	C B	C C	C D	C E	C F	D A	D B	D C	D D	D E	D F
199	199	34	169	199	169	35	169	35	34	35	34

E A	E B	E C	E D	E E	E F	F A	F B	F C	F D	F E	F F
34	141	141	141	141	222	118	169	118	169	35	118

50 Matthew Scadding

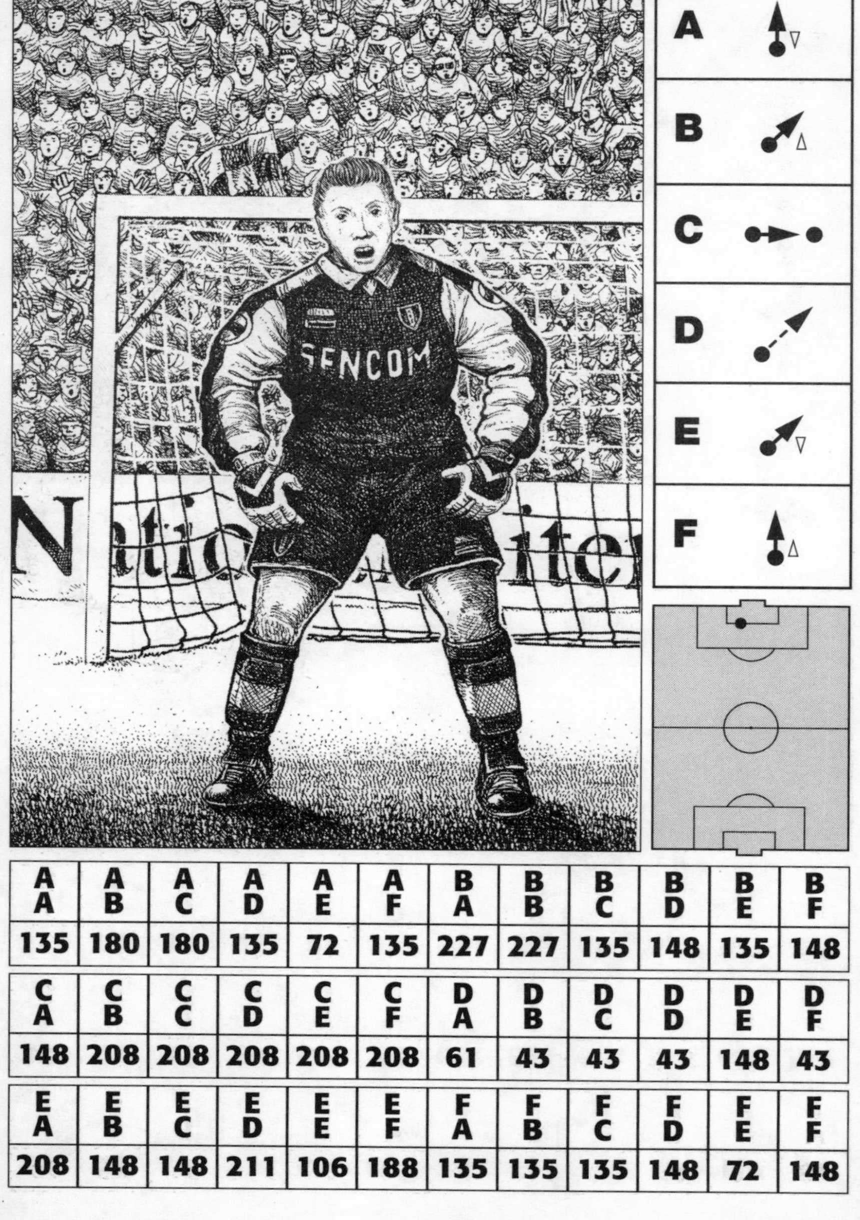

A A	A B	A C	A D	A E	A F	B A	B B	B C	B D	B E	B F
135	180	180	135	72	135	227	227	135	148	135	148

C A	C B	C C	C D	C E	C F	D A	D B	D C	D D	D E	D F
148	208	208	208	208	208	61	43	43	43	148	43

E A	E B	E C	E D	E E	E F	F A	F B	F C	F D	F E	F F
208	148	148	211	106	188	135	135	135	148	72	148

Terry Hiner 51

A A	A B	A C	A D	A E	A F	B A	B B	B C	B D	B E	B F
51	128	128	86	69	69	3	128	3	3	3	3

C A	C B	C C	C D	C E	C F	D A	D B	D C	D D	D E	D F
17	86	128	51	17	17	86	86	128	51	237	237

E A	E B	E C	E D	E E	E F	F A	F B	F C	F D	F E	F F
48	48	48	48	118	25	11	86	128	51	86	11

52 Aaron Hall

A	B	C	D	E	F

AA	AB	AC	AD	AE	AF	BA	BB	BC	BD	BE	BF
48	187	48	48	48	179	149	33	33	33	33	33

CA	CB	CC	CD	CE	CF	DA	DB	DC	DD	DE	DF
18	18	164	18	18	18	52	187	133	146	146	133

EA	EB	EC	ED	EE	EF	FA	FB	FC	FD	FE	FF
19	125	19	167	167	167	145	40	146	164	145	164

Fabien Deschamps 53

A A	A B	A C	A D	A E	A F	B A	B B	B C	B D	B E	B F
59	97	59	53	54	158	67	81	159	67	41	158

C A	C B	C C	C D	C E	C F	D A	D B	D C	D D	D E	D F
97	6	6	129	6	6	26	158	42	158	97	158

E A	E B	E C	E D	E E	E F	F A	F B	F C	F D	F E	F F
21	122	21	21	122	122	42	23	23	226	23	23

54 Pierre Pasqualle / Throw-in

A A	A B	A C	A D	A E	A F	B A	B B	B C	B D	B E	B F
151	90	41	90	90	90	108	41	83	83	83	83

C A	C B	C C	C D	C E	C F	D A	D B	D C	D D	D E	D F
40	40	40	174	90	174	12	83	12	104	12	104

E A	E B	E C	E D	E E	E F	F A	F B	F C	F D	F E	F F
28	28	151	115	28	115	41	21	21	21	54	21

A A	A B	A C	A D	A E	A F	B A	B B	B C	B D	B E	B F
80	80	80	94	80	55	64	13	13	13	64	166

C A	C B	C C	C D	C E	C F	D A	D B	D C	D D	D E	D F
5	39	5	94	5	242	56	56	136	94	56	136

E A	E B	E C	E D	E E	E F	F A	F B	F C	F D	F E	F F
35	8	117	8	35	166	105	241	65	65	105	166

56 Laurencio

A A	A B	A C	A D	A E	A F	B A	B B	B C	B D	B E	B F
49	208	208	208	211	208	75	75	141	232	56	117

C A	C B	C C	C D	C E	C F	D A	D B	D C	D D	D E	D F
198	141	217	232	56	136	56	34	232	49	49	232

E A	E B	E C	E D	E E	E F	F A	F B	F C	F D	F E	F F
141	177	199	232	56	49	63	63	232	63	63	117

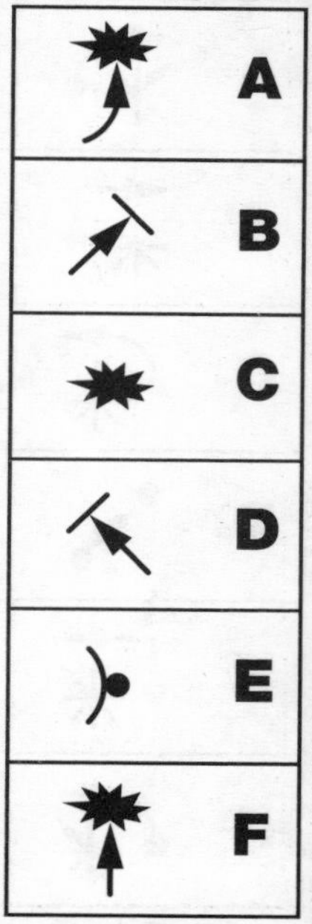

Brett Green 57

A

B

C

D

E

F

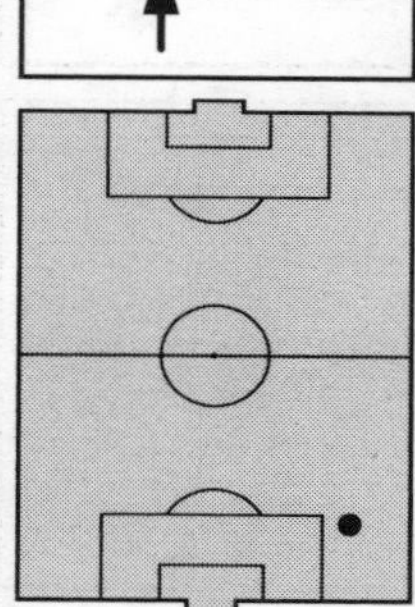

A A	A B	A C	A D	A E	A F	B A	B B	B C	B D	B E	B F
173	201	173	57	201	173	172	112	173	29	112	29

C A	C B	C C	C D	C E	C F	D A	D B	D C	D D	D E	D F
70	29	156	156	156	156	102	29	116	219	219	29

E A	E B	E C	E D	E E	E F	F A	F B	F C	F D	F E	F F
203	203	203	30	172	203	3	171	77	171	171	29

58 Ross Hewitt

A A	A B	A C	A D	A E	A F	B A	B B	B C	B D	B E	B F
151	104	12	12	209	12	115	174	40	40	209	174

C A	C B	C C	C D	C E	C F	D A	D B	D C	D D	D E	D F
20	125	20	20	209	20	221	9	9	9	209	9

E A	E B	E C	E D	E E	E F	F A	F B	F C	F D	F E	F F
24	7	76	24	209	32	11	25	32	11	209	11

Fabien Deschamps 59

A

B

C

D

E

F

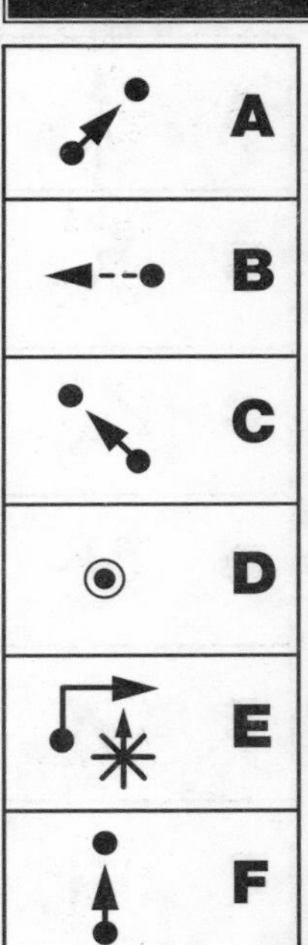

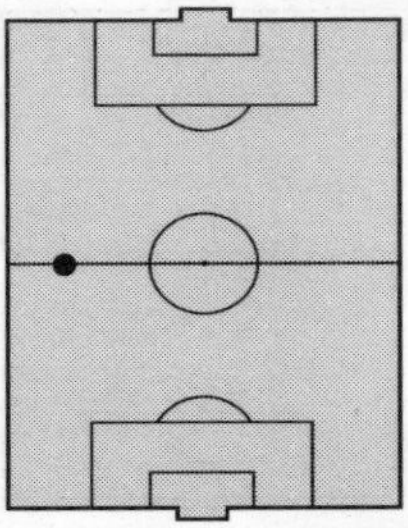

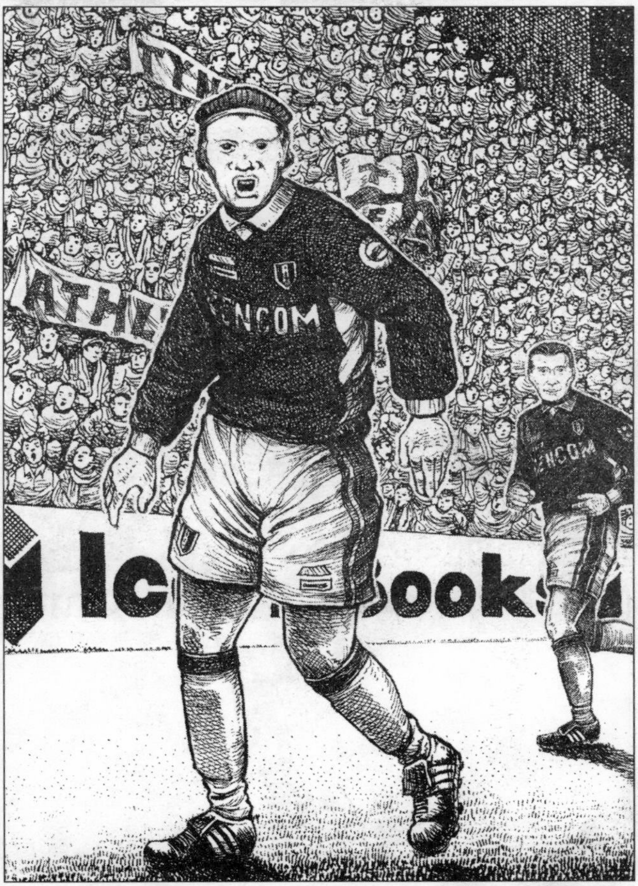

A A	A B	A C	A D	A E	A F	B A	B B	B C	B D	B E	B F
104	97	123	129	123	123	54	53	158	122	53	59

C A	C B	C C	C D	C E	C F	D A	D B	D C	D D	D E	D F
81	67	67	159	67	97	23	179	23	23	95	23

E A	E B	E C	E D	E E	E F	F A	F B	F C	F D	F E	F F
124	14	124	124	134	124	108	26	42	97	26	26

60 Ross Hewitt

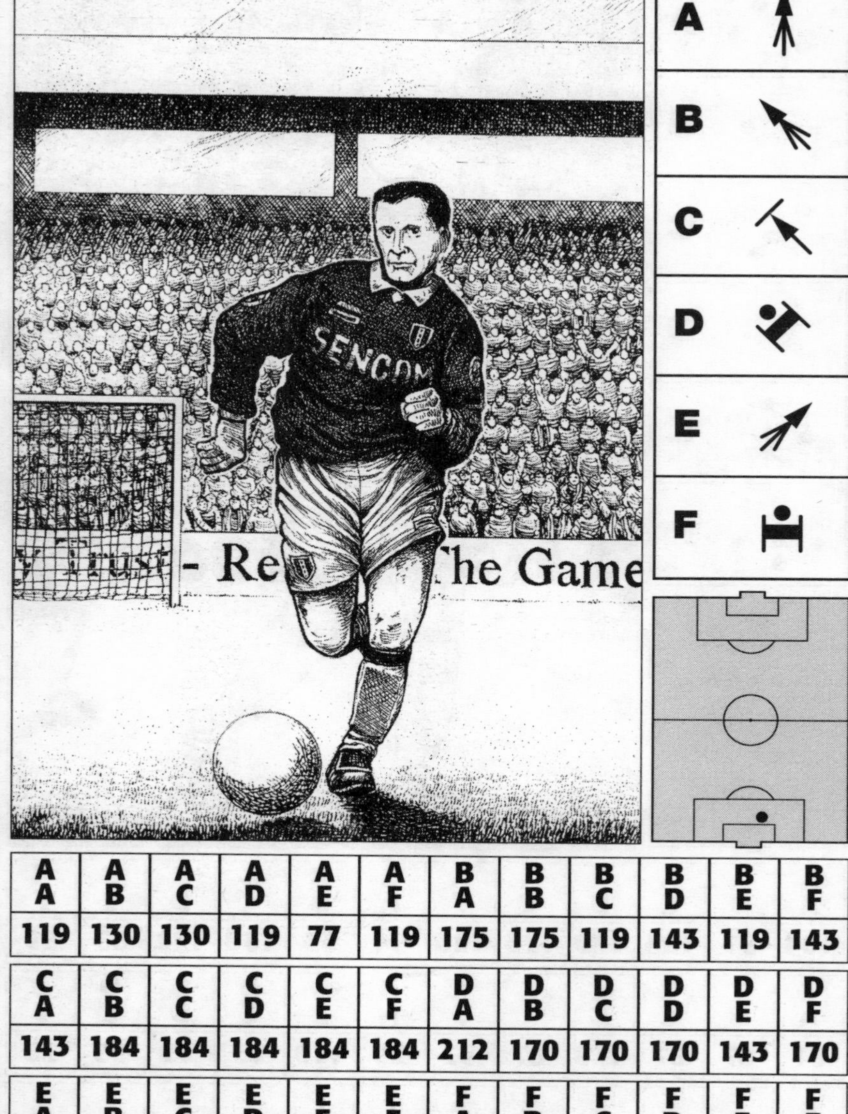

A A	A B	A C	A D	A E	A F	B A	B B	B C	B D	B E	B F
119	130	130	119	77	119	175	175	119	143	119	143

C A	C B	C C	C D	C E	C F	D A	D B	D C	D D	D E	D F
143	184	184	184	184	184	212	170	170	170	143	170

E A	E B	E C	E D	E E	E F	F A	F B	F C	F D	F E	F F
184	143	143	144	31	204	119	119	119	143	77	143

A A	A B	A C	A D	A E	A F	B A	B B	B C	B D	B E	B F
135	227	227	135	227	148	180	135	135	180	135	135

C A	C B	C C	C D	C E	C F	D A	D B	D C	D D	D E	D F
135	180	135	148	135	135	148	135	43	208	50	135

E A	E B	E C	E D	E E	E F	F A	F B	F C	F D	F E	F F
227	135	148	135	135	227	135	148	135	135	135	180

62 Laurencio

A A	A B	A C	A D	A E	A F	B A	B B	B C	B D	B E	B F
84	37	110	134	37	37	134	124	110	6	124	124

C A	C B	C C	C D	C E	C F	D A	D B	D C	D D	D E	D F
208	110	208	208	208	208	110	62	96	95	96	96

E A	E B	E C	E D	E E	E F	F A	F B	F C	F D	F E	F F
35	8	8	13	110	8	223	34	34	223	62	49

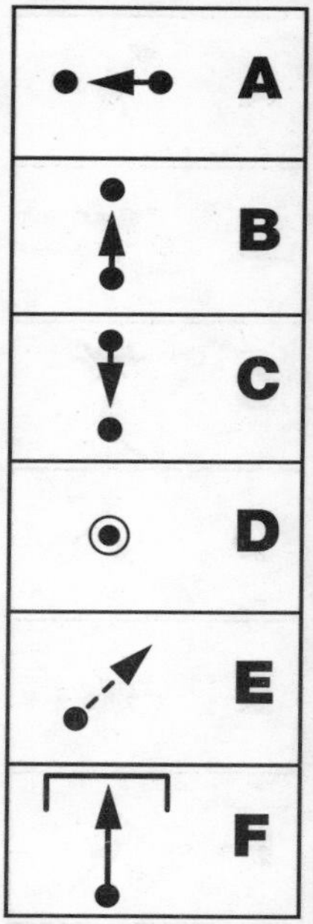

A
B
C
D
E
F

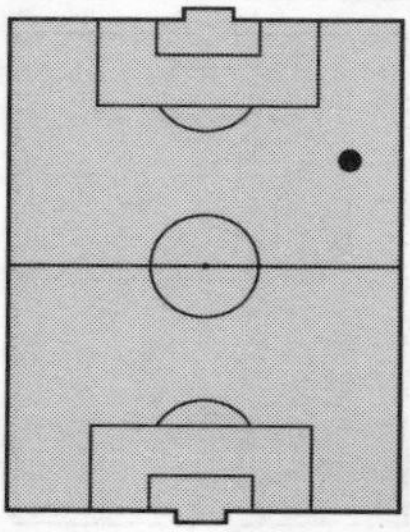

A A	A B	A C	A D	A E	A F	B A	B B	B C	B D	B E	B F
117	8	8	232	8	64	56	117	63	166	56	39

C A	C B	C C	C D	C E	C F	D A	D B	D C	D D	D E	D F
5	166	5	5	5	166	35	62	110	62	62	62

E A	E B	E C	E D	E E	E F	F A	F B	F C	F D	F E	F F
107	166	107	166	63	166	49	74	126	74	74	74

Laurencio

A A	A B	A C	A D	A E	A F	B A	B B	B C	B D	B E	B F
117	13	238	64	13	117	179	238	95	179	13	13

C A	C B	C C	C D	C E	C F	D A	D B	D C	D D	D E	D F
39	238	117	13	13	39	64	13	8	118	238	118

E A	E B	E C	E D	E E	E F	F A	F B	F C	F D	F E	F F
16	146	146	146	146	15	35	238	8	35	238	35

Fabien Deschamps 65

A A	A B	A C	A D	A E	A F	B A	B B	B C	B D	B E	B F
11	11	11	11	105	166	5	105	166	5	39	242

C A	C B	C C	C D	C E	C F	D A	D B	D C	D D	D E	D F
13	13	166	13	64	166	33	33	33	105	118	155

E A	E B	E C	E D	E E	E F	F A	F B	F C	F D	F E	F F
64	8	8	8	8	8	179	23	23	64	23	23

66 Helmut Bremen

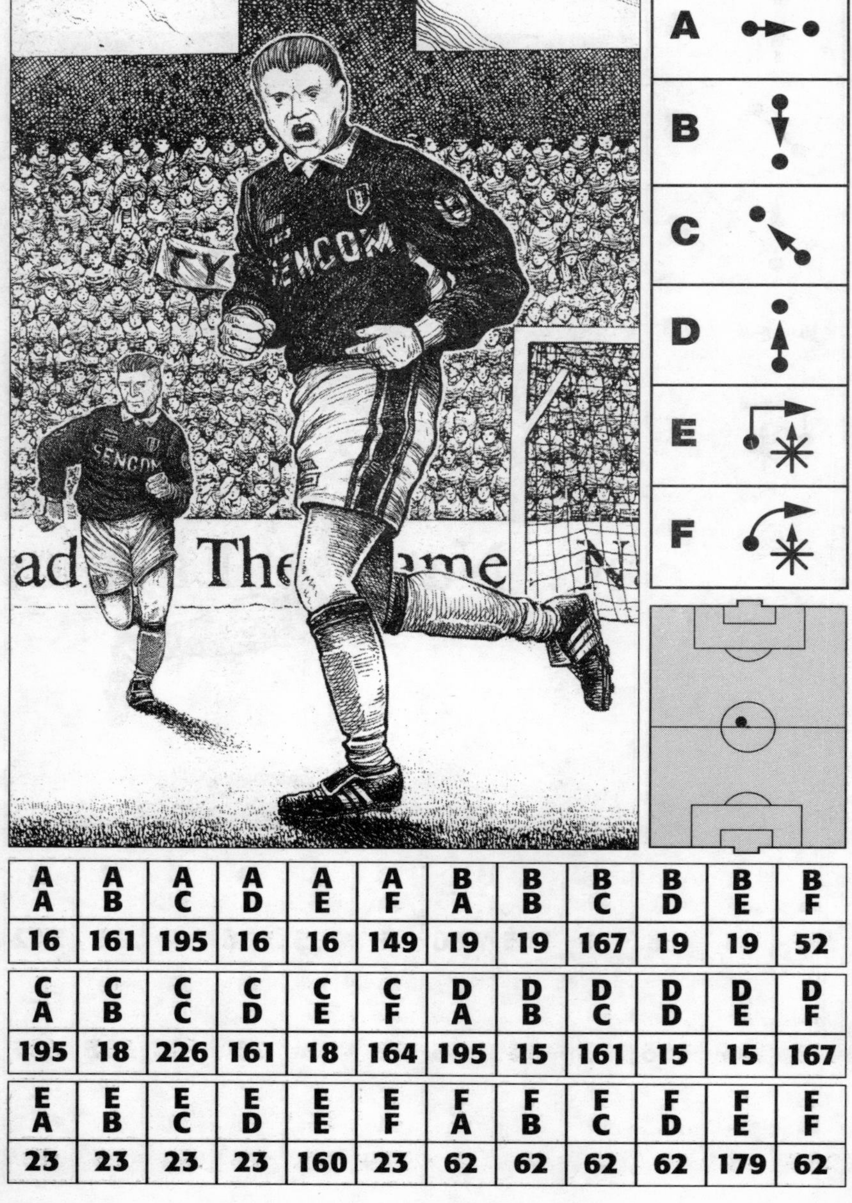

A A	A B	A C	A D	A E	A F	B A	B B	B C	B D	B E	B F
16	161	195	16	16	149	19	19	167	19	19	52

C A	C B	C C	C D	C E	C F	D A	D B	D C	D D	D E	D F
195	18	226	161	18	164	195	15	161	15	15	167

E A	E B	E C	E D	E E	E F	F A	F B	F C	F D	F E	F F
23	23	23	23	160	23	62	62	62	62	179	62

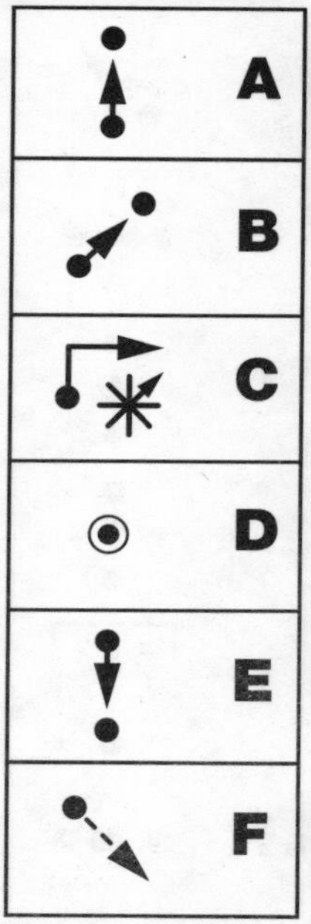

A

B

C

D

E

F

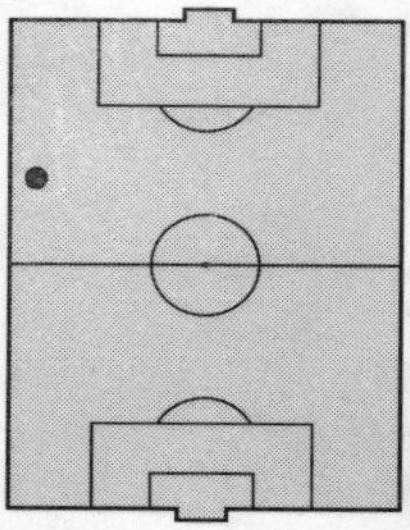

A A	A B	A C	A D	A E	A F	B A	B B	B C	B D	B E	B F
239	38	225	159	225	67	81	38	127	159	22	67

C A	C B	C C	C D	C E	C F	D A	D B	D C	D D	D E	D F
124	124	14	124	134	124	62	62	95	62	110	62

E A	E B	E C	E D	E E	E F	F A	F B	F C	F D	F E	F F
239	53	53	38	53	53	38	26	67	38	26	67

68 Laurencio

A A	A B	A C	A D	A E	A F	B A	B B	B C	B D	B E	B F
68	61	126	74	202	61	202	232	34	34	49	35

C A	C B	C C	C D	C E	C F	D A	D B	D C	D D	D E	D F
208	61	68	208	211	110	62	62	62	62	110	223

E A	E B	E C	E D	E E	E F	F A	F B	F C	F D	F E	F F
181	181	181	181	181	218	96	154	96	202	218	134

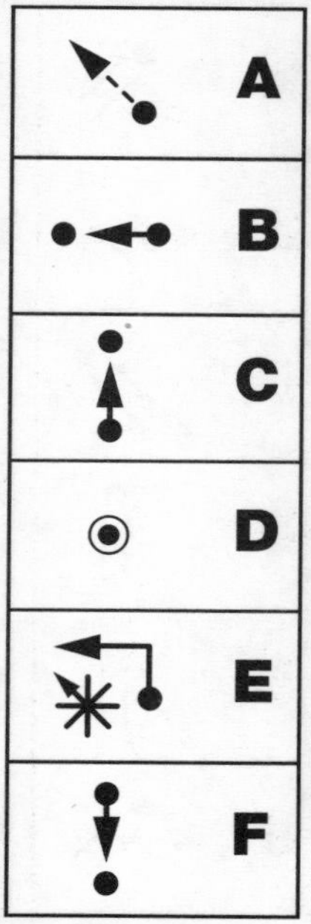

A

B

C

D

E

F

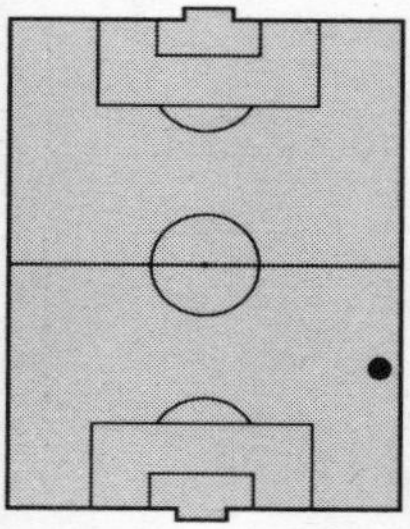

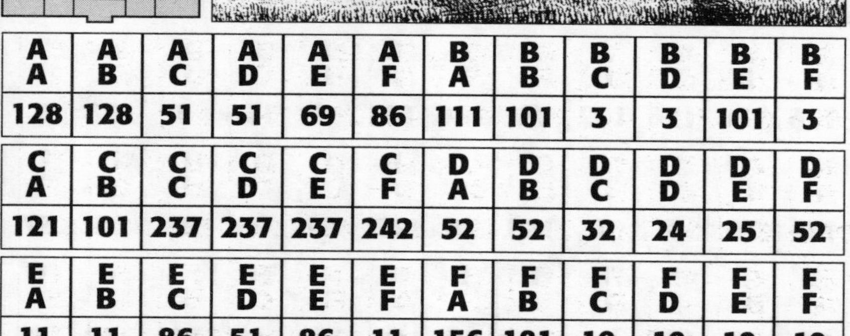

AA	AB	AC	AD	AE	AF	BA	BB	BC	BD	BE	BF
128	128	51	51	69	86	111	101	3	3	101	3

CA	CB	CC	CD	CE	CF	DA	DB	DC	DD	DE	DF
121	101	237	237	237	242	52	52	32	24	25	52

EA	EB	EC	ED	EE	EF	FA	FB	FC	FD	FE	FF
11	11	86	51	86	11	156	101	10	10	10	10

70 Aaron Hall / Throw-in

A A	A B	A C	A D	A E	A F	B A	B B	B C	B D	B E	B F
116	116	156	102	70	116	121	3	156	3	128	3

C A	C B	C C	C D	C E	C F	D A	D B	D C	D D	D E	D F
111	76	7	7	139	76	29	57	29	29	45	57

E A	E B	E C	E D	E E	E F	F A	F B	F C	F D	F E	F F
10	10	156	10	102	10	46	112	46	171	130	112

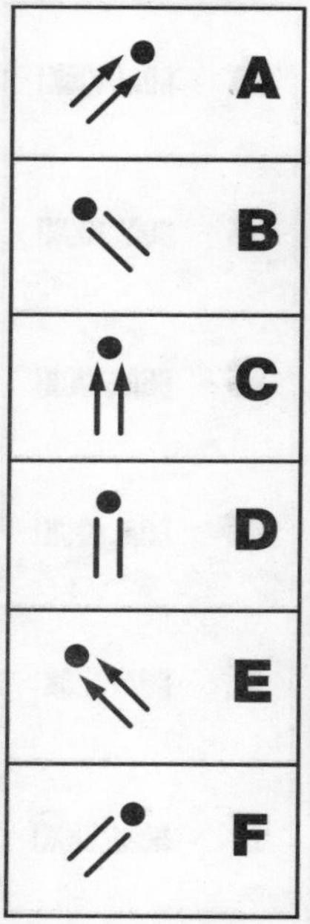

A

B

C

D

E

F

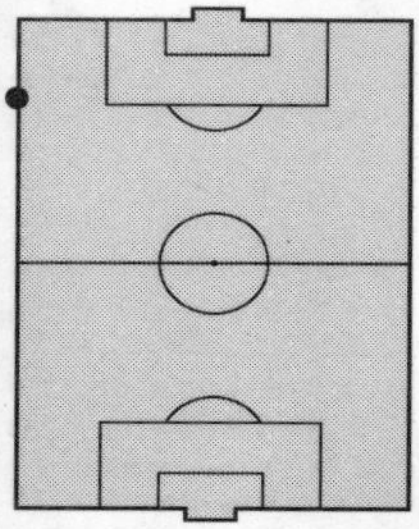

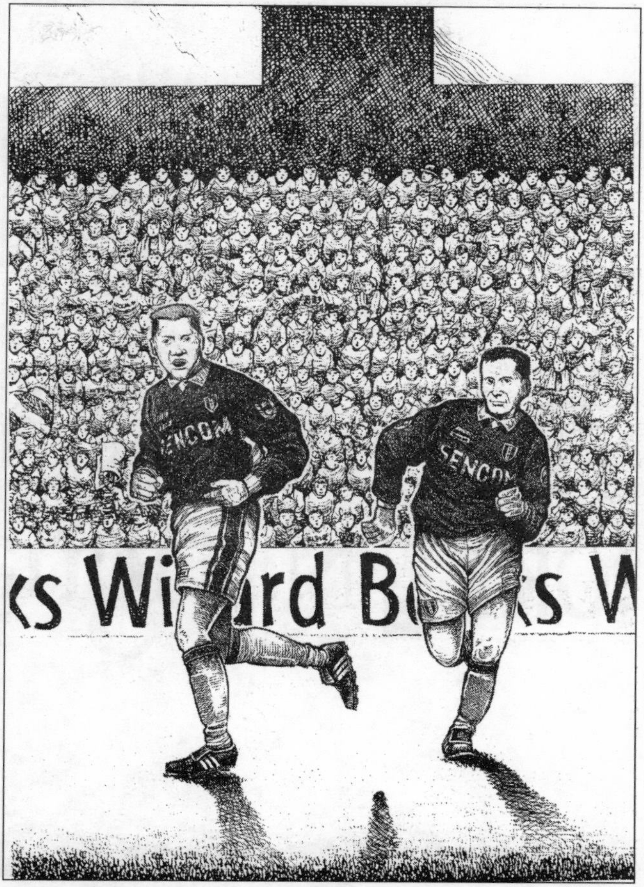

A A	A B	A C	A D	A E	A F	B A	B B	B C	B D	B E	B F
14	159	6	6	26	14	215	207	178	168	71	207

C A	C B	C C	C D	C E	C F	D A	D B	D C	D D	D E	D F
134	124	124	124	154	134	71	225	225	234	178	225

E A	E B	E C	E D	E E	E F	F A	F B	F C	F D	F E	F F
206	193	73	193	180	206	124	159	22	127	38	22

72 Goal Kick!

A A	A B	A C	A D	A E	A F	B A	B B	B C	B D	B E	B F
106	106	106	106	106	106	106	106	106	106	106	106

C A	C B	C C	C D	C E	C F	D A	D B	D C	D D	D E	D F
106	106	106	106	106	106	106	106	106	106	106	106

E A	E B	E C	E D	E E	E F	F A	F B	F C	F D	F E	F F
106	106	106	106	106	106	106	106	106	106	106	106

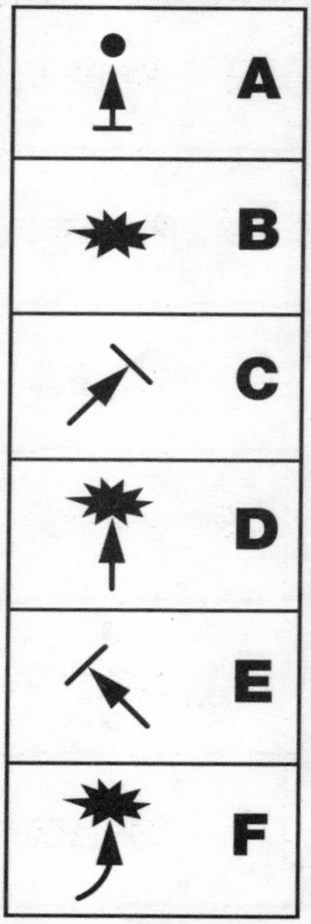

A

B

C

D

E

F

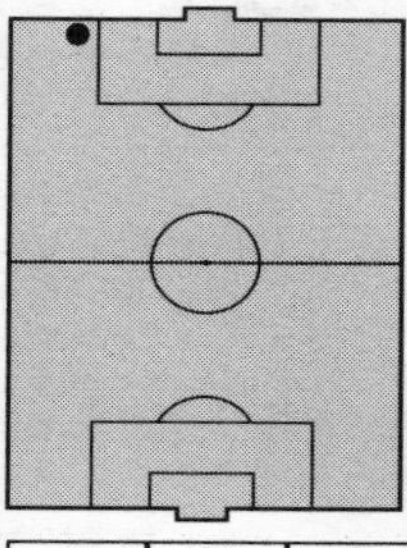

A A	A B	A C	A D	A E	A F	B A	B B	B C	B D	B E	B F
193	233	206	36	206	180	134	134	134	134	134	134

C A	C B	C C	C D	C E	C F	D A	D B	D C	D D	D E	D F
14	14	14	14	14	14	73	180	147	36	36	72

E A	E B	E C	E D	E E	E F	F A	F B	F C	F D	F E	F F
234	234	234	234	72	234	159	159	159	159	239	159

74 Matthew Scadding

A A	A B	A C	A D	A E	A F	B A	B B	B C	B D	B E	B F
231	148	135	61	227	135	126	208	211	202	208	208

C A	C B	C C	C D	C E	C F	D A	D B	D C	D D	D E	D F
208	85	148	68	50	180	126	194	135	74	148	135

E A	E B	E C	E D	E E	E F	F A	F B	F C	F D	F E	F F
148	194	194	199	148	194	135	148	211	135	180	148

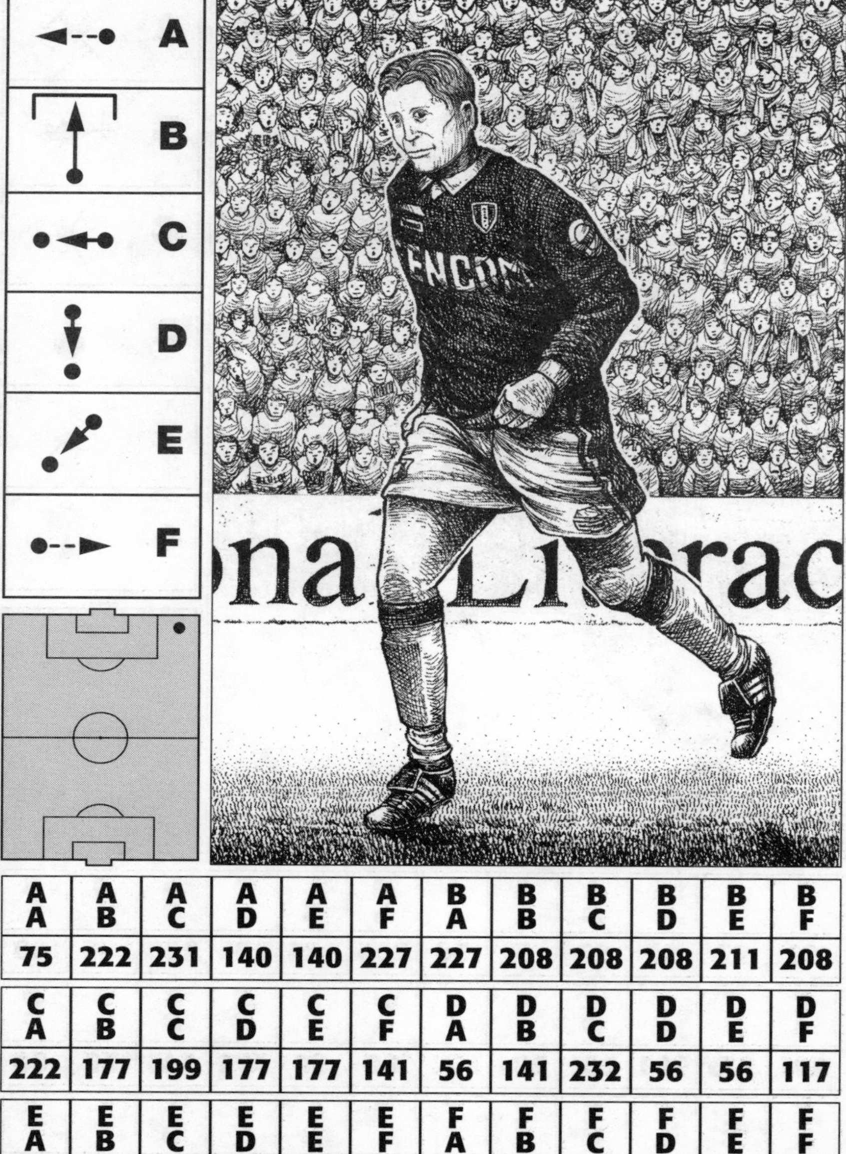

A A	A B	A C	A D	A E	A F	B A	B B	B C	B D	B E	B F
75	222	231	140	140	227	227	208	208	208	211	208

C A	C B	C C	C D	C E	C F	D A	D B	D C	D D	D E	D F
222	177	199	177	177	141	56	141	232	56	56	117

E A	E B	E C	E D	E E	E F	F A	F B	F C	F D	F E	F F
199	232	232	34	34	35	189	231	189	75	189	153

76 Henri Le Clerc

A

B

C

D

E

F

A A	A B	A C	A D	A E	A F	B A	B B	B C	B D	B E	B F
92	92	92	92	7	30	203	173	203	203	7	88

C A	C B	C C	C D	C E	C F	D A	D B	D C	D D	D E	D F
201	173	201	201	201	7	60	60	172	143	30	60

E A	E B	E C	E D	E E	E F	F A	F B	F C	F D	F E	F F
7	173	57	57	57	29	7	111	111	111	111	3

GOAL KICK!	A
GOAL KICK!	B
GOAL KICK!	C
GOAL KICK!	D
GOAL KICK!	E
GOAL KICK!	F

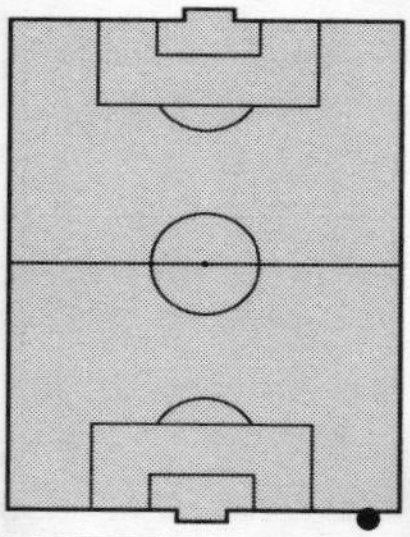

A A	A B	A C	A D	A E	A F	B A	B B	B C	B D	B E	B F
31	31	31	31	31	31	31	31	31	31	31	31

C A	C B	C C	C D	C E	C F	D A	D B	D C	D D	D E	D F
31	31	31	31	31	31	31	31	31	31	31	31

E A	E B	E C	E D	E E	E F	F A	F B	F C	F D	F E	F F
31	31	31	31	31	31	31	31	31	31	31	31

78 Pierre Pasqualle

A	A	A	A	A	A	B	B	B	B	B	B
A	B	C	D	E	F	A	B	C	D	E	F
78	91	78	9	9	221	100	221	28	28	28	28

C	C	C	C	C	C	D	D	D	D	D	D
A	B	C	D	E	F	A	B	C	D	E	F
21	137	21	100	21	21	90	152	151	90	90	100

E	E	E	E	E	E	F	F	F	F	F	F
A	B	C	D	E	F	A	B	C	D	E	F
174	12	12	12	151	12	132	175	132	132	132	152

- A
- B
- C
- D
- E
- F

A A	A B	A C	A D	A E	A F	B A	B B	B C	B D	B E	B F
200	183	200	200	200	79	113	78	113	99	113	103

C A	C B	C C	C D	C E	C F	D A	D B	D C	D D	D E	D F
221	183	221	221	221	183	58	212	79	89	89	175

E A	E B	E C	E D	E E	E F	F A	F B	F C	F D	F E	F F
157	144	99	162	162	212	184	184	58	184	144	184

80 Brett Green

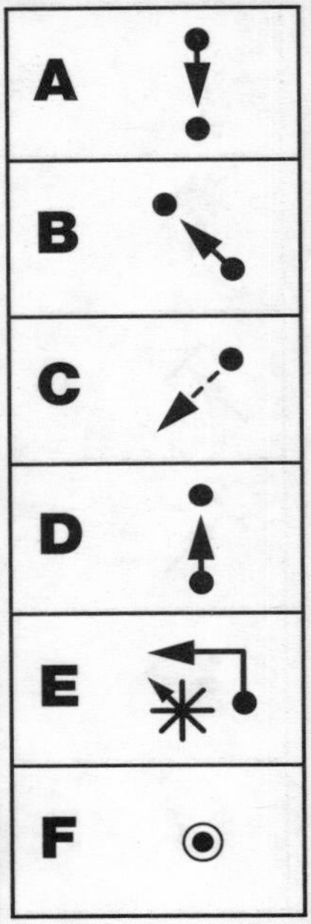

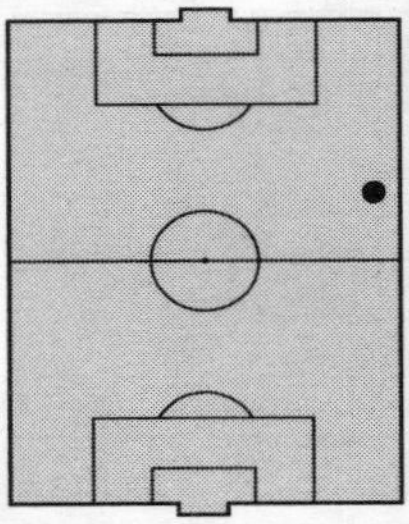

A

B

C

D

E

F

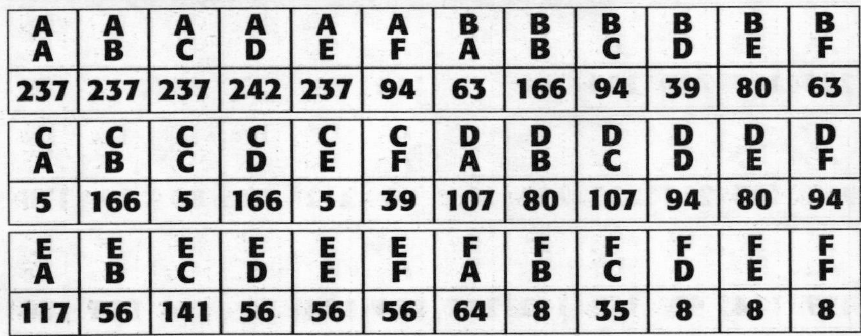

AA	AB	AC	AD	AE	AF	BA	BB	BC	BD	BE	BF
237	237	237	242	237	94	63	166	94	39	80	63

CA	CB	CC	CD	CE	CF	DA	DB	DC	DD	DE	DF
5	166	5	166	5	39	107	80	107	94	80	94

EA	EB	EC	ED	EE	EF	FA	FB	FC	FD	FE	FF
117	56	141	56	56	56	64	8	35	8	8	8

Throw-in / Dave Chell 81

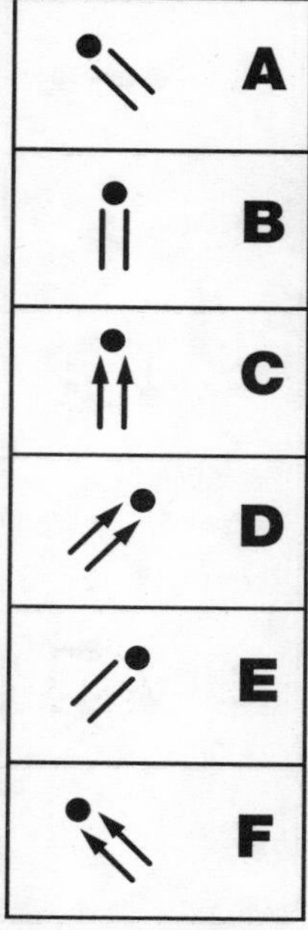

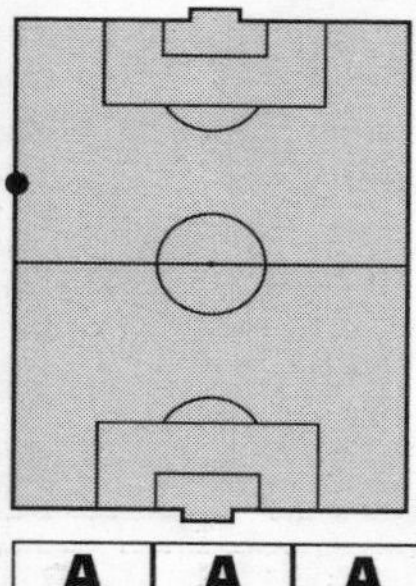

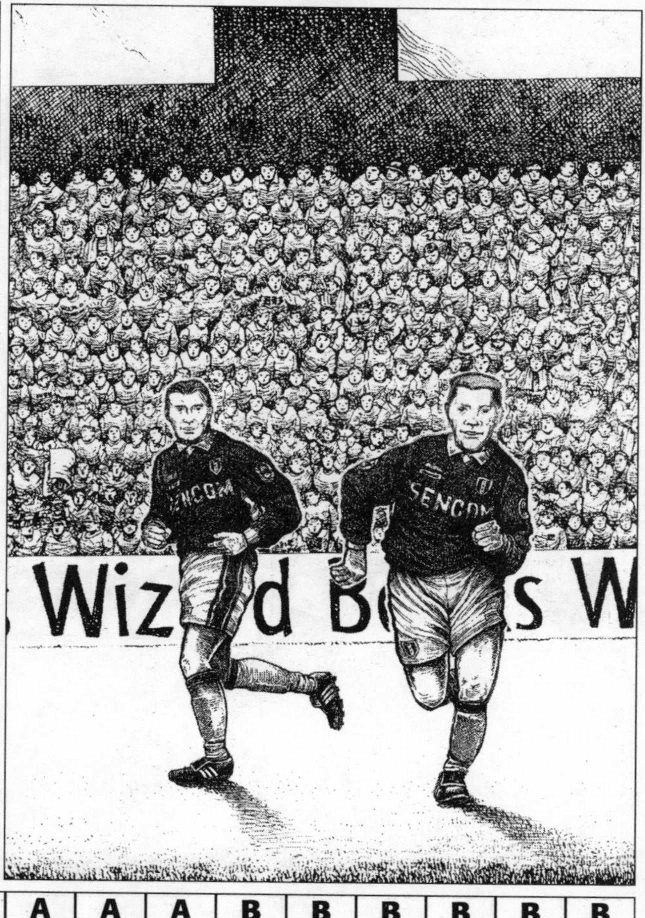

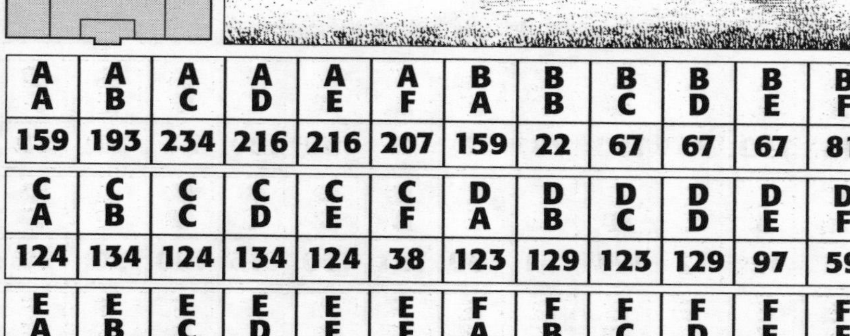

A A	A B	A C	A D	A E	A F	B A	B B	B C	B D	B E	B F
159	193	234	216	216	207	159	22	67	67	67	81

C A	C B	C C	C D	C E	C F	D A	D B	D C	D D	D E	D F
124	134	124	134	124	38	123	129	123	129	97	59

E A	E B	E C	E D	E E	E F	F A	F B	F C	F D	F E	F F
159	123	26	26	158	67	37	84	224	84	37	154

82 Fabien Deschamps

A A	A B	A C	A D	A E	A F	B A	B B	B C	B D	B E	B F
78	150	79	100	78	78	41	150	120	21	21	21

C A	C B	C C	C D	C E	C F	D A	D B	D C	D D	D E	D F
12	12	12	174	151	150	151	150	115	100	90	90

E A	E B	E C	E D	E E	E F	F A	F B	F C	F D	F E	F F
18	18	18	164	226	18	47	152	137	47	47	47

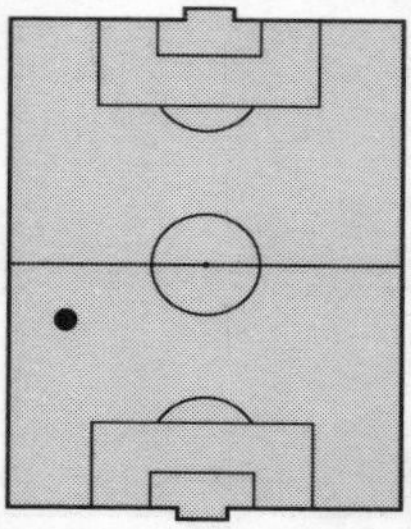

Ross Hewitt 83

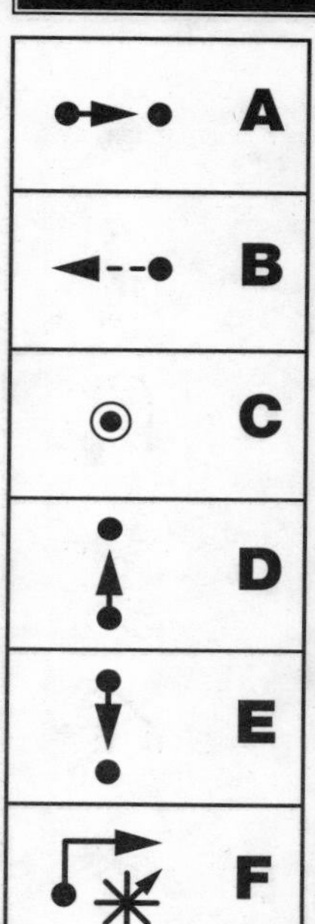

A A	A B	A C	A D	A E	A F	B A	B B	B C	B D	B E	B F
12	174	12	104	12	12	41	152	21	152	21	108

C A	C B	C C	C D	C E	C F	D A	D B	D C	D D	D E	D F
15	15	164	15	160	15	83	151	59	108	97	59

E A	E B	E C	E D	E E	E F	F A	F B	F C	F D	F E	F F
90	152	90	152	90	90	18	18	104	18	226	18

84 Dave Chell

A A	A B	A C	A D	A E	A F	B A	B B	B C	B D	B E	B F
110	37	110	68	110	37	23	62	48	179	179	179

C A	C B	C C	C D	C E	C F	D A	D B	D C	D D	D E	D F
224	224	224	233	84	37	218	84	218	236	218	37

E A	E B	E C	E D	E E	E F	F A	F B	F C	F D	F E	F F
134	134	134	193	134	37	206	206	206	180	206	233

A

B

C

D

E

F

A A	A B	A C	A D	A E	A F	B A	B B	B C	B D	B E	B F
160	48	160	160	160	160	95	62	95	208	95	240

C A	C B	C C	C D	C E	C F	D A	D B	D C	D D	D E	D F
50	134	84	50	84	240	37	224	127	127	127	127

E A	E B	E C	E D	E E	E F	F A	F B	F C	F D	F E	F F
117	5	34	117	117	117	49	177	74	68	49	240

86 Terry Hiner

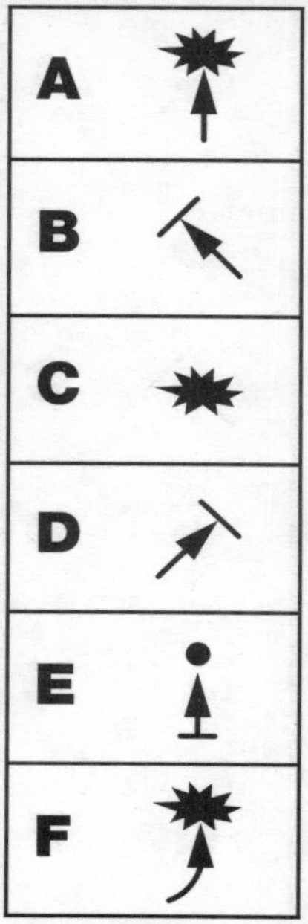

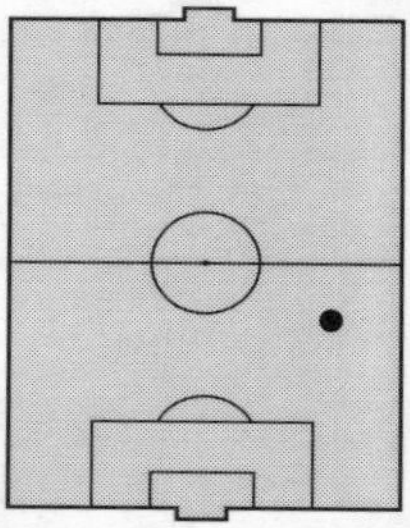

A

B

C

D

E

F

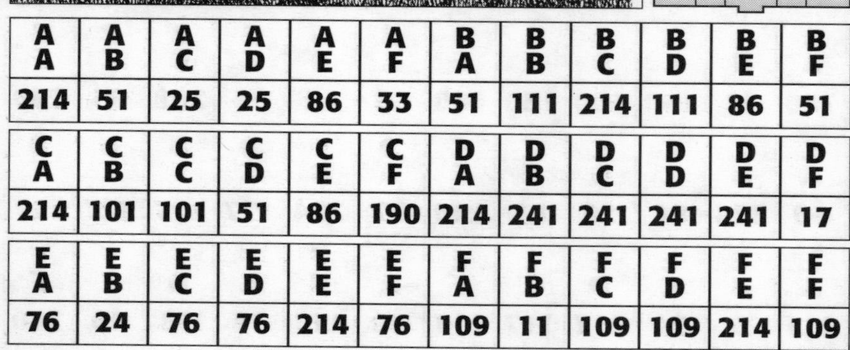

A A	A B	A C	A D	A E	A F	B A	B B	B C	B D	B E	B F
214	51	25	25	86	33	51	111	214	111	86	51

C A	C B	C C	C D	C E	C F	D A	D B	D C	D D	D E	D F
214	101	101	51	86	190	214	241	241	241	241	17

E A	E B	E C	E D	E E	E F	F A	F B	F C	F D	F E	F F
76	24	76	76	214	76	109	11	109	109	214	109

A A	A B	A C	A D	A E	A F	B A	B B	B C	B D	B E	B F
52	52	52	52	187	187	66	87	66	161	195	195

C A	C B	C C	C D	C E	C F	D A	D B	D C	D D	D E	D F
19	93	19	19	93	146	155	16	16	155	93	167

E A	E B	E C	E D	E E	E F	F A	F B	F C	F D	F E	F F
33	33	93	118	93	149	133	133	93	133	93	25

88 Henri Le Clerc

A A	A B	A C	A D	A E	A F	B A	B B	B C	B D	B E	B F
139	172	88	88	139	139	203	203	192	192	186	89

C A	C B	C C	C D	C E	C F	D A	D B	D C	D D	D E	D F
11	11	11	32	11	11	203	7	76	203	139	201

E A	E B	E C	E D	E E	E F	F A	F B	F C	F D	F E	F F
203	30	92	30	186	144	28	28	28	28	28	28

A A	A B	A C	A D	A E	A F	B A	B B	B C	B D	B E	B F
103	143	119	212	175	119	58	184	144	192	184	184

C A	C B	C C	C D	C E	C F	D A	D B	D C	D D	D E	D F
184	131	143	197	60	130	58	162	119	89	143	119

E A	E B	E C	E D	E E	E F	F A	F B	F C	F D	F E	F F
143	162	162	99	143	162	119	143	144	119	130	143

90 Fabien Deschamps

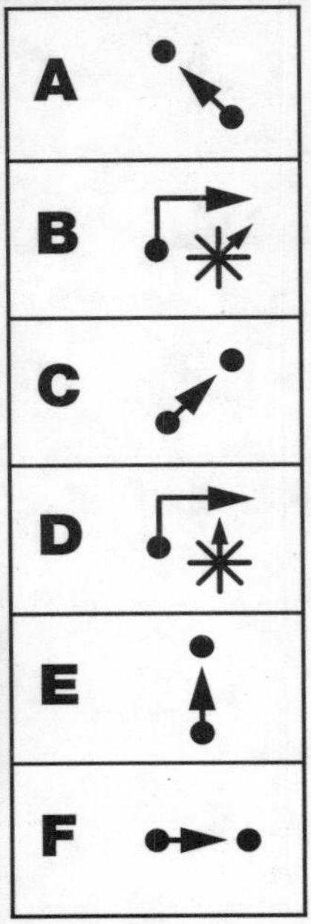

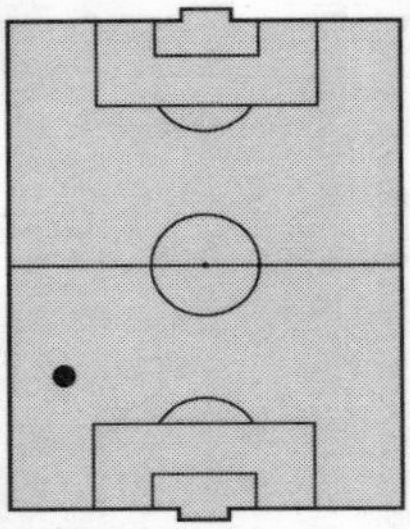

A

B

C

D

E

F

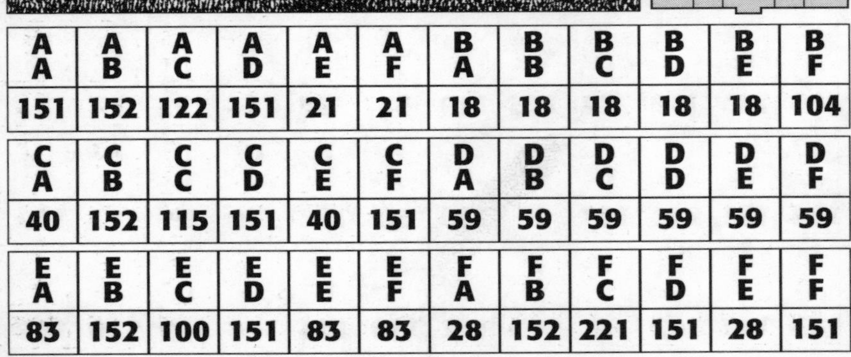

A A	A B	A C	A D	A E	A F	B A	B B	B C	B D	B E	B F
151	152	122	151	21	21	18	18	18	18	18	104

C A	C B	C C	C D	C E	C F	D A	D B	D C	D D	D E	D F
40	152	115	151	40	151	59	59	59	59	59	59

E A	E B	E C	E D	E E	E F	F A	F B	F C	F D	F E	F F
83	152	100	151	83	83	28	152	221	151	28	151

A	A	A	A	A	A	B	B	B	B	B	B
A	B	C	D	E	F	A	B	C	D	E	F
123	6	123	123	129	123	146	87	52	52	146	52

C	C	C	C	C	C	D	D	D	D	D	D
A	B	C	D	E	F	A	B	C	D	E	F
125	109	174	20	125	20	83	174	151	41	108	83

E	E	E	E	E	E	F	F	F	F	F	F
A	B	C	D	E	F	A	B	C	D	E	F
78	78	78	221	78	9	221	30	30	30	30	192

92 Fabien Deschamps

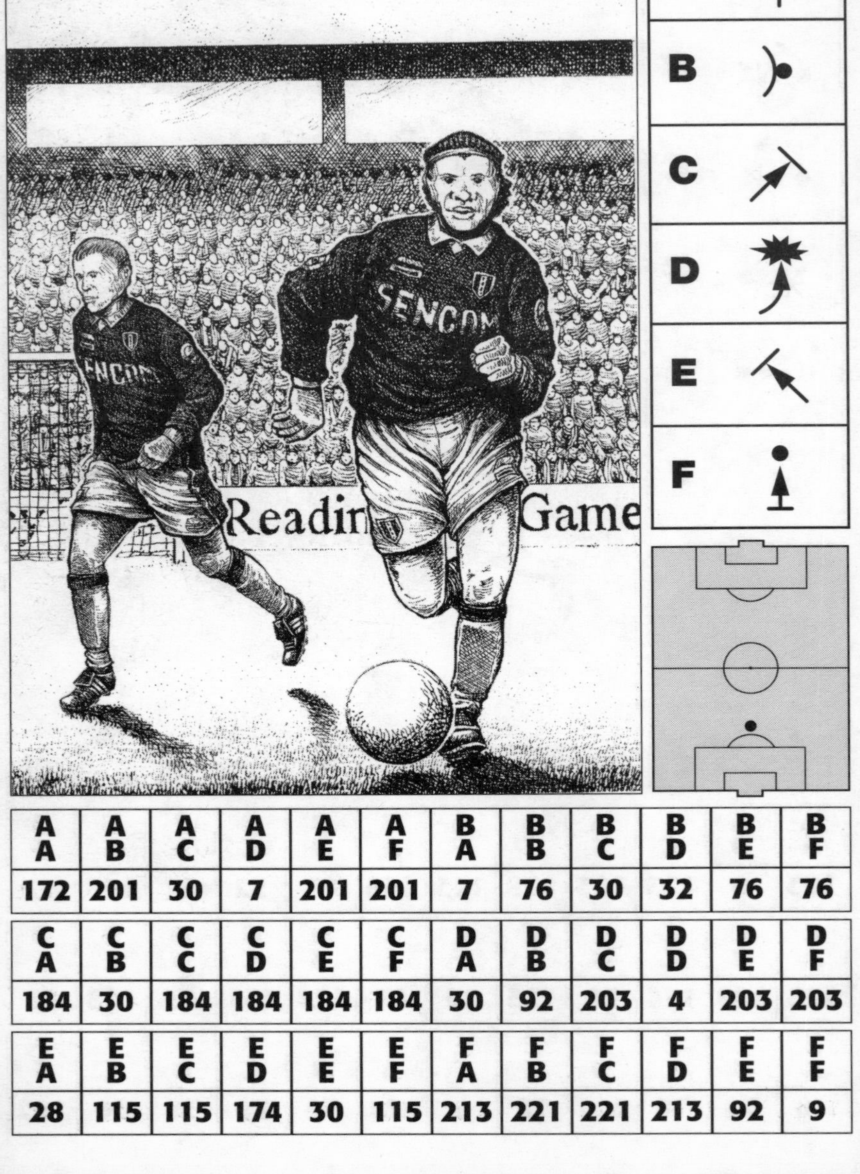

A A	A B	A C	A D	A E	A F	B A	B B	B C	B D	B E	B F
172	201	30	7	201	201	7	76	30	32	76	76

C A	C B	C C	C D	C E	C F	D A	D B	D C	D D	D E	D F
184	30	184	184	184	184	30	92	203	4	203	203

E A	E B	E C	E D	E E	E F	F A	F B	F C	F D	F E	F F
28	115	115	174	30	115	213	221	221	213	92	9

Helmut Bremen 93

A A	A B	A C	A D	A E	A F	B A	B B	B C	B D	B E	B F
167	87	196	167	167	18	155	155	16	155	155	160

C A	C B	C C	C D	C E	C F	D A	D B	D C	D D	D E	D F
196	149	133	87	149	33	196	146	87	146	146	16

E A	E B	E C	E D	E E	E F	F A	F B	F C	F D	F E	F F
109	109	109	109	52	109	92	92	92	92	20	92

94 Brett Green

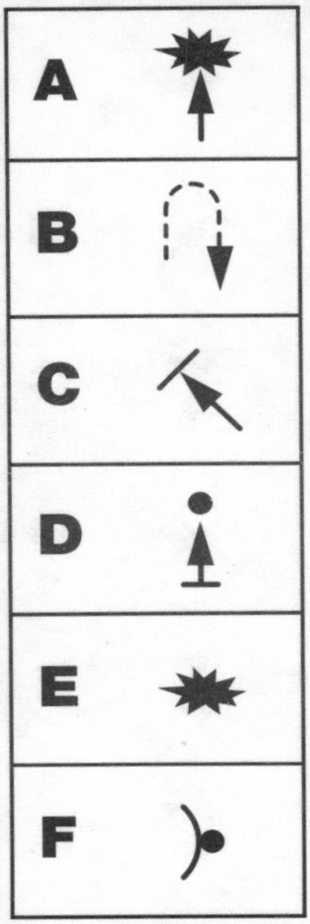

A	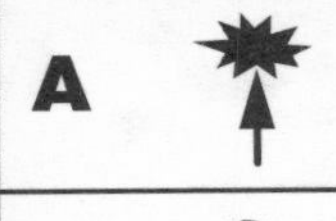
B	
C	
D	
E	
F	

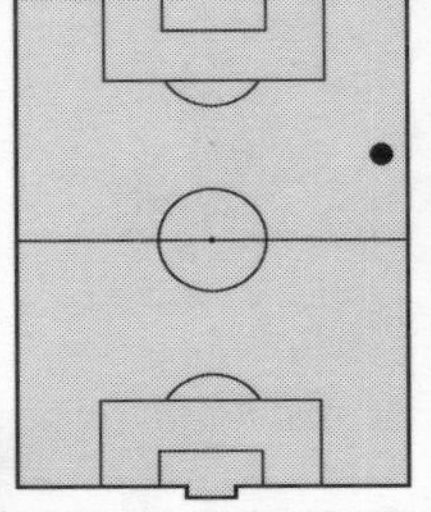

A A	A B	A C	A D	A E	A F	B A	B B	B C	B D	B E	B F
80	5	94	80	238	39	63	117	80	94	117	117

C A	C B	C C	C D	C E	C F	D A	D B	D C	D D	D E	D F
238	136	136	136	136	136	80	237	242	94	238	80

E A	E B	E C	E D	E E	E F	F A	F B	F C	F D	F E	F F
111	111	111	111	238	80	32	32	5	32	238	117

A A	A B	A C	A D	A E	A F	B A	B B	B C	B D	B E	B F
14	14	14	95	23	95	110	110	110	110	236	236

C A	C B	C C	C D	C E	C F	D A	D B	D C	D D	D E	D F
179	23	179	179	95	179	23	95	64	64	64	236

E A	E B	E C	E D	E E	E F	F A	F B	F C	F D	F E	F F
48	23	8	118	236	236	226	23	124	6	236	236

96 Dave Chell

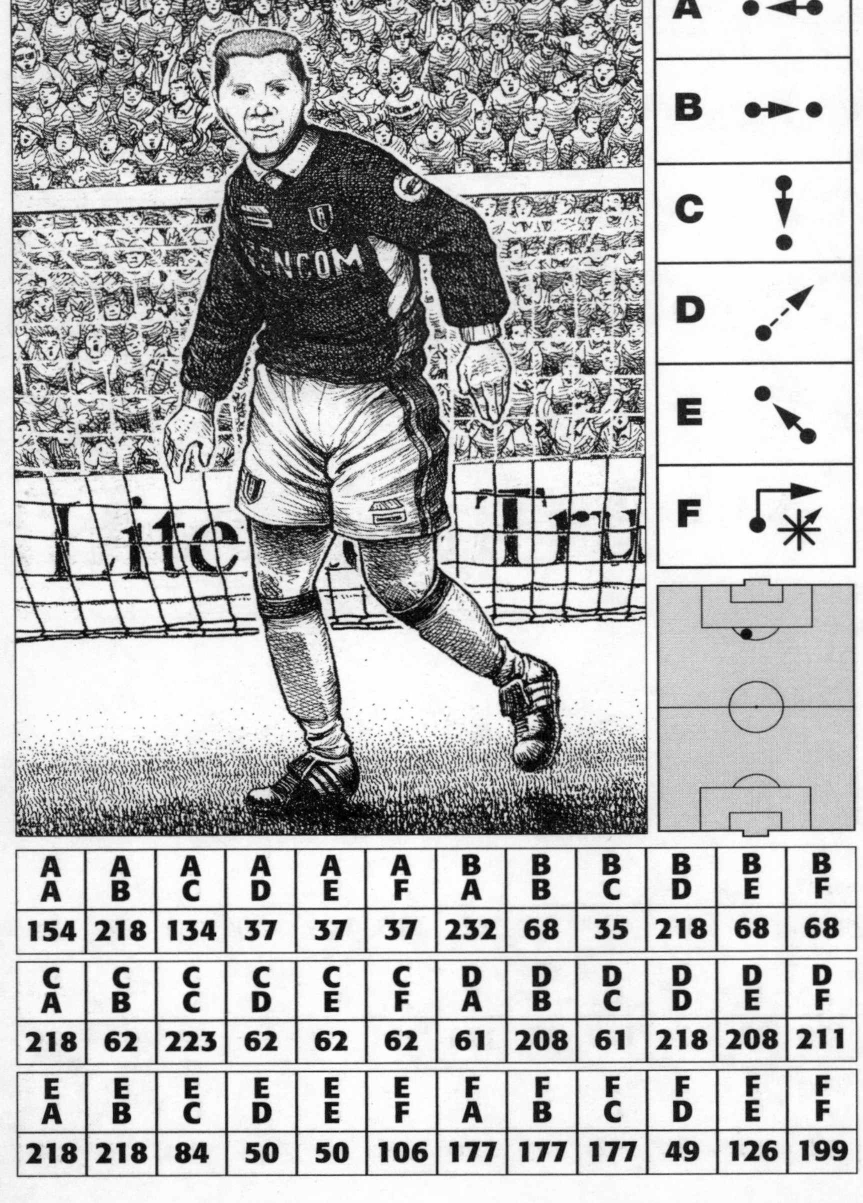

A A	A B	A C	A D	A E	A F	B A	B B	B C	B D	B E	B F
154	218	134	37	37	37	232	68	35	218	68	68

C A	C B	C C	C D	C E	C F	D A	D B	D C	D D	D E	D F
218	62	223	62	62	62	61	208	61	218	208	211

E A	E B	E C	E D	E E	E F	F A	F B	F C	F D	F E	F F
218	218	84	50	50	106	177	177	177	49	126	199

Fabien Deschamps 97

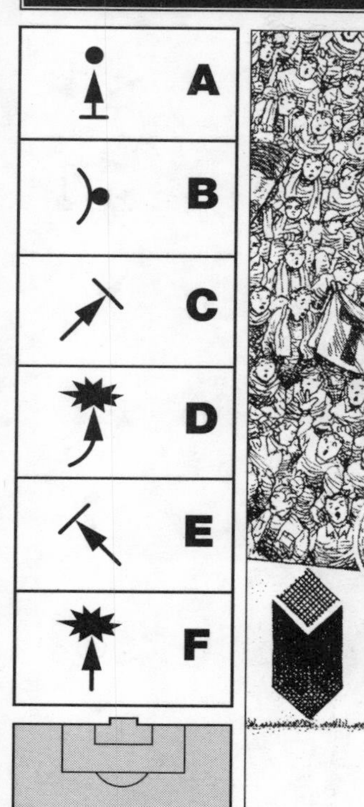

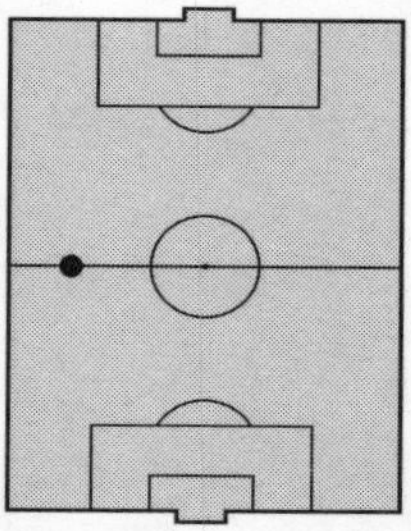

A A	A B	A C	A D	A E	A F	B A	B B	B C	B D	B E	B F
109	109	104	44	109	44	42	42	42	26	42	44

C A	C B	C C	C D	C E	C F	D A	D B	D C	D D	D E	D F
97	104	59	129	104	123	59	158	158	239	97	59

E A	E B	E C	E D	E E	E F	F A	F B	F C	F D	F E	F F
97	108	108	42	122	59	115	59	12	44	115	44

98 Aaron Hall

A

B

C

D

E

F

A A	A B	A C	A D	A E	A F	B A	B B	B C	B D	B E	B F
24	57	3	3	3	111	4	172	7	7	7	76

C A	C B	C C	C D	C E	C F	D A	D B	D C	D D	D E	D F
45	98	130	130	77	230	70	10	10	10	10	156

E A	E B	E C	E D	E E	E F	F A	F B	F C	F D	F E	F F
116	116	77	102	230	219	25	24	11	11	11	25

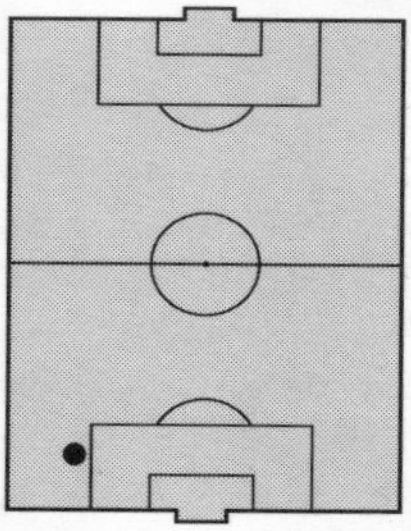

Ross Hewitt 99

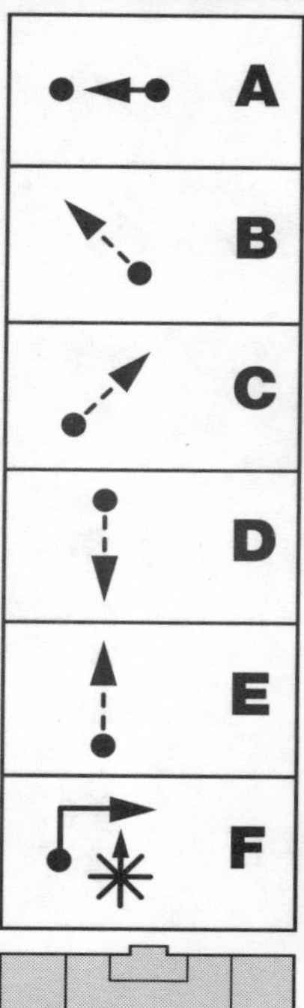

A A	A B	A C	A D	A E	A F	B A	B B	B C	B D	B E	B F
91	79	103	132	175	132	79	91	99	78	91	79

C A	C B	C C	C D	C E	C F	D A	D B	D C	D D	D E	D F
79	91	192	79	186	79	91	79	191	191	175	191

E A	E B	E C	E D	E E	E F	F A	F B	F C	F D	F E	F F
91	221	9	9	91	79	145	145	145	145	145	99

100 Pierre Pasqualle

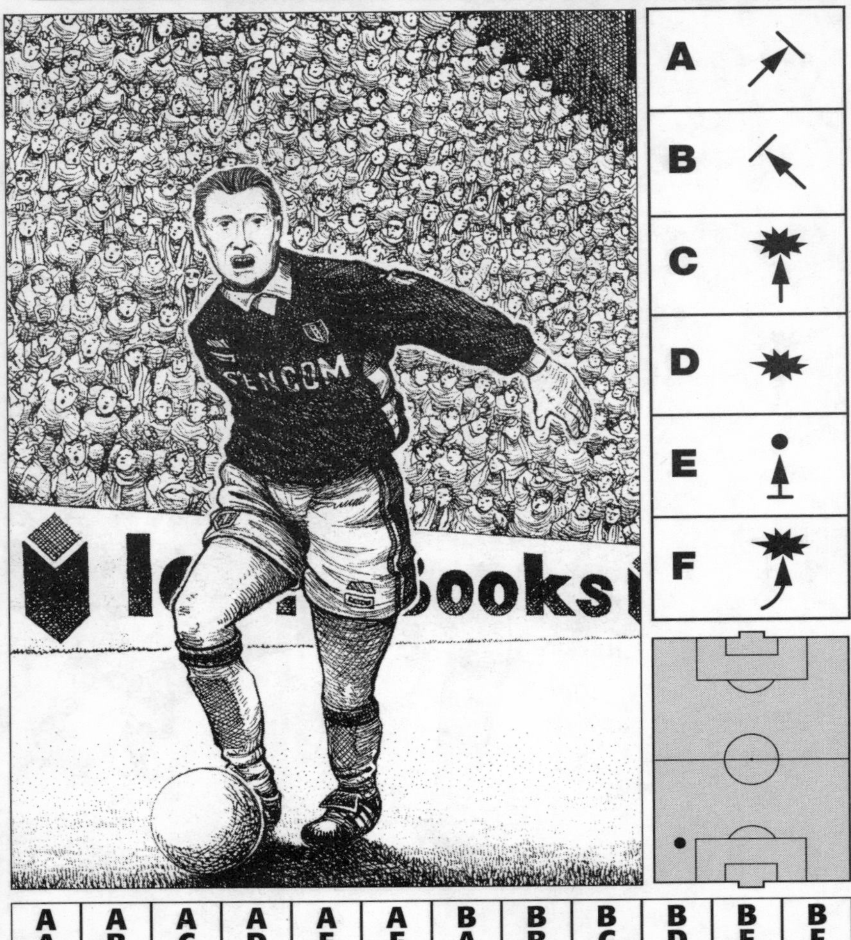

A A	A B	A C	A D	A E	A F	B A	B B	B C	B D	B E	B F
9	184	184	184	144	184	113	113	78	183	100	90

C A	C B	C C	C D	C E	C F	D A	D B	D C	D D	D E	D F
120	78	47	183	100	82	100	221	183	9	9	183

E A	E B	E C	E D	E E	E F	F A	F B	F C	F D	F E	F F
78	79	99	183	100	9	151	151	183	151	151	90

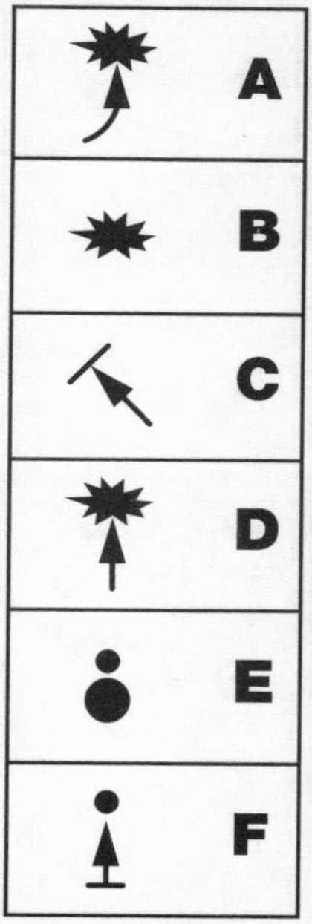

A

B

C

D

E

F

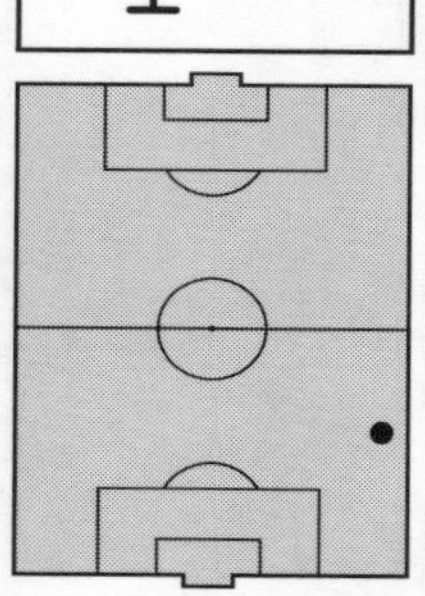

A A	A B	A C	A D	A E	A F	B A	B B	B C	B D	B E	B F
121	214	156	69	156	101	190	214	3	69	111	101

C A	C B	C C	C D	C E	C F	D A	D B	D C	D D	D E	D F
76	76	24	76	7	76	92	92	4	92	30	92

E A	E B	E C	E D	E E	E F	F A	F B	F C	F D	F E	F F
121	242	242	214	242	242	214	86	101	214	86	101

102 Brett Green / Throw-in

A A	A B	A C	A D	A E	A F	B A	B B	B C	B D	B E	B F
24	69	32	32	86	24	171	219	70	116	102	219

C A	C B	C C	C D	C E	C F	D A	D B	D C	D D	D E	D F
7	76	76	76	173	7	102	156	156	10	70	156

E A	E B	E C	E D	E E	E F	F A	F B	F C	F D	F E	F F
46	112	163	112	130	46	76	69	111	3	214	111

GOAL KICK!	A
GOAL KICK!	B
GOAL KICK!	C
GOAL KICK!	D
GOAL KICK!	E
GOAL KICK!	F

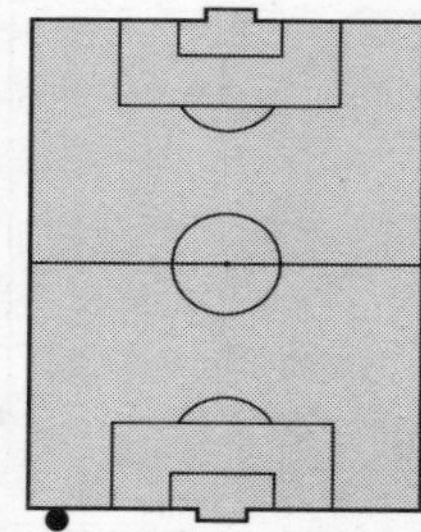

A A	A B	A C	A D	A E	A F	B A	B B	B C	B D	B E	B F
58	58	58	58	58	58	58	58	58	58	58	58

C A	C B	C C	C D	C E	C F	D A	D B	D C	D D	D E	D F
58	58	58	58	58	58	58	58	58	58	58	58

E A	E B	E C	E D	E E	E F	F A	F B	F C	F D	F E	F F
58	58	58	58	58	58	58	58	58	58	58	58

104 Aaron Hall

A A	A B	A C	A D	A E	A F	B A	B B	B C	B D	B E	B F
129	129	129	129	12	44	108	12	44	108	83	53

C A	C B	C C	C D	C E	C F	D A	D B	D C	D D	D E	D F
174	174	44	174	40	44	164	164	164	12	145	19

E A	E B	E C	E D	E E	E F	F A	F B	F C	F D	F E	F F
40	115	115	115	115	115	20	109	109	40	109	109

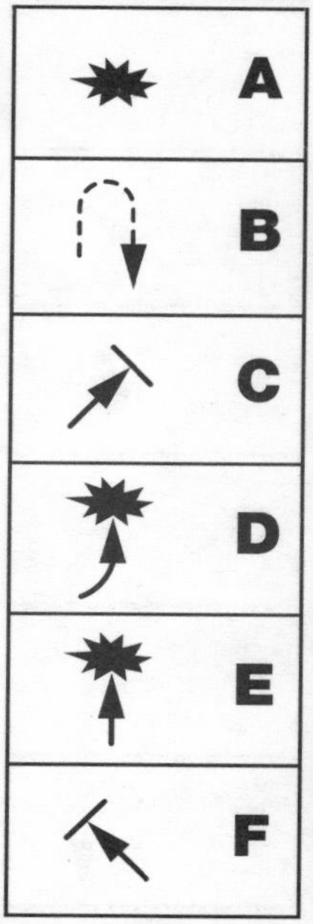

A

B

C

D

E

F

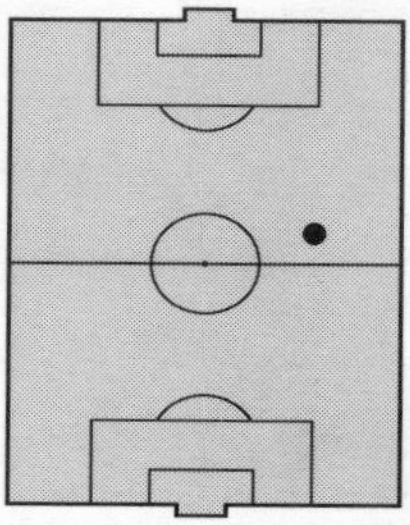

A A	A B	A C	A D	A E	A F	B A	B B	B C	B D	B E	B F
64	64	64	235	64	64	241	11	65	39	241	241

C A	C B	C C	C D	C E	C F	D A	D B	D C	D D	D E	D F
118	118	118	160	118	65	65	11	25	235	65	25

E A	E B	E C	E D	E E	E F	F A	F B	F C	F D	F E	F F
149	133	149	118	149	65	92	92	92	92	235	33

106 Matthew Scadding

A A	A B	A C	A D	A E	A F	B A	B B	B C	B D	B E	B F
129	129	6	129	129	123	105	105	13	105	105	65

C A	C B	C C	C D	C E	C F	D A	D B	D C	D D	D E	D F
37	14	134	224	240	6	34	96	35	64	240	13

E A	E B	E C	E D	E E	E F	F A	F B	F C	F D	F E	F F
160	160	48	160	160	15	84	84	84	50	233	84

A

B

C

D

E

F

A A	A B	A C	A D	A E	A F	B A	B B	B C	B D	B E	B F
166	107	107	166	63	166	35	56	136	107	56	136

C A	C B	C C	C D	C E	C F	D A	D B	D C	D D	D E	D F
232	136	222	141	75	227	182	80	80	166	80	182

E A	E B	E C	E D	E E	E F	F A	F B	F C	F D	F E	F F
94	217	198	153	198	136	177	177	49	177	141	177

108 Ross Hewitt

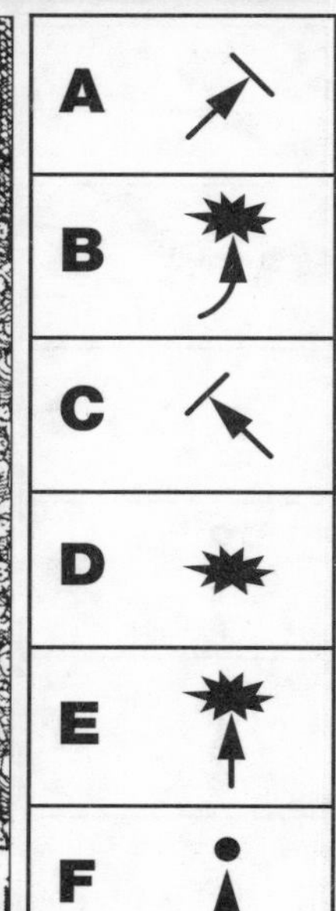

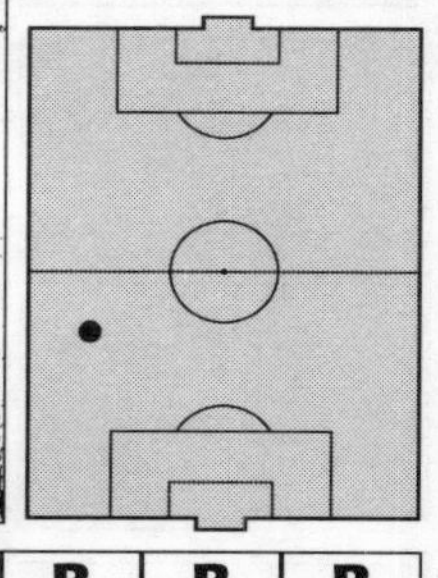

A A	A B	A C	A D	A E	A F	B A	B B	B C	B D	B E	B F
83	12	174	108	104	108	83	104	104	104	104	108

C A	C B	C C	C D	C E	C F	D A	D B	D C	D D	D E	D F
97	44	97	97	44	97	41	158	83	108	158	108

E A	E B	E C	E D	E E	E F	F A	F B	F C	F D	F E	F F
151	44	151	44	83	108	104	44	92	92	44	92

A

B

C

D

E

F

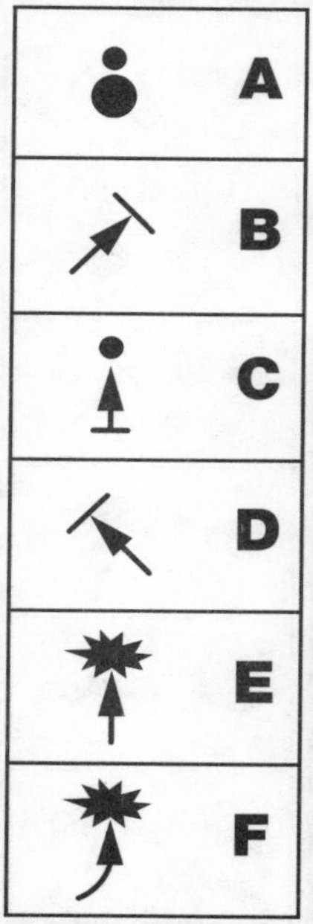

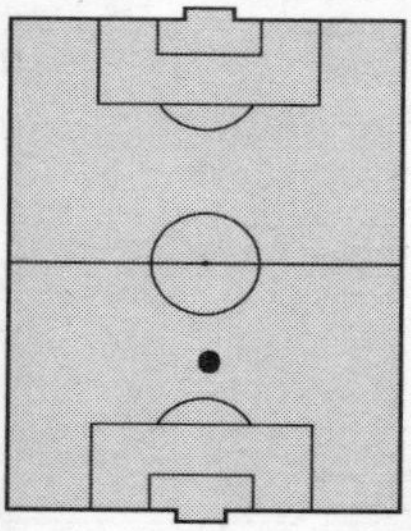

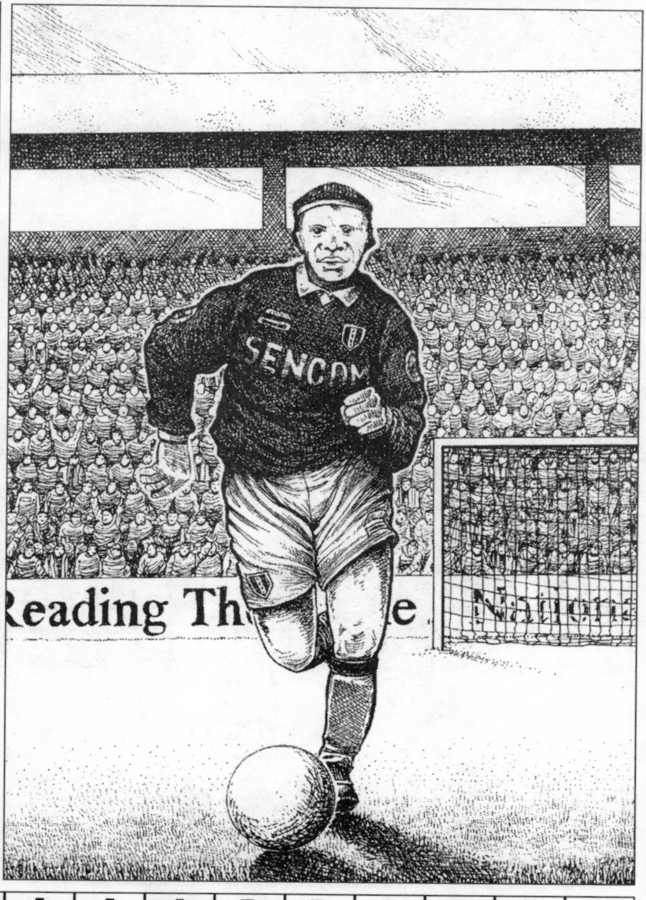

A A	A B	A C	A D	A E	A F	B A	B B	B C	B D	B E	B F
115	115	115	4	4	174	76	4	76	76	4	32

C A	C B	C C	C D	C E	C F	D A	D B	D C	D D	D E	D F
125	125	125	125	213	20	92	92	92	92	4	109

E A	E B	E C	E D	E E	E F	F A	F B	F C	F D	F E	F F
32	109	4	32	214	213	4	221	221	40	221	213

110 Laurencio

A A	A B	A C	A D	A E	A F	B A	B B	B C	B D	B E	B F
160	62	160	236	160	160	134	134	62	124	236	84

C A	C B	C C	C D	C E	C F	D A	D B	D C	D D	D E	D F
202	202	202	62	236	68	95	95	95	62	62	96

E A	E B	E C	E D	E E	E F	F A	F B	F C	F D	F E	F F
62	35	35	8	236	49	179	23	179	236	236	236

A

B

C

D

E

F

A A	A B	A C	A D	A E	A F	B A	B B	B C	B D	B E	B F
3	32	76	76	76	214	86	51	86	86	86	214

C A	C B	C C	C D	C E	C F	D A	D B	D C	D D	D E	D F
156	101	156	3	156	214	101	190	101	3	101	214

E A	E B	E C	E D	E E	E F	F A	F B	F C	F D	F E	F F
3	76	201	201	201	214	57	214	57	57	57	3

112 Henri Le Clerc

A

B

C

D

E

F

A A	A B	A C	A D	A E	A F	B A	B B	B C	B D	B E	B F
212	212	112	228	46	143	173	172	185	185	46	185

C A	C B	C C	C D	C E	C F	D A	D B	D C	D D	D E	D F
170	170	143	170	170	143	212	88	46	60	46	60

E A	E B	E C	E D	E E	E F	F A	F B	F C	F D	F E	F F
173	173	201	201	173	201	171	116	171	46	46	171

Fabien Deschamps 113

A A	A B	A C	A D	A E	A F	B A	B B	B C	B D	B E	B F
113	132	103	200	200	175	175	184	184	184	144	184

C A	C B	C C	C D	C E	C F	D A	D B	D C	D D	D E	D F
132	79	99	79	79	78	100	78	183	100	100	90

E A	E B	E C	E D	E E	E F	F A	F B	F C	F D	F E	F F
99	183	183	221	221	28	138	103	138	113	138	176

114 Fabien Deschamps

A A	A B	A C	A D	A E	A F	B A	B B	B C	B D	B E	B F
175	114	103	132	175	113	28	113	28	221	28	115

C A	C B	C C	C D	C E	C F	D A	D B	D C	D D	D E	D F
90	90	90	115	90	151	138	47	175	47	103	120

E A	E B	E C	E D	E E	E F	F A	F B	F C	F D	F E	F F
12	103	12	104	12	104	52	103	52	146	52	146

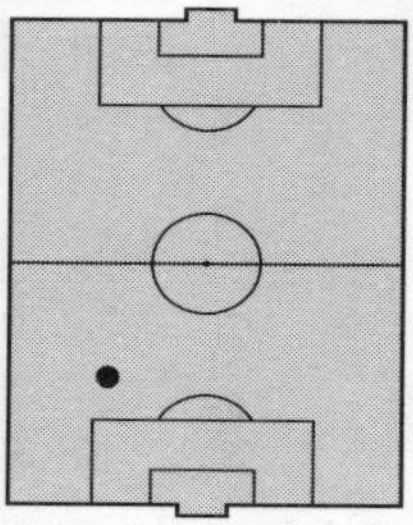

Henri Le Clerc 115

A A	A B	A C	A D	A E	A F	B A	B B	B C	B D	B E	B F
100	100	100	90	28	100	92	28	92	4	92	92

C A	C B	C C	C D	C E	C F	D A	D B	D C	D D	D E	D F
184	192	9	183	184	28	203	92	88	183	203	28

E A	E B	E C	E D	E E	E F	F A	F B	F C	F D	F E	F F
183	174	174	183	174	174	183	151	151	90	90	151

116 Terry Hiner

A A	A B	A C	A D	A E	A F	B A	B B	B C	B D	B E	B F
98	102	98	130	98	98	45	219	171	77	45	45

C A	C B	C C	C D	C E	C F	D A	D B	D C	D D	D E	D F
57	219	201	112	29	29	237	237	237	237	156	121

E A	E B	E C	E D	E E	E F	F A	F B	F C	F D	F E	F F
3	3	57	3	219	32	156	219	10	70	10	10

Laurencio 117

A

B

C

D

E

F

A A	A B	A C	A D	A E	A F	B A	B B	B C	B D	B E	B F
63	238	55	63	94	94	149	149	149	149	149	65

C A	C B	C C	C D	C E	C F	D A	D B	D C	D D	D E	D F
64	238	8	63	64	63	241	241	241	241	241	241

E A	E B	E C	E D	E E	E F	F A	F B	F C	F D	F E	F F
39	238	56	63	39	39	35	238	34	63	35	63

118 Henri Le Clerc

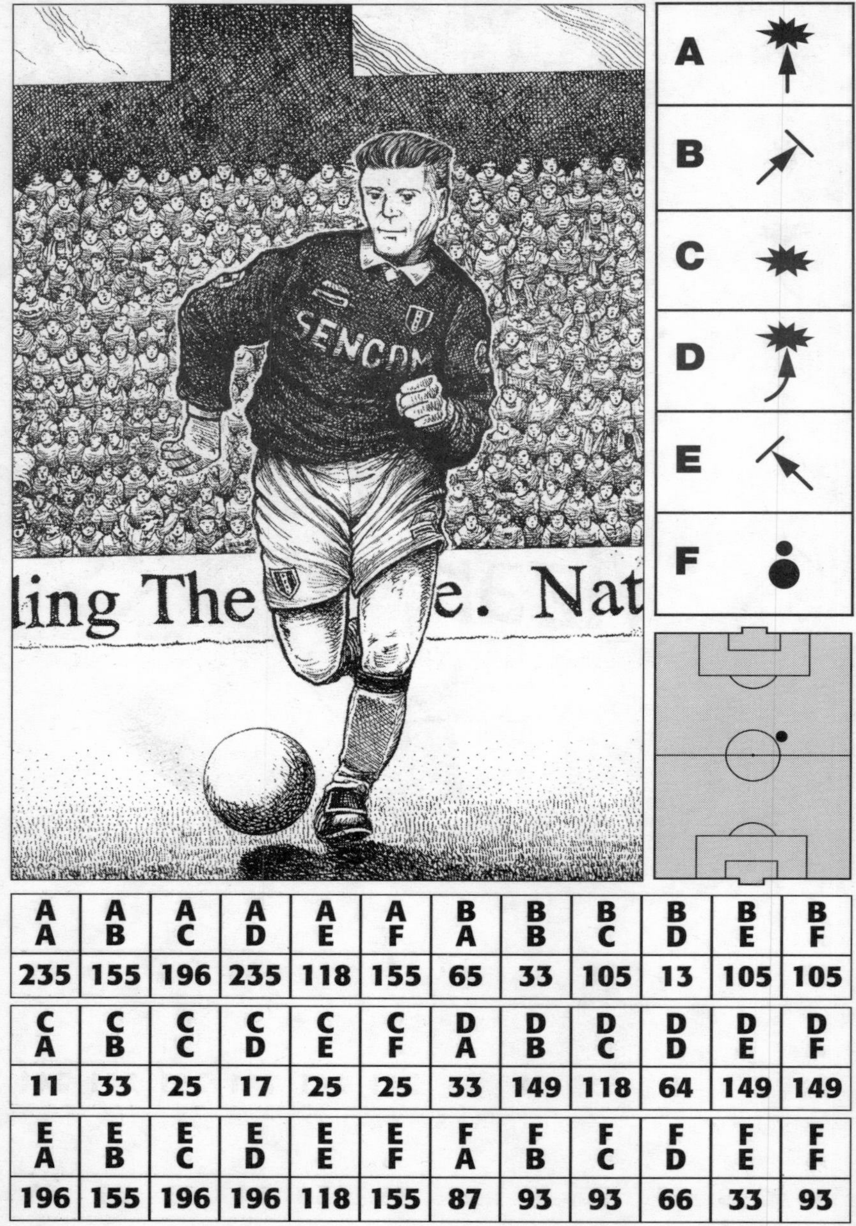

A A	A B	A C	A D	A E	A F	B A	B B	B C	B D	B E	B F
235	155	196	235	118	155	65	33	105	13	105	105

C A	C B	C C	C D	C E	C F	D A	D B	D C	D D	D E	D F
11	33	25	17	25	25	33	149	118	64	149	149

E A	E B	E C	E D	E E	E F	F A	F B	F C	F D	F E	F F
196	155	196	196	118	155	87	93	93	66	33	93

GOAL!	A
GOAL!	B
GOAL!	C
GOAL!	D
GOAL!	E
GOAL!	F

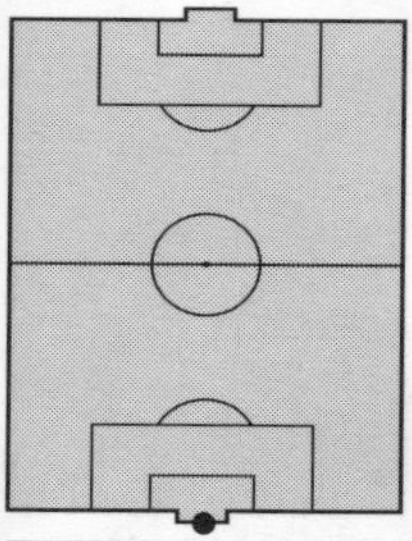

A A	A B	A C	A D	A E	A F	B A	B B	B C	B D	B E	B F
1	1	1	1	1	1	1	1	1	1	1	1

C A	C B	C C	C D	C E	C F	D A	D B	D C	D D	D E	D F
1	1	1	1	1	1	1	1	1	1	1	1

E A	E B	E C	E D	E E	E F	F A	F B	F C	F D	F E	F F
1	1	1	1	1	1	1	1	1	1	1	1

120 Ross Hewitt

A A	A B	A C	A D	A E	A F	B A	B B	B C	B D	B E	B F
176	150	150	150	137	150	79	79	9	78	79	79

C A	C B	C C	C D	C E	C F	D A	D B	D C	D D	D E	D F
82	176	138	138	47	114	78	132	47	113	47	113

E A	E B	E C	E D	E E	E F	F A	F B	F C	F D	F E	F F
183	44	47	100	183	100	221	221	221	28	221	221

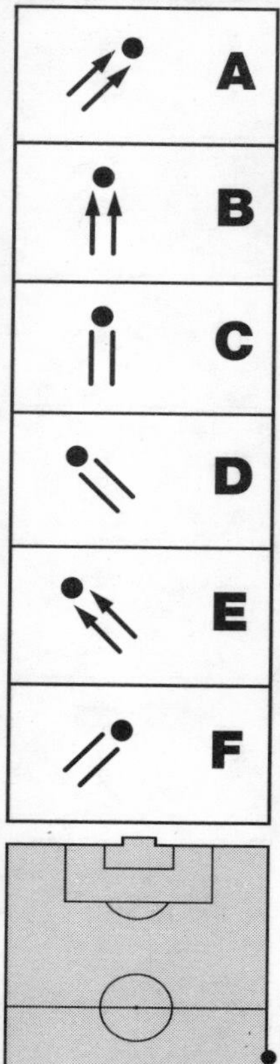

A

B

C

D

E

F

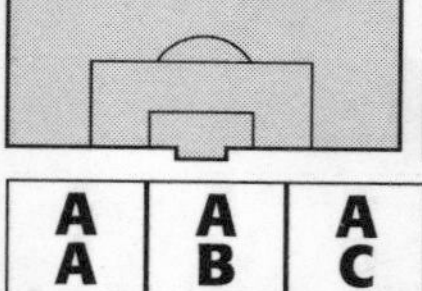

A A	A B	A C	A D	A E	A F	B A	B B	B C	B D	B E	B F
241	25	11	118	11	11	3	111	3	32	3	3

C A	C B	C C	C D	C E	C F	D A	D B	D C	D D	D E	D F
69	69	69	51	69	101	29	29	156	10	29	101

E A	E B	E C	E D	E E	E F	F A	F B	F C	F D	F E	F F
7	76	111	109	7	7	242	51	51	69	51	101

122 Ross Hewitt / Throw-in

A A	A B	A C	A D	A E	A F	B A	B B	B C	B D	B E	B F
41	41	41	21	41	122	40	174	174	174	40	44

C A	C B	C C	C D	C E	C F	D A	D B	D C	D D	D E	D F
108	83	108	21	108	53	100	100	82	21	100	82

E A	E B	E C	E D	E E	E F	F A	F B	F C	F D	F E	F F
28	115	90	115	28	44	12	59	104	104	12	44

A A	A B	A C	A D	A E	A F	B A	B B	B C	B D	B E	B F
12	12	104	12	129	12	18	18	164	18	18	129

C A	C B	C C	C D	C E	C F	D A	D B	D C	D D	D E	D F
124	129	124	124	124	124	62	14	62	62	62	95

E A	E B	E C	E D	E E	E F	F A	F B	F C	F D	F E	F F
26	26	97	129	42	26	38	6	104	6	14	6

124 Ross Hewitt

A A	A B	A C	A D	A E	A F	B A	B B	B C	B D	B E	B F
62	62	62	62	134	110	96	154	96	96	134	218

C A	C B	C C	C D	C E	C F	D A	D B	D C	D D	D E	D F
37	154	37	37	37	134	50	50	84	148	110	50

E A	E B	E C	E D	E E	E F	F A	F B	F C	F D	F E	F F
134	154	216	216	216	224	134	22	22	22	22	127

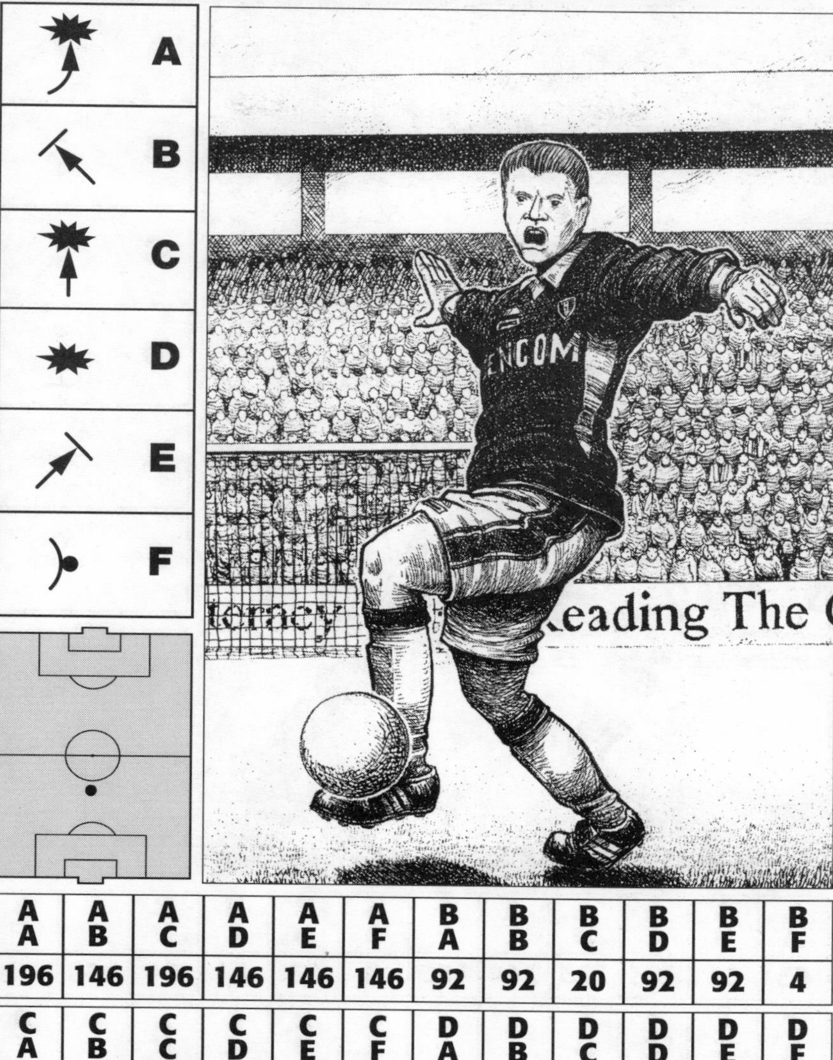

A A	A B	A C	A D	A E	A F	B A	B B	B C	B D	B E	B F
196	146	196	146	146	146	92	92	20	92	92	4

C A	C B	C C	C D	C E	C F	D A	D B	D C	D D	D E	D F
164	20	40	125	174	174	52	109	4	196	109	20

E A	E B	E C	E D	E E	E F	F A	F B	F C	F D	F E	F F
133	32	24	125	20	32	76	76	76	76	24	24

Matthew Scadding / Goal Kick

A A	A B	A C	A D	A E	A F	B A	B B	B C	B D	B E	B F
63	65	105	105	240	105	8	13	64	64	240	13

C A	C B	C C	C D	C E	C F	D A	D B	D C	D D	D E	D F
179	48	179	179	240	179	34	49	49	49	240	49

E A	E B	E C	E D	E E	E F	F A	F B	F C	F D	F E	F F
14	134	124	14	240	6	129	123	6	129	240	129

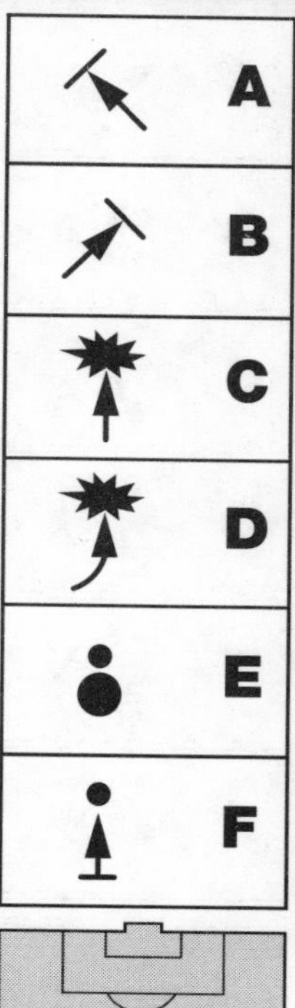

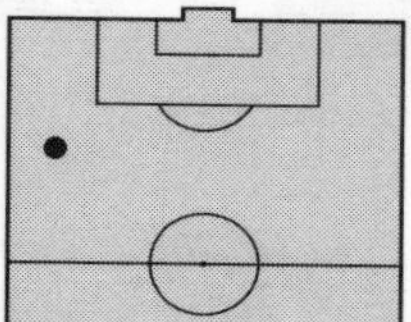

A A	A B	A C	A D	A E	A F	B A	B B	B C	B D	B E	B F
224	224	165	22	224	224	134	127	22	165	134	127

C A	C B	C C	C D	C E	C F	D A	D B	D C	D D	D E	D F
42	42	22	159	42	42	14	6	14	134	14	14

E A	E B	E C	E D	E E	E F	F A	F B	F C	F D	F E	F F
97	97	97	165	26	97	67	159	159	127	159	159

Aaron Hall / Free Kick

A A	A B	A C	A D	A E	A F	B A	B B	B C	B D	B E	B F
146	52	125	52	164	52	160	15	161	15	226	15

C A	C B	C C	C D	C E	C F	D A	D B	D C	D D	D E	D F
69	69	69	190	69	111	118	32	149	33	48	33

E A	E B	E C	E D	E E	E F	F A	F B	F C	F D	F E	F F
64	13	25	13	95	13	117	63	63	63	141	63

Aaron Hall 129

A A	A B	A C	A D	A E	A F	B A	B B	B C	B D	B E	B F
226	226	15	123	226	226	164	123	226	123	164	164

C A	C B	C C	C D	C E	C F	D A	D B	D C	D D	D E	D F
97	123	42	97	97	123	123	104	235	104	235	104

E A	E B	E C	E D	E E	E F	F A	F B	F C	F D	F E	F F
235	14	6	14	14	14	109	109	109	109	123	109

130 Aaron Hall / Corner

A	A	A	A	A	A	B	B	B	B	B	B
A	B	C	D	E	F	A	B	C	D	E	F
143	184	88	184	184	184	184	162	162	9	162	143

C	C	C	C	C	C	D	D	D	D	D	D
A	B	C	D	E	F	A	B	C	D	E	F
184	46	228	228	143	228	203	203	203	203	203	203

E	E	E	E	E	E	F	F	F	F	F	F
A	B	C	D	E	F	A	B	C	D	E	F
197	197	197	197	197	197	57	57	57	57	57	57

A

B

C

D

E

F

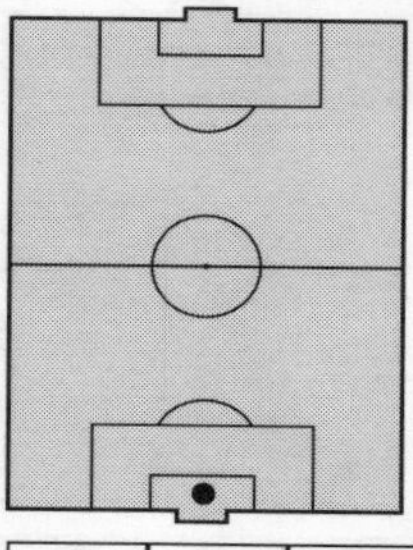

A A	A B	A C	A D	A E	A F	B A	B B	B C	B D	B E	B F
52	125	52	52	52	52	4	92	4	184	4	209

C A	C B	C C	C D	C E	C F	D A	D B	D C	D D	D E	D F
60	7	172	60	172	209	201	29	3	3	3	3

E A	E B	E C	E D	E E	E F	F A	F B	F C	F D	F E	F F
90	108	221	90	90	90	9	79	89	197	9	209

132 Fabien Deschamps

A
B
C
D
E
F

A A	A B	A C	A D	A E	A F	B A	B B	B C	B D	B E	B F
99	99	113	91	99	175	28	91	221	28	28	28

C A	C B	C C	C D	C E	C F	D A	D B	D C	D D	D E	D F
40	40	115	40	40	40	113	47	47	137	47	137

E A	E B	E C	E D	E E	E F	F A	F B	F C	F D	F E	F F
113	113	82	176	150	137	78	113	78	132	100	103

A A	A B	A C	A D	A E	A F	B A	B B	B C	B D	B E	B F
52	52	187	52	187	52	65	105	241	65	105	149

C A	C B	C C	C D	C E	C F	D A	D B	D C	D D	D E	D F
87	87	187	133	187	87	16	155	167	149	155	16

E A	E B	E C	E D	E E	E F	F A	F B	F C	F D	F E	F F
11	11	86	11	25	149	118	118	149	33	149	33

134 Ross Hewitt

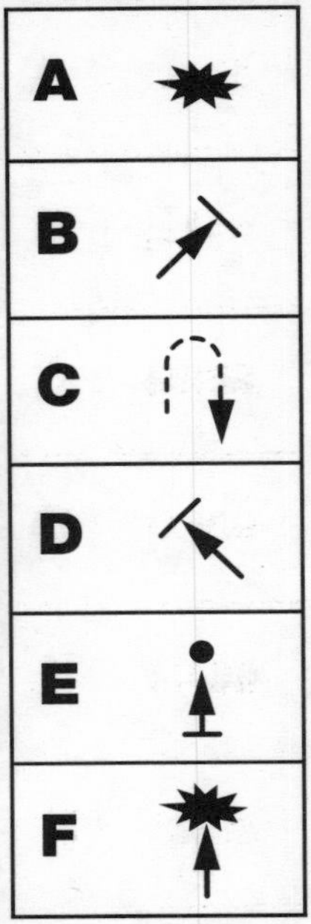

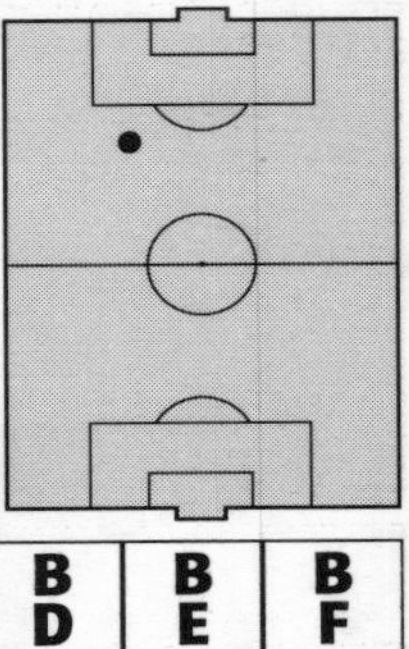

A

B

C

D

E

F

A A	A B	A C	A D	A E	A F	B A	B B	B C	B D	B E	B F
95	124	95	95	95	236	165	84	84	84	84	165

C A	C B	C C	C D	C E	C F	D A	D B	D C	D D	D E	D F
165	127	134	124	124	124	134	14	6	14	134	124

E A	E B	E C	E D	E E	E F	F A	F B	F C	F D	F E	F F
179	95	179	179	179	179	97	97	97	26	97	97

GOAL!	A
GOAL!	B
GOAL!	C
GOAL!	D
GOAL!	E
GOAL!	F

A A	A B	A C	A D	A E	A F	B A	B B	B C	B D	B E	B F
2	2	2	2	2	2	2	2	2	2	2	2

C A	C B	C C	C D	C E	C F	D A	D B	D C	D D	D E	D F
2	2	2	2	2	2	2	2	2	2	2	2

E A	E B	E C	E D	E E	E F	F A	F B	F C	F D	F E	F F
2	2	2	2	2	2	2	2	2	2	2	2

136 Terry Hiner

A A	A B	A C	A D	A E	A F	B A	B B	B C	B D	B E	B F
141	107	177	56	141	141	80	107	198	94	94	94

C A	C B	C C	C D	C E	C F	D A	D B	D C	D D	D E	D F
105	105	105	13	63	107	63	107	8	56	117	117

E A	E B	E C	E D	E E	E F	F A	F B	F C	F D	F E	F F
149	149	149	33	133	149	217	238	182	217	217	217

A A	A B	A C	A D	A E	A F	B A	B B	B C	B D	B E	B F
78	78	78	120	78	100	21	40	164	40	174	40

C A	C B	C C	C D	C E	C F	D A	D B	D C	D D	D E	D F
28	28	109	28	115	28	99	99	103	113	79	99

E A	E B	E C	E D	E E	E F	F A	F B	F C	F D	F E	F F
82	82	82	82	82	150	54	90	90	90	90	151

138 Fabien Deschamps

A A	A B	A C	A D	A E	A F	B A	B B	B C	B D	B E	B F
120	120	120	176	137	114	9	184	100	184	184	184

C A	C B	C C	C D	C E	C F	D A	D B	D C	D D	D E	D F
138	114	113	137	103	114	100	79	78	79	79	79

E A	E B	E C	E D	E E	E F	F A	F B	F C	F D	F E	F F
82	100	90	150	100	100	30	197	92	197	197	197

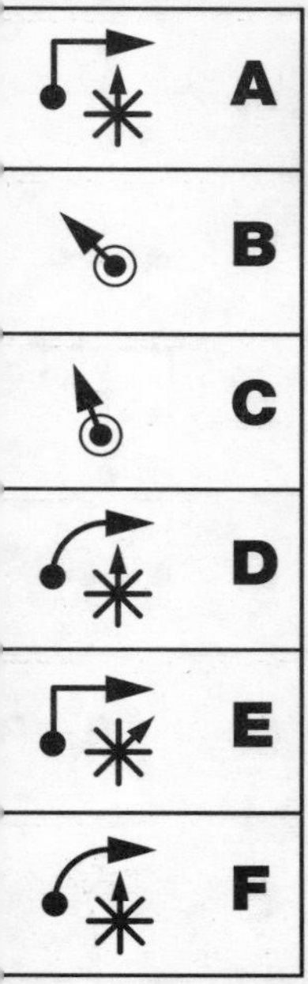

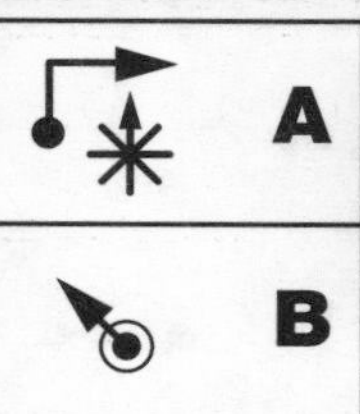

A

B

C

D

E

F

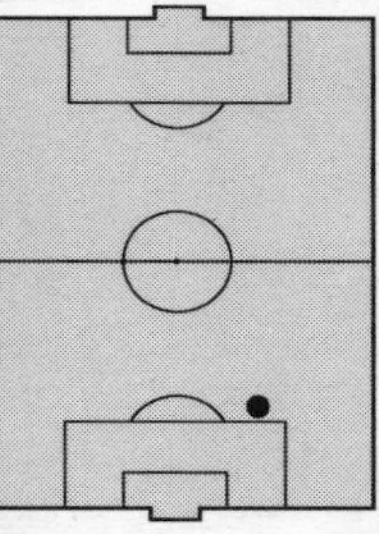

A A	A B	A C	A D	A E	A F	B A	B B	B C	B D	B E	B F
7	24	24	24	32	24	167	20	52	52	146	146

C A	C B	C C	C D	C E	C F	D A	D B	D C	D D	D E	D F
179	66	15	15	160	160	64	33	33	33	33	118

E A	E B	E C	E D	E E	E F	F A	F B	F C	F D	F E	F F
242	51	51	111	86	86	39	17	17	101	17	241

140 Laurencio

A A	A B	A C	A D	A E	A F	B A	B B	B C	B D	B E	B F
232	177	177	232	177	56	220	220	194	199	194	61

C A	C B	C C	C D	C E	C F	D A	D B	D C	D D	D E	D F
208	202	208	208	208	208	231	75	222	231	140	227

E A	E B	E C	E D	E E	E F	F A	F B	F C	F D	F E	F F
61	126	74	232	74	34	68	110	68	68	68	68

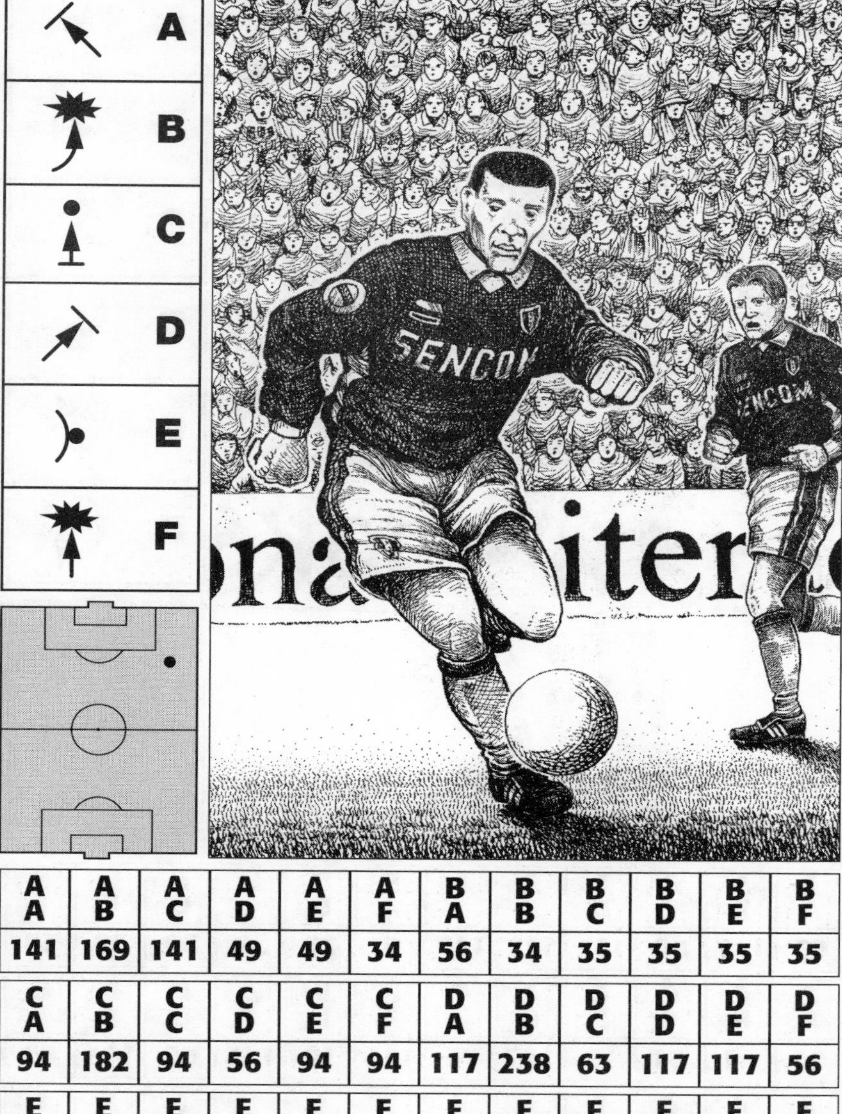

A A	A B	A C	A D	A E	A F	B A	B B	B C	B D	B E	B F
141	169	141	49	49	34	56	34	35	35	35	35

C A	C B	C C	C D	C E	C F	D A	D B	D C	D D	D E	D F
94	182	94	56	94	94	117	238	63	117	117	56

E A	E B	E C	E D	E E	E F	F A	F B	F C	F D	F E	F F
13	105	105	105	63	105	222	227	222	222	222	238

142 Terry Hiner / Throw-in

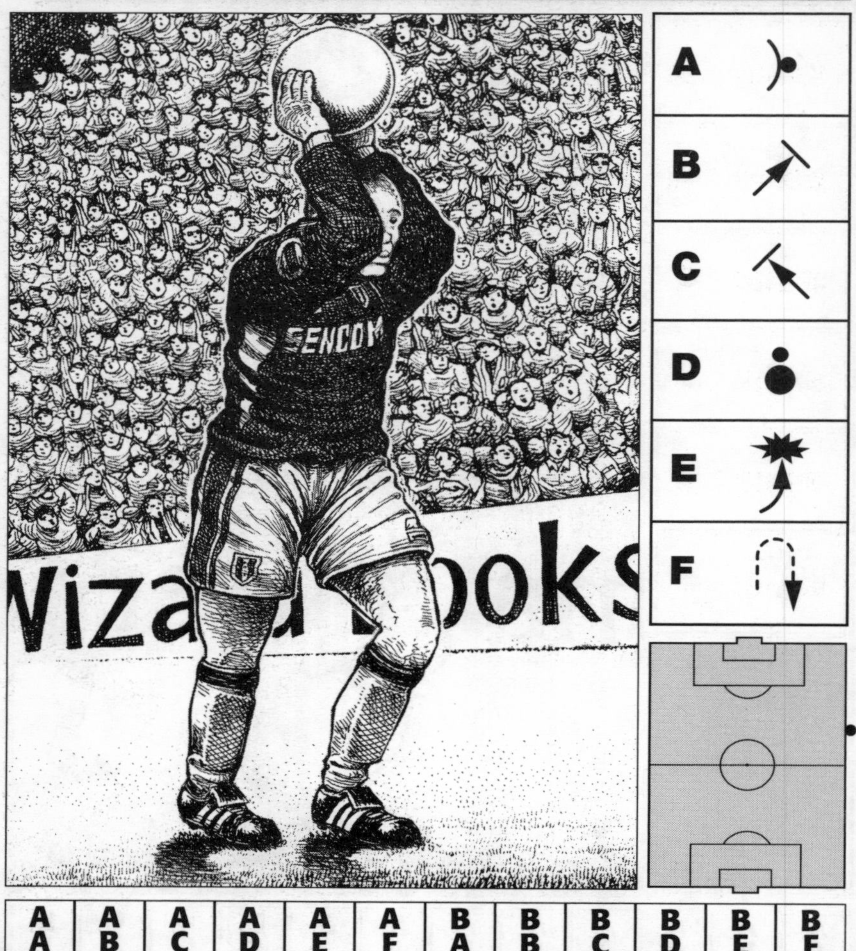

A A	A B	A C	A D	A E	A F	B A	B B	B C	B D	B E	B F
63	117	80	117	117	117	5	80	39	39	39	39

C A	C B	C C	C D	C E	C F	D A	D B	D C	D D	D E	D F
64	64	64	13	117	13	105	39	105	65	105	65

E A	E B	E C	E D	E E	E F	F A	F B	F C	F D	F E	F F
35	35	63	8	35	8	80	94	94	94	142	94

Keeper's Ball! 143

KEEPER'S BALL	A
KEEPER'S BALL	B
KEEPER'S BALL	C
KEEPER'S BALL	D
KEEPER'S BALL	E
KEEPER'S BALL	F

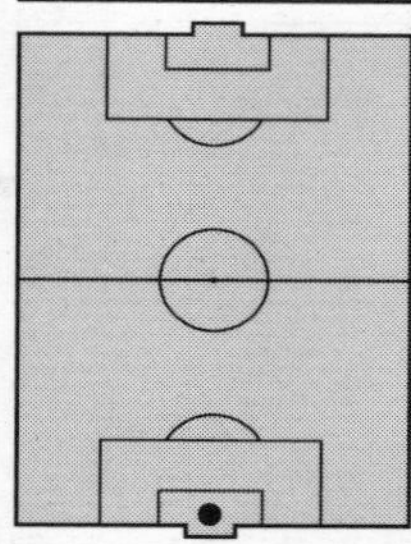

A A	A B	A C	A D	A E	A F	B A	B B	B C	B D	B E	B F
209	209	209	209	209	209	209	209	209	209	209	209

C A	C B	C C	C D	C E	C F	D A	D B	D C	D D	D E	D F
209	209	209	209	209	209	209	209	209	209	209	209

E A	E B	E C	E D	E E	E F	F A	F B	F C	F D	F E	F F
209	209	209	209	209	209	209	209	209	209	209	209

144 Henri Le Clerc / Goal Kick

A A	A B	A C	A D	A E	A F	B A	B B	B C	B D	B E	B F
88	88	144	184	88	60	52	167	52	52	146	209

C A	C B	C C	C D	C E	C F	D A	D B	D C	D D	D E	D F
51	242	51	76	86	209	115	158	83	83	151	209

E A	E B	E C	E D	E E	E F	F A	F B	F C	F D	F E	F F
184	192	144	192	192	89	4	92	4	4	109	209

Fabien Deschamps 145

A A	A B	A C	A D	A E	A F	B A	B B	B C	B D	B E	B F
187	19	195	187	145	19	104	164	12	174	12	12

C A	C B	C C	C D	C E	C F	D A	D B	D C	D D	D E	D F
129	164	123	97	123	123	164	18	145	40	18	18

E A	E B	E C	E D	E E	E F	F A	F B	F C	F D	F E	F F
195	19	195	195	145	19	161	66	66	93	164	66

146 Aaron Hall

A A	A B	A C	A D	A E	A F	B A	B B	B C	B D	B E	B F
149	93	149	52	149	149	52	196	52	164	164	52

C A	C B	C C	C D	C E	C F	D A	D B	D C	D D	D E	D F
174	196	115	115	40	115	76	196	76	149	24	76

E A	E B	E C	E D	E E	E F	F A	F B	F C	F D	F E	F F
125	52	20	125	125	146	93	196	93	93	93	93

A A	A B	A C	A D	A E	A F	B A	B B	B C	B D	B E	B F
229	229	229	229	215	180	206	206	215	206	233	72

C A	C B	C C	C D	C E	C F	D A	D B	D C	D D	D E	D F
147	84	215	37	233	193	147	215	234	207	165	178

E A	E B	E C	E D	E E	E F	F A	F B	F C	F D	F E	F F
168	215	168	168	165	178	215	224	224	22	215	180

148 Keeper's Ball!

A A	A B	A C	A D	A E	A F	B A	B B	B C	B D	B E	B F
240	240	240	240	240	240	240	240	240	240	240	240

C A	C B	C C	C D	C E	C F	D A	D B	D C	D D	D E	D F
240	240	240	240	240	240	240	240	240	240	240	240

E A	E B	E C	E D	E E	E F	F A	F B	F C	F D	F E	F F
240	240	240	240	240	240	240	240	240	240	240	240

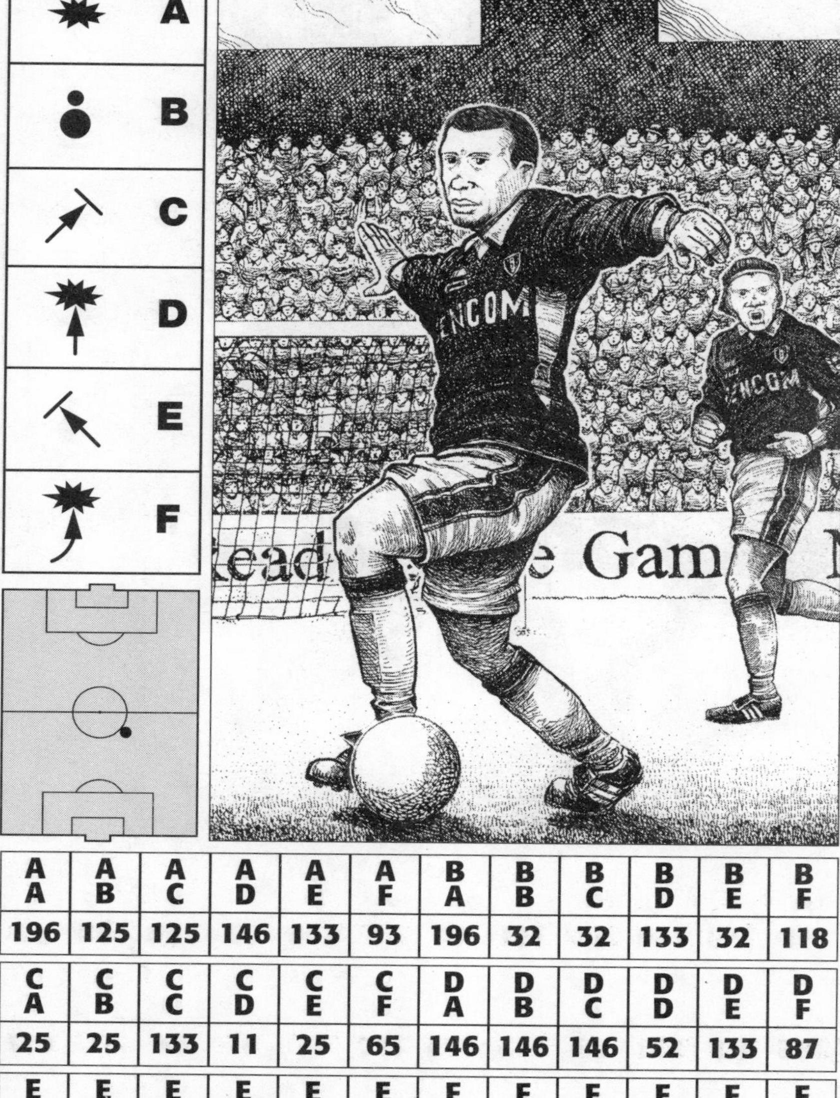

A A	A B	A C	A D	A E	A F	B A	B B	B C	B D	B E	B F
196	125	125	146	133	93	196	32	32	133	32	118

C A	C B	C C	C D	C E	C F	D A	D B	D C	D D	D E	D F
25	25	133	11	25	65	146	146	146	52	133	87

E A	E B	E C	E D	E E	E F	F A	F B	F C	F D	F E	F F
196	32	76	196	76	196	196	52	115	196	125	196

150 Fabien Deschamps

A A	A B	A C	A D	A E	A F	B A	B B	B C	B D	B E	B F
44	150	150	44	151	44	28	100	82	150	100	82

C A	C B	C C	C D	C E	C F	D A	D B	D C	D D	D E	D F
183	82	132	78	113	175	137	41	41	44	41	137

E A	E B	E C	E D	E E	E F	F A	F B	F C	F D	F E	F F
21	47	120	176	120	82	79	79	9	79	78	79

A A	A B	A C	A D	A E	A F	B A	B B	B C	B D	B E	B F
90	115	115	183	115	40	100	90	151	44	100	83

C A	C B	C C	C D	C E	C F	D A	D B	D C	D D	D E	D F
108	44	108	108	108	44	28	92	30	92	92	92

E A	E B	E C	E D	E E	E F	F A	F B	F C	F D	F E	F F
150	44	150	44	151	44	9	89	58	89	89	89

152 Fabien Deschamps / Free Kick

A A	A B	A C	A D	A E	A F	B A	B B	B C	B D	B E	B F
52	146	52	87	174	52	15	160	15	48	164	15

C A	C B	C C	C D	C E	C F	D A	D B	D C	D D	D E	D F
59	97	108	104	59	59	26	42	26	127	26	26

E A	E B	E C	E D	E E	E F	F A	F B	F C	F D	F E	F F
108	83	83	83	83	83	41	21	21	21	21	54

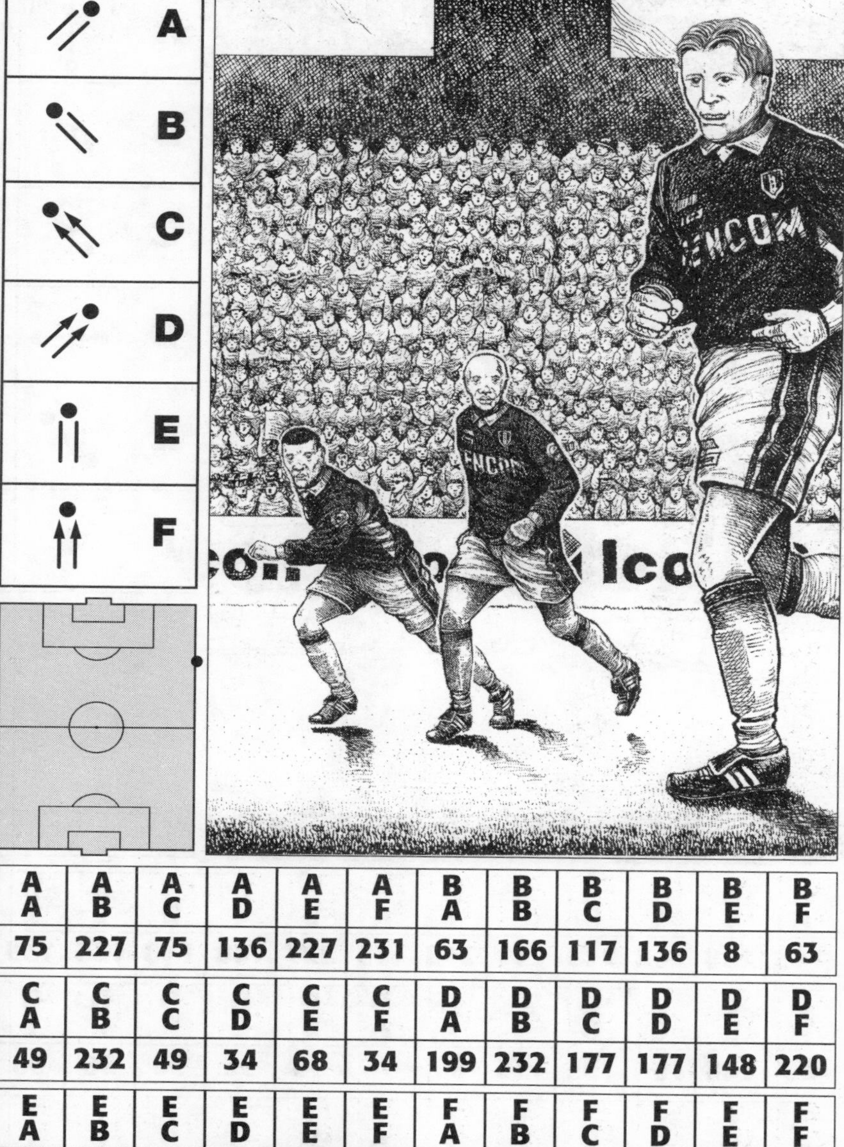

A A	A B	A C	A D	A E	A F	B A	B B	B C	B D	B E	B F
75	227	75	136	227	231	63	166	117	136	8	63

C A	C B	C C	C D	C E	C F	D A	D B	D C	D D	D E	D F
49	232	49	34	68	34	199	232	177	177	148	220

E A	E B	E C	E D	E E	E F	F A	F B	F C	F D	F E	F F
107	182	107	136	153	107	35	223	8	8	110	8

154 Matthew Scadding / Free Kick

A A	A B	A C	A D	A E	A F	B A	B B	B C	B D	B E	B F
148	208	208	211	211	218	135	227	148	148	135	135

C A	C B	C C	C D	C E	C F	D A	D B	D C	D D	D E	D F
85	148	106	135	135	85	96	96	96	96	96	96

E A	E B	E C	E D	E E	E F	F A	F B	F C	F D	F E	F F
106	50	50	50	61	50	193	193	193	193	193	193

A A	A B	A C	A D	A E	A F	B A	B B	B C	B D	B E	B F
167	167	235	16	155	155	93	93	160	155	93	235

C A	C B	C C	C D	C E	C F	D A	D B	D C	D D	D E	D F
161	161	15	235	16	235	16	118	235	16	118	235

E A	E B	E C	E D	E E	E F	F A	F B	F C	F D	F E	F F
160	160	15	235	160	160	125	15	235	125	125	125

156 Aaron Hall

A

B

C

D

E

F

A A	A B	A C	A D	A E	A F	B A	B B	B C	B D	B E	B F
101	101	101	101	101	102	171	171	45	156	171	70

C A	C B	C C	C D	C E	C F	D A	D B	D C	D D	D E	D F
219	219	156	219	116	10	57	57	57	10	57	10

E A	E B	E C	E D	E E	E F	F A	F B	F C	F D	F E	F F
111	111	3	3	111	214	29	7	201	3	201	201

A A	A B	A C	A D	A E	A F	B A	B B	B C	B D	B E	B F
99	99	99	103	79	99	52	146	52	209	52	167

C A	C B	C C	C D	C E	C F	D A	D B	D C	D D	D E	D F
221	115	28	209	151	9	197	92	203	209	30	192

E A	E B	E C	E D	E E	E F	F A	F B	F C	F D	F E	F F
12	104	12	209	174	129	203	76	201	209	7	92

158 Fabien Deschamps

A A	A B	A C	A D	A E	A F	B A	B B	B C	B D	B E	B F
97	97	158	42	59	59	108	108	53	12	53	108

C A	C B	C C	C D	C E	C F	D A	D B	D C	D D	D E	D F
104	40	12	174	174	174	41	41	41	122	53	41

E A	E B	E C	E D	E E	E F	F A	F B	F C	F D	F E	F F
97	12	59	104	104	104	9	115	174	115	115	115

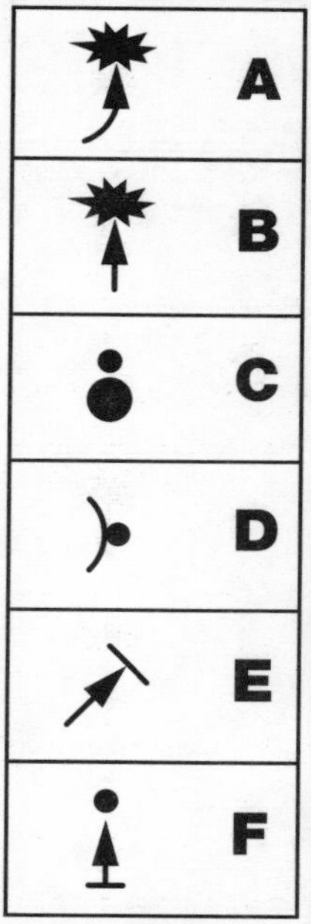

Pierre Pasqualle

A

B

C

D

E

F

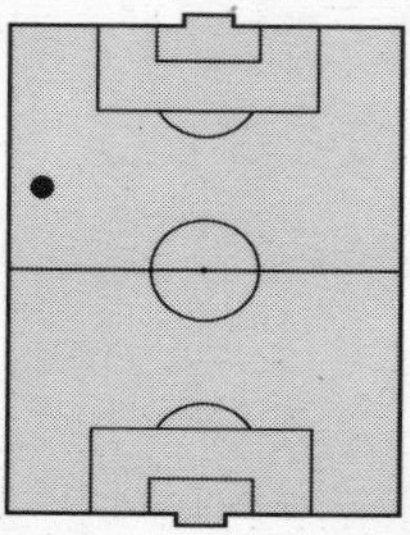

A A	A B	A C	A D	A E	A F	B A	B B	B C	B D	B E	B F
165	165	42	42	159	26	22	67	127	127	67	127

C A	C B	C C	C D	C E	C F	D A	D B	D C	D D	D E	D F
239	67	158	158	158	53	160	160	6	14	123	160

E A	E B	E C	E D	E E	E F	F A	F B	F C	F D	F E	F F
129	129	26	42	26	129	225	67	234	234	234	234

160 Helmut Bremen

A A	A B	A C	A D	A E	A F	B A	B B	B C	B D	B E	B F
125	235	125	125	125	20	18	164	164	164	164	164

C A	C B	C C	C D	C E	C F	D A	D B	D C	D D	D E	D F
149	149	33	149	149	149	160	235	226	15	15	226

E A	E B	E C	E D	E E	E F	F A	F B	F C	F D	F E	F F
155	48	155	16	16	16	118	64	15	33	118	33

Helmut Bremen 161

A A	A B	A C	A D	A E	A F	B A	B B	B C	B D	B E	B F
160	160	160	160	235	235	93	161	93	87	196	196

C A	C B	C C	C D	C E	C F	D A	D B	D C	D D	D E	D F
155	66	155	155	66	15	19	167	167	19	66	16

E A	E B	E C	E D	E E	E F	F A	F B	F C	F D	F E	F F
164	164	66	145	66	18	226	226	66	226	66	123

162 Henri Le Clerc

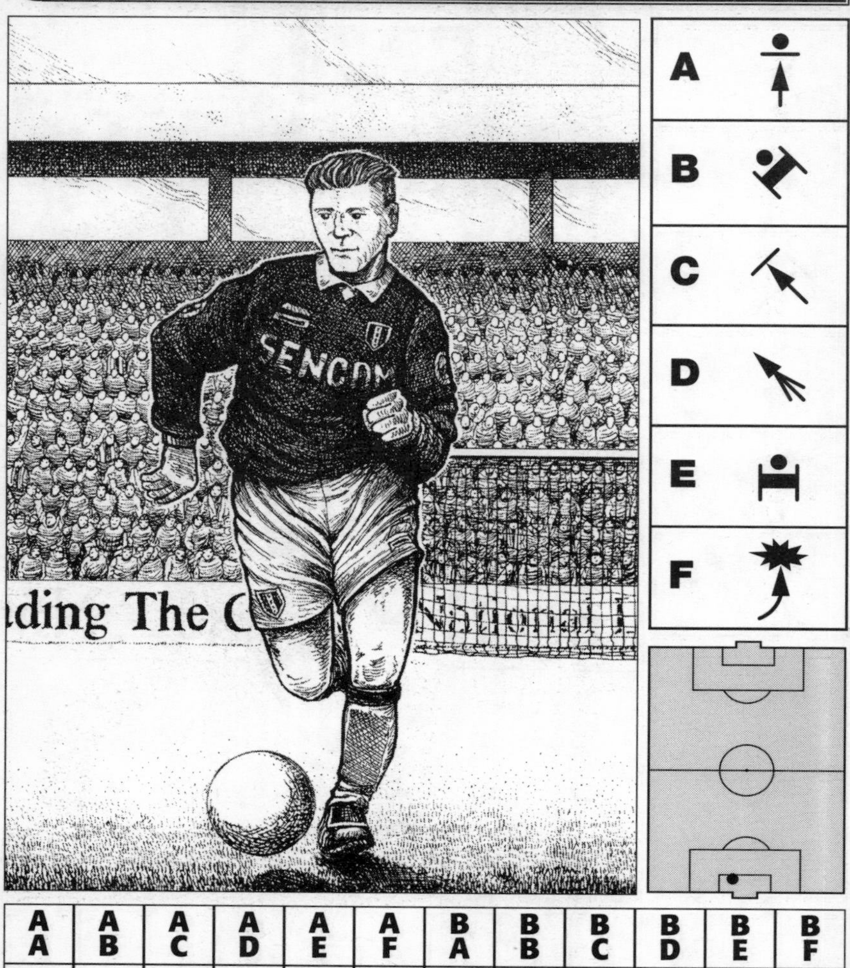

A A	A B	A C	A D	A E	A F	B A	B B	B C	B D	B E	B F
184	143	119	143	119	197	143	170	170	143	170	212

C A	C B	C C	C D	C E	C F	D A	D B	D C	D D	D E	D F
130	143	119	119	143	119	143	119	119	143	119	79

E A	E B	E C	E D	E E	E F	F A	F B	F C	F D	F E	F F
119	143	175	119	143	119	89	89	89	157	89	192

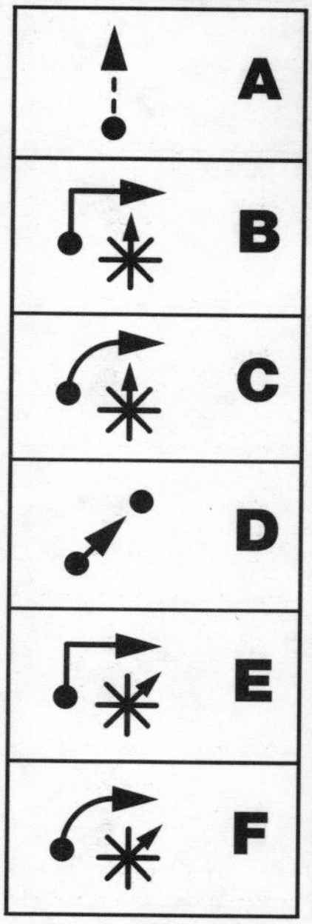

Aaron Hall 163

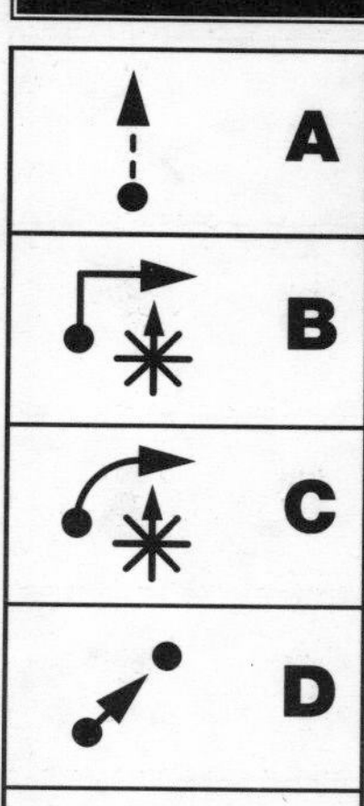

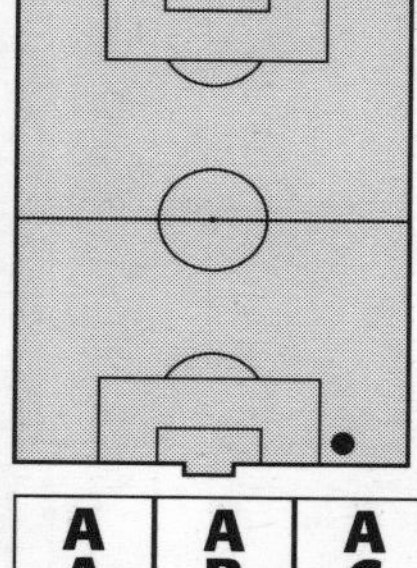

A A	A B	A C	A D	A E	A F	B A	B B	B C	B D	B E	B F
112	139	46	185	46	130	7	7	7	7	7	7

C A	C B	C C	C D	C E	C F	D A	D B	D C	D D	D E	D F
24	24	24	24	24	24	163	130	45	185	185	77

E A	E B	E C	E D	E E	E F	F A	F B	F C	F D	F E	F F
10	10	10	10	77	10	69	69	69	69	121	69

164 Fabien Deschamps

A

B

C

D

E

F

A A	A B	A C	A D	A E	A F	B A	B B	B C	B D	B E	B F
104	145	104	97	164	145	164	196	146	196	145	146

C A	C B	C C	C D	C E	C F	D A	D B	D C	D D	D E	D F
145	145	125	20	164	125	174	145	174	18	164	174

E A	E B	E C	E D	E E	E F	F A	F B	F C	F D	F E	F F
52	92	20	92	92	92	226	196	226	196	226	226

A A	A B	A C	A D	A E	A F	B A	B B	B C	B D	B E	B F
15	160	48	160	33	160	52	146	87	146	133	146

C A	C B	C C	C D	C E	C F	D A	D B	D C	D D	D E	D F
159	159	159	81	159	22	145	6	18	164	125	164

E A	E B	E C	E D	E E	E F	F A	F B	F C	F D	F E	F F
40	174	123	174	4	174	90	151	151	151	78	151

166 Brett Green / Free Kick

A A	A B	A C	A D	A E	A F	B A	B B	B C	B D	B E	B F
35	208	110	208	211	208	8	8	117	8	8	64

C A	C B	C C	C D	C E	C F	D A	D B	D C	D D	D E	D F
35	117	202	34	49	232	95	62	35	62	110	223

E A	E B	E C	E D	E E	E F	F A	F B	F C	F D	F E	F F
56	56	56	56	56	117	64	23	179	23	95	48

Henri Le Clerc 167

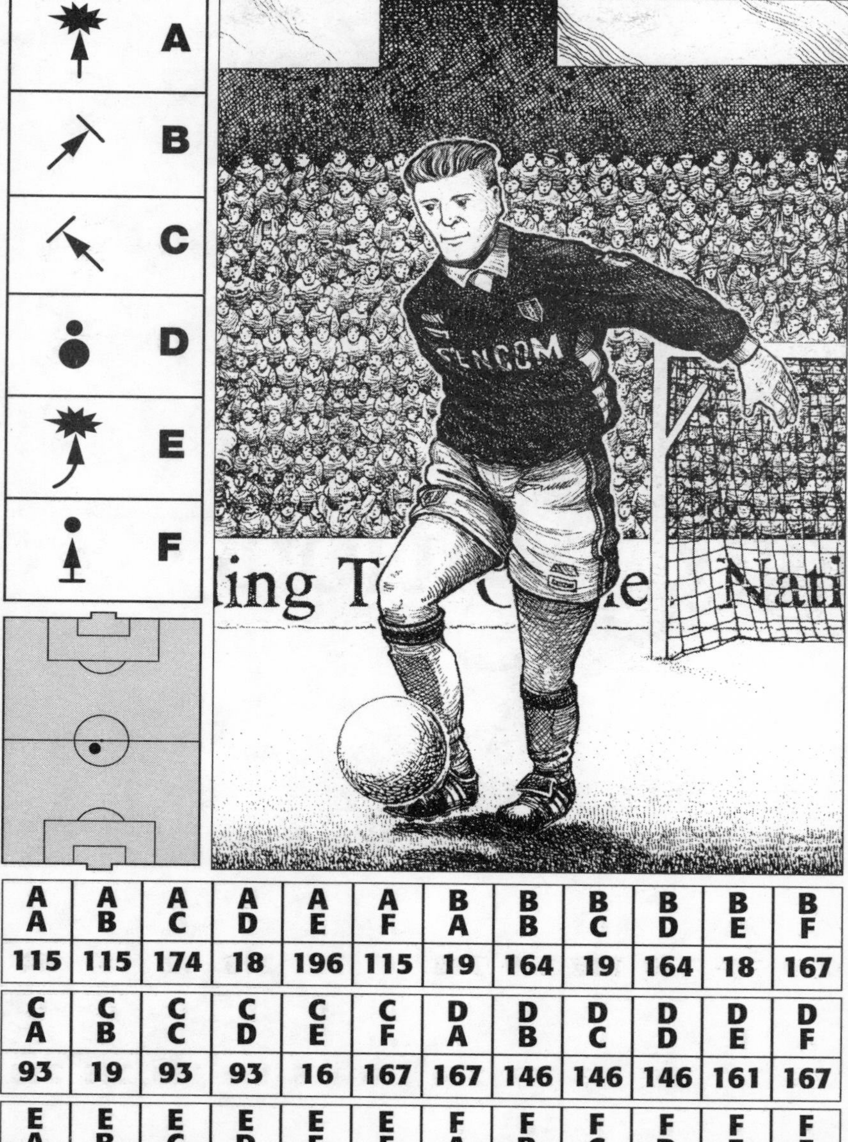

AA	AB	AC	AD	AE	AF	BA	BB	BC	BD	BE	BF
115	115	174	18	196	115	19	164	19	164	18	167

CA	CB	CC	CD	CE	CF	DA	DB	DC	DD	DE	DF
93	19	93	93	16	167	167	146	146	146	161	167

EA	EB	EC	ED	EE	EF	FA	FB	FC	FD	FE	FF
125	125	125	155	196	125	196	161	161	161	66	161

168 Ross Hewitt

A A	A B	A C	A D	A E	A F	B A	B B	B C	B D	B E	B F
229	71	229	180	229	229	147	207	215	72	147	147

C A	C B	C C	C D	C E	C F	D A	D B	D C	D D	D E	D F
216	207	37	193	224	224	158	158	158	158	225	239

E A	E B	E C	E D	E E	E F	F A	F B	F C	F D	F E	F F
127	127	216	127	207	6	225	207	234	178	234	234

A A	A B	A C	A D	A E	A F	B A	B B	B C	B D	B E	B F
25	32	25	25	11	25	15	161	160	160	15	160

C A	C B	C C	C D	C E	C F	D A	D B	D C	D D	D E	D F
48	23	13	179	48	179	39	13	63	80	5	39

E A	E B	E C	E D	E E	E F	F A	F B	F C	F D	F E	F F
141	141	141	34	141	49	34	110	110	110	110	202

170 Ross Hewitt

A

B

C

D

E

F

A A	A B	A C	A D	A E	A F	B A	B B	B C	B D	B E	B F
175	119	175	143	119	119	130	143	119	119	130	119

C A	C B	C C	C D	C E	C F	D A	D B	D C	D D	D E	D F
119	162	119	119	143	130	143	119	130	175	119	175

E A	E B	E C	E D	E E	E F	F A	F B	F C	F D	F E	F F
119	175	119	119	175	143	119	119	143	175	119	175

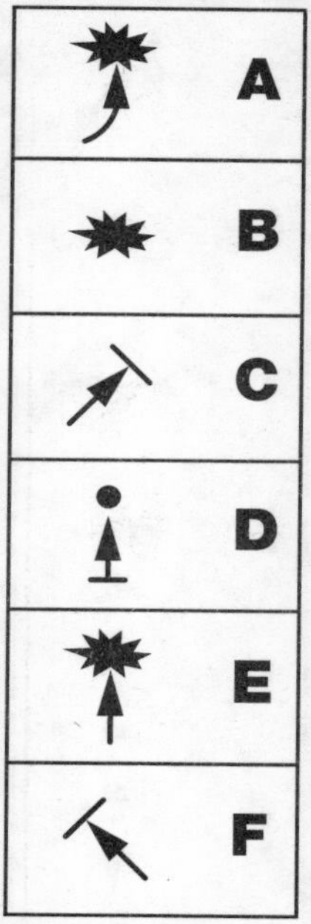

A

B

C

D

E

F

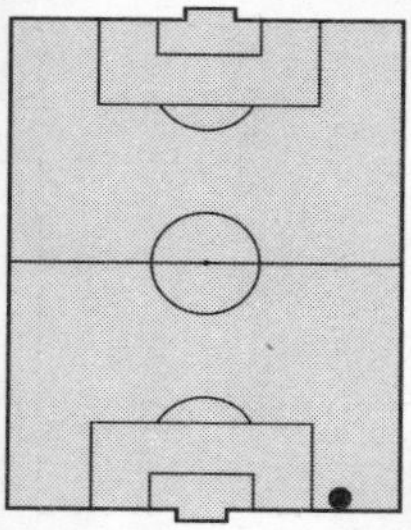

A A	A B	A C	A D	A E	A F	B A	B B	B C	B D	B E	B F
57	77	112	112	45	45	130	130	185	163	77	171

C A	C B	C C	C D	C E	C F	D A	D B	D C	D D	D E	D F
184	184	184	184	184	130	173	201	201	201	172	45

E A	E B	E C	E D	E E	E F	F A	F B	F C	F D	F E	F F
77	130	45	98	130	230	3	57	57	57	29	57

172 Brett Green

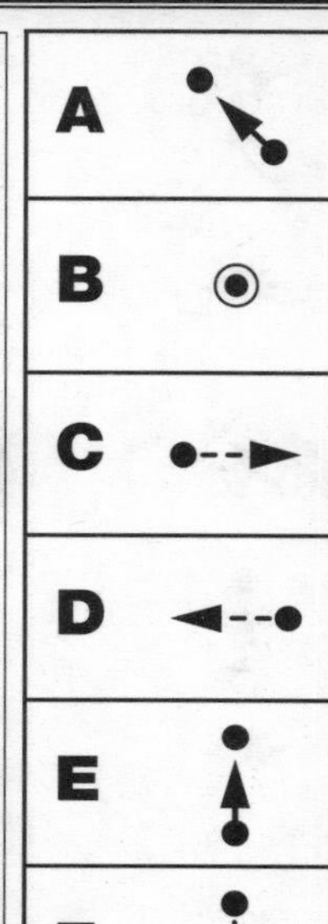

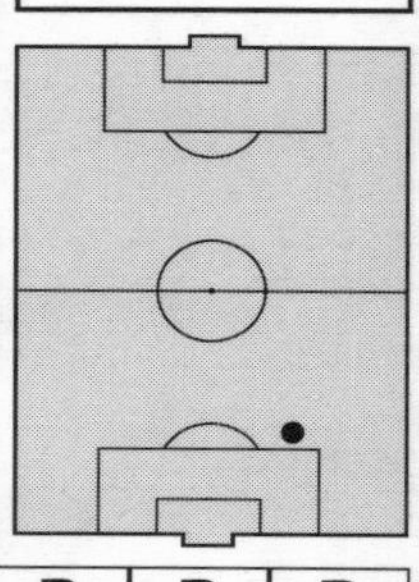

A A	A B	A C	A D	A E	A F	B A	B B	B C	B D	B E	B F
30	201	30	197	30	201	109	92	125	20	20	20

C A	C B	C C	C D	C E	C F	D A	D B	D C	D D	D E	D F
29	29	29	139	172	201	88	172	88	186	88	201

E A	E B	E C	E D	E E	E F	F A	F B	F C	F D	F E	F F
7	7	7	112	7	201	46	46	46	130	46	139

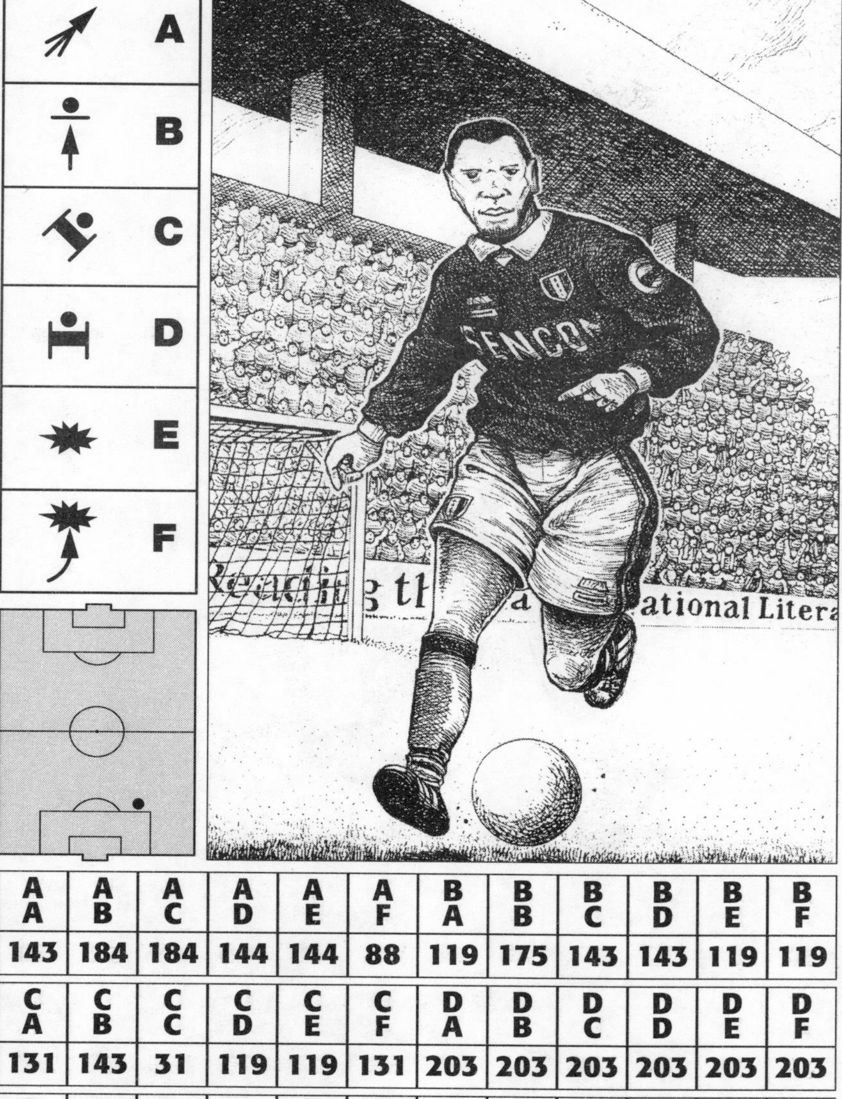

A A	A B	A C	A D	A E	A F	B A	B B	B C	B D	B E	B F
143	184	184	144	144	88	119	175	143	143	119	119

C A	C B	C C	C D	C E	C F	D A	D B	D C	D D	D E	D F
131	143	31	119	119	131	203	203	203	203	203	203

E A	E B	E C	E D	E E	E F	F A	F B	F C	F D	F E	F F
31	60	60	60	212	60	112	112	112	112	112	112

174 Aaron Hall

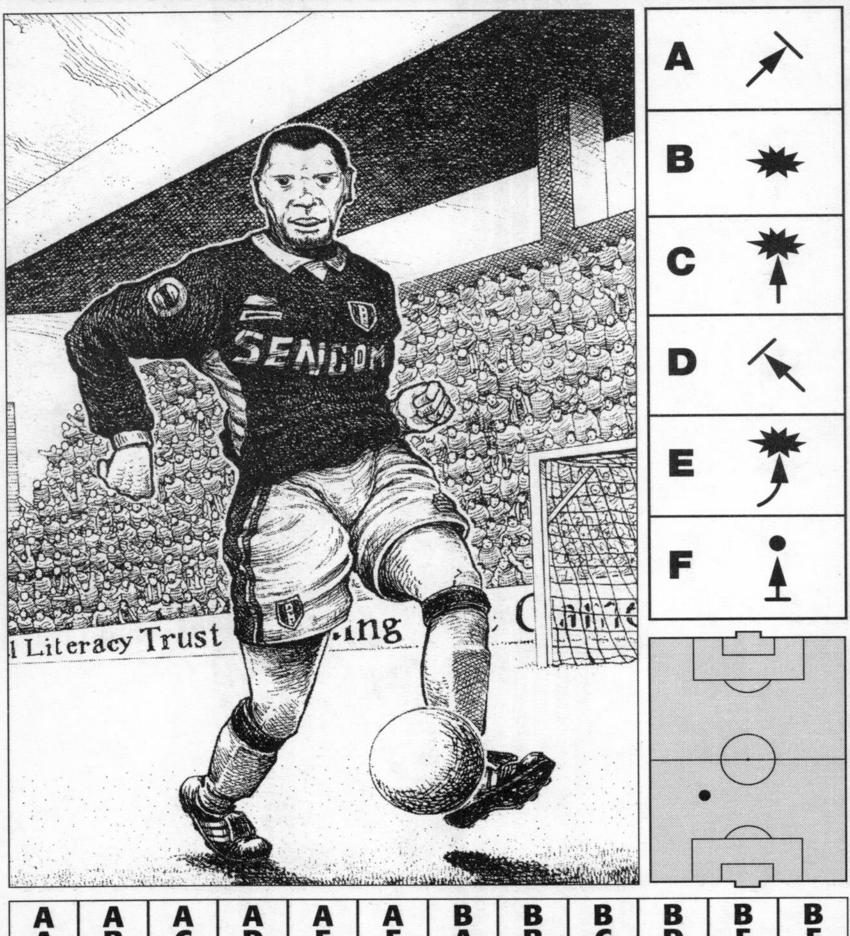

A A	A B	A C	A D	A E	A F	B A	B B	B C	B D	B E	B F
151	151	151	40	108	40	40	109	109	109	125	40

C A	C B	C C	C D	C E	C F	D A	D B	D C	D D	D E	D F
115	44	164	109	145	40	92	92	213	92	44	92

E A	E B	E C	E D	E E	E F	F A	F B	F C	F D	F E	F F
104	44	40	104	59	104	164	44	44	164	196	164

A A	A B	A C	A D	A E	A F	B A	B B	B C	B D	B E	B F
79	79	79	79	79	79	143	143	184	143	209	184
C A	**C B**	**C C**	**C D**	**C E**	**C F**	**D A**	**D B**	**D C**	**D D**	**D E**	**D F**
170	143	184	143	209	170	100	100	100	100	100	100
E A	**E B**	**E C**	**E D**	**E E**	**E F**	**F A**	**F B**	**F C**	**F D**	**F E**	**F F**
221	221	221	221	221	221	197	197	197	197	197	197

176 Pierre Pasqualle / Throw-in

A A	A B	A C	A D	A E	A F	B A	B B	B C	B D	B E	B F
113	175	113	82	175	103	151	44	90	82	115	151

C A	C B	C C	C D	C E	C F	D A	D B	D C	D D	D E	D F
9	183	9	221	197	221	99	183	79	79	143	191

E A	E B	E C	E D	E E	E F	F A	F B	F C	F D	F E	F F
150	137	150	82	176	150	28	213	115	115	30	115

Laurencio 177

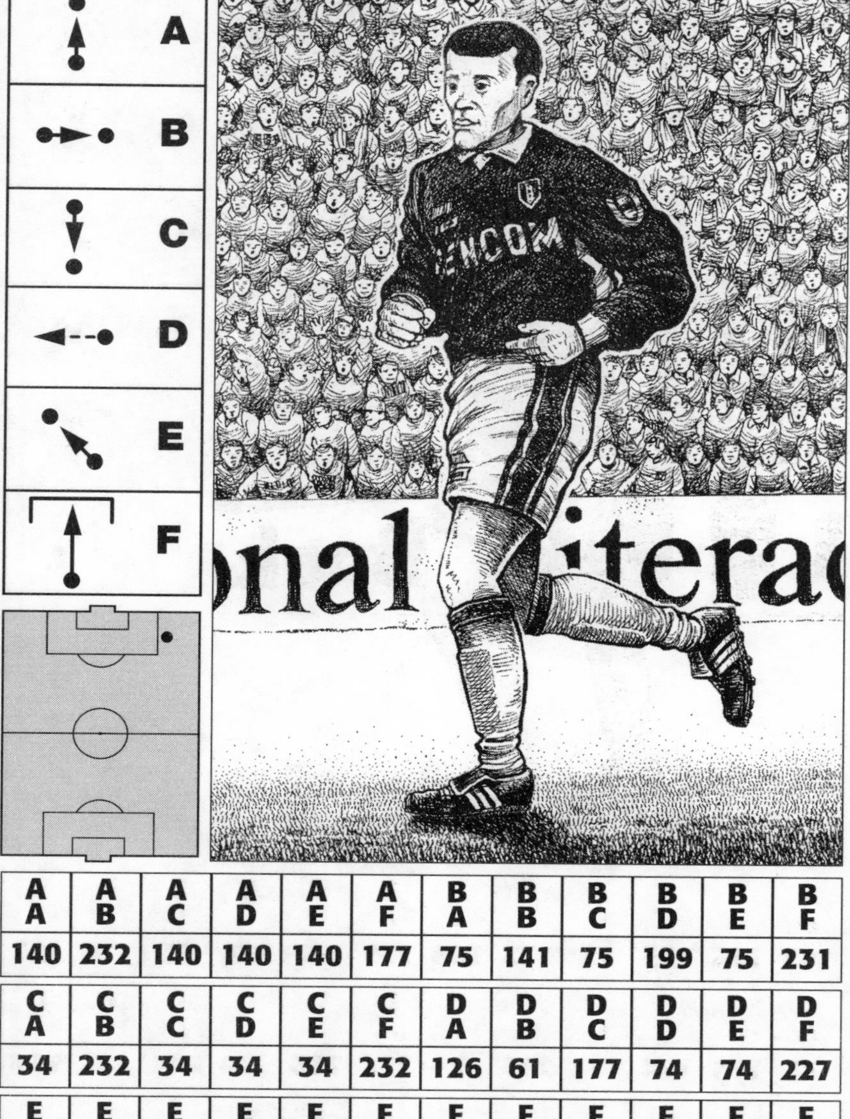

A A	A B	A C	A D	A E	A F	B A	B B	B C	B D	B E	B F
140	232	140	140	140	177	75	141	75	199	75	231

C A	C B	C C	C D	C E	C F	D A	D B	D C	D D	D E	D F
34	232	34	34	34	232	126	61	177	74	74	227

E A	E B	E C	E D	E E	E F	F A	F B	F C	F D	F E	F F
27	211	199	194	194	61	208	208	126	208	211	208

178 Pierre Pasqualle / Throw-in

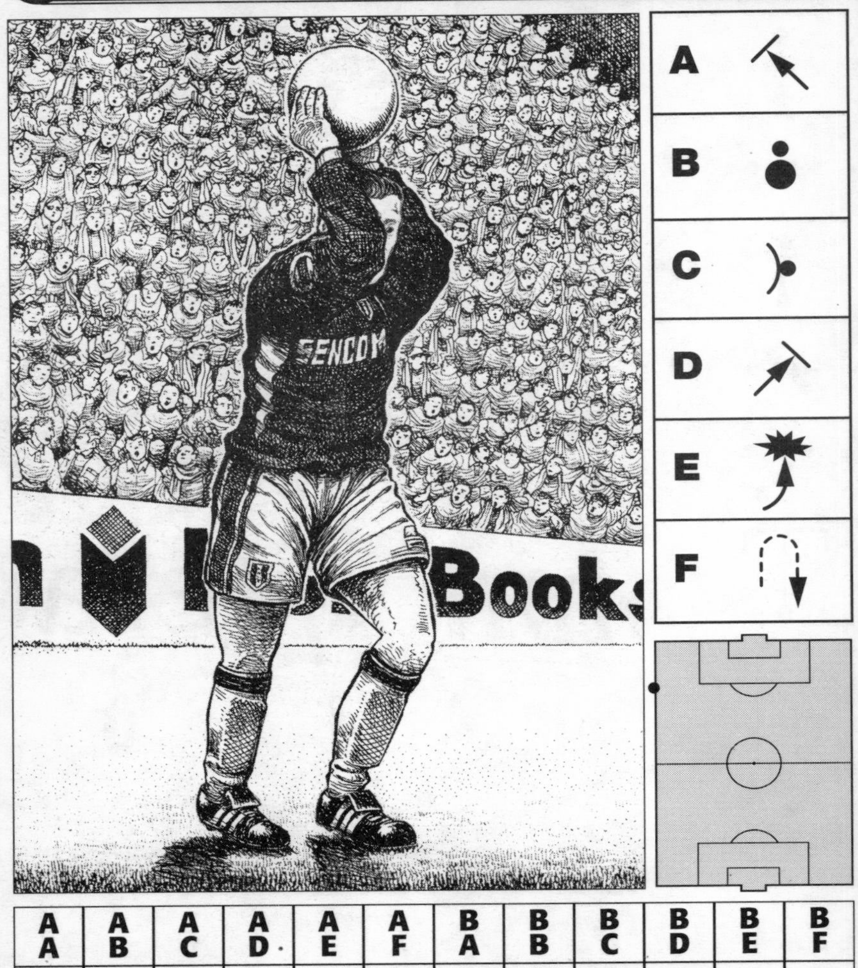

A A	A B	A C	A D	A E	A F	B A	B B	B C	B D	B E	B F
168	168	225	71	178	168	239	127	225	127	165	127

C A	C B	C C	C D	C E	C F	D A	D B	D C	D D	D E	D F
22	124	134	134	233	124	224	216	224	224	147	216

E A	E B	E C	E D	E E	E F	F A	F B	F C	F D	F E	F F
234	234	225	234	71	234	206	193	206	215	180	193

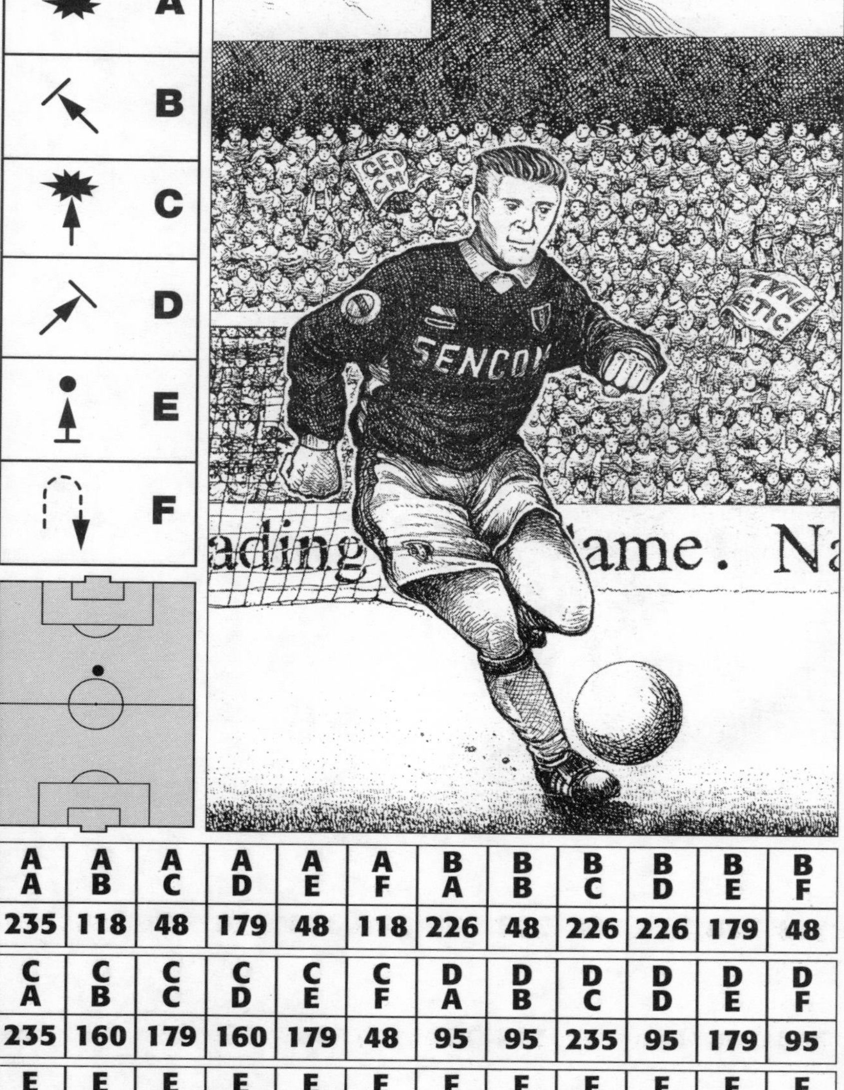

A A	A B	A C	A D	A E	A F	B A	B B	B C	B D	B E	B F
235	118	48	179	48	118	226	48	226	226	179	48

C A	C B	C C	C D	C E	C F	D A	D B	D C	D D	D E	D F
235	160	179	160	179	48	95	95	235	95	179	95

E A	E B	E C	E D	E E	E F	F A	F B	F C	F D	F E	F F
241	241	235	33	241	241	97	18	235	97	97	97

180 Matthew Scadding / Corner

A A	A B	A C	A D	A E	A F	B A	B B	B C	B D	B E	B F
148	208	218	208	208	208	208	194	194	49	194	148

C A	C B	C C	C D	C E	C F	D A	D B	D C	D D	D E	D F
208	206	181	181	148	181	96	96	96	96	96	96

E A	E B	E C	E D	E E	E F	F A	F B	F C	F D	F E	F F
68	68	68	68	68	68	216	216	216	216	216	216

A A	A B	A C	A D	A E	A F	B A	B B	B C	B D	B E	B F
135	148	227	135	84	148	43	43	148	43	43	43

C A	C B	C C	C D	C E	C F	D A	D B	D C	D D	D E	D F
50	208	135	180	148	135	148	148	180	135	227	180

E A	E B	E C	E D	E E	E F	F A	F B	F C	F D	F E	F F
135	135	148	135	194	148	50	50	50	50	50	50

Brett Green / Throw-in

A A	A B	A C	A D	A E	A F	B A	B B	B C	B D	B E	B F
141	141	141	198	141	56	94	64	33	64	13	64

C A	C B	C C	C D	C E	C F	D A	D B	D C	D D	D E	D F
35	35	23	35	8	35	199	199	231	75	177	199

E A	E B	E C	E D	E E	E F	F A	F B	F C	F D	F E	F F
136	136	136	136	136	107	142	117	117	117	117	63

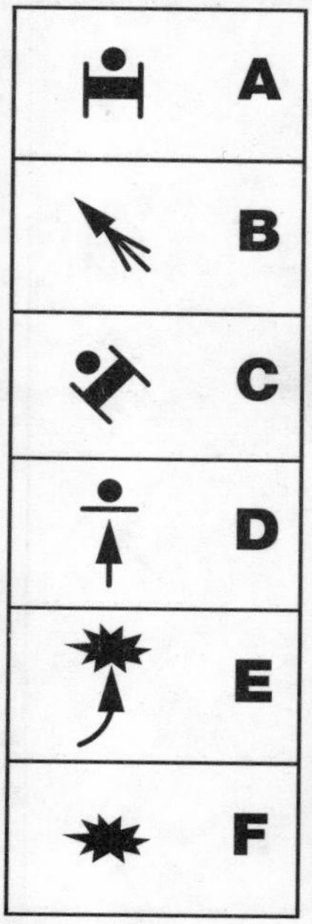

	A
	B
	C
	D
	E
	F

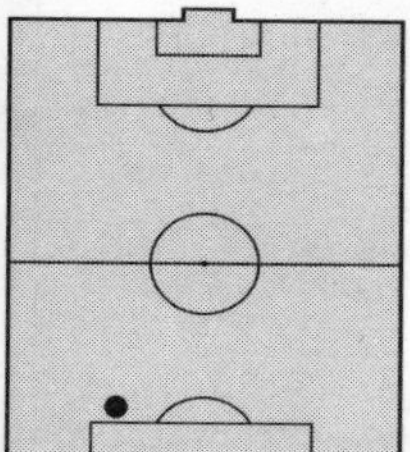

A A	A B	A C	A D	A E	A F	B A	B B	B C	B D	B E	B F
143	119	119	175	119	209	79	79	79	79	79	79

C A	C B	C C	C D	C E	C F	D A	D B	D C	D D	D E	D F
197	197	197	197	197	197	119	143	119	143	119	212

E A	E B	E C	E D	E E	E F	F A	F B	F C	F D	F E	F F
89	89	89	143	212	209	143	143	184	184	88	209

184 Henri Le Clerc

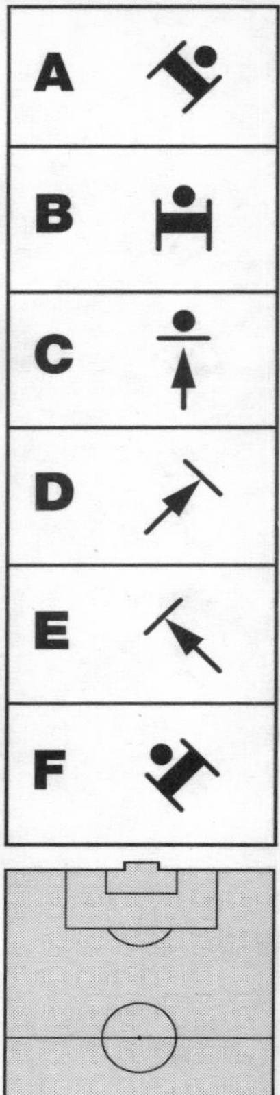

A

B

C

D

E

F

A A	A B	A C	A D	A E	A F	B A	B B	B C	B D	B E	B F
119	175	119	119	130	143	130	119	130	143	119	119

C A	C B	C C	C D	C E	C F	D A	D B	D C	D D	D E	D F
77	143	175	130	119	175	119	119	143	130	175	119

E A	E B	E C	E D	E E	E F	F A	F B	F C	F D	F E	F F
119	119	175	175	143	175	143	130	119	119	119	119

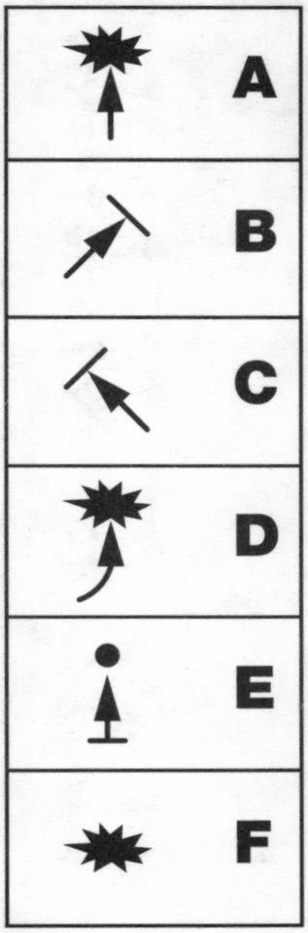

Aaron Hall 185

A

B

C

D

E

F

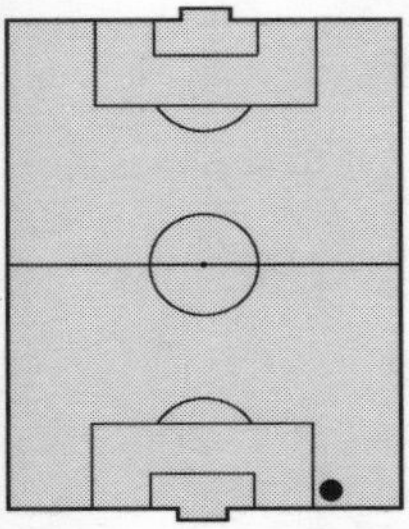

AA	AB	AC	AD	AE	AF	BA	BB	BC	BD	BE	BF
112	112	112	172	112	173	77	130	171	173	163	173

CA	CB	CC	CD	CE	CF	DA	DB	DC	DD	DE	DF
130	228	163	60	185	228	163	60	60	31	60	46

EA	EB	EC	ED	EE	EF	FA	FB	FC	FD	FE	FF
170	170	31	170	170	170	92	92	88	92	92	92

186 Fabien Deschamps / Free Kick

A A	A B	A C	A D	A E	A F	B A	B B	B C	B D	B E	B F
15	15	179	15	160	15	11	32	24	149	11	11

C A	C B	C C	C D	C E	C F	D A	D B	D C	D D	D E	D F
65	133	39	65	105	65	52	52	20	125	146	52

E A	E B	E C	E D	E E	E F	F A	F B	F C	F D	F E	F F
12	123	14	123	129	123	174	12	40	164	12	12

Free Kick / Helmut Bremen 187

A A	A B	A C	A D	A E	A F	B A	B B	B C	B D	B E	B F
23	23	23	95	110	23	33	149	33	118	16	149

C A	C B	C C	C D	C E	C F	D A	D B	D C	D D	D E	D F
8	64	8	35	49	8	123	123	164	129	145	129

E A	E B	E C	E D	E E	E F	F A	F B	F C	F D	F E	F F
124	124	14	134	84	124	15	15	15	160	66	160

188 Matthew Scadding

A A	A B	A C	A D	A E	A F	B A	B B	B C	B D	B E	B F
206	206	206	193	206	206	95	110	95	95	23	62

C A	C B	C C	C D	C E	C F	D A	D B	D C	D D	D E	D F
179	15	179	179	48	179	134	84	134	37	124	62

E A	E B	E C	E D	E E	E F	F A	F B	F C	F D	F E	F F
127	67	127	124	22	127	73	73	73	36	73	73

A A	A B	A C	A D	A E	A F	B A	B B	B C	B D	B E	B F
198	198	198	153	182	210	49	208	56	208	208	208

C A	C B	C C	C D	C E	C F	D A	D B	D C	D D	D E	D F
189	210	75	182	231	210	56	177	141	177	177	177

E A	E B	E C	E D	E E	E F	F A	F B	F C	F D	F E	F F
136	56	117	107	56	56	110	68	62	68	68	68

190 Terry Hiner / Throw-in

A A	A B	A C	A D	A E	A F	B A	B B	B C	B D	B E	B F
69	112	10	57	57	219	69	111	101	101	101	190

C A	C B	C C	C D	C E	C F	D A	D B	D C	D D	D E	D F
76	7	76	7	76	214	25	11	25	11	17	241

E A	E B	E C	E D	E E	E F	F A	F B	F C	F D	F E	F F
69	25	86	86	237	101	201	172	29	172	201	173

Fabien Deschamps 191

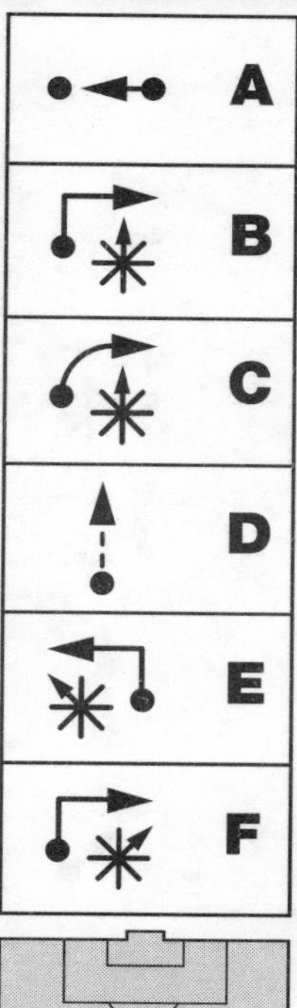

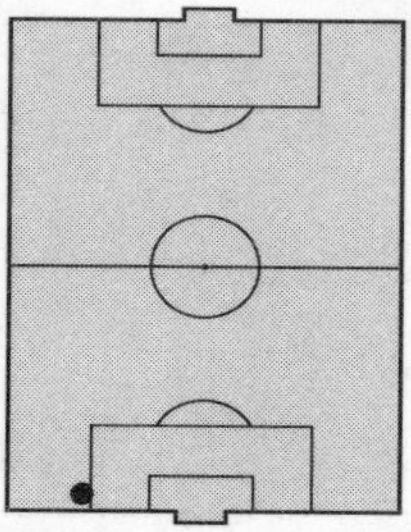

A A	A B	A C	A D	A E	A F	B A	B B	B C	B D	B E	B F
103	132	103	200	132	103	28	115	28	28	28	28

C A	C B	C C	C D	C E	C F	D A	D B	D C	D D	D E	D F
12	104	12	12	12	12	91	99	175	99	99	175

E A	E B	E C	E D	E E	E F	F A	F B	F C	F D	F E	F F
82	150	82	137	82	82	4	109	4	4	92	4

192 Ross Hewitt

A A	A B	A C	A D	A E	A F	B A	B B	B C	B D	B E	B F
88	88	197	88	197	60	192	192	91	9	9	91

C A	C B	C C	C D	C E	C F	D A	D B	D C	D D	D E	D F
4	4	4	30	4	4	52	52	52	20	52	52

E A	E B	E C	E D	E E	E F	F A	F B	F C	F D	F E	F F
197	30	186	93	30	186	28	197	197	28	28	221

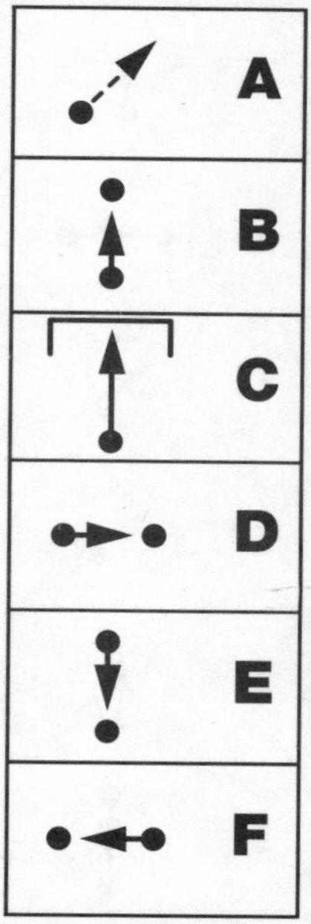

A

B

C

D

E

F

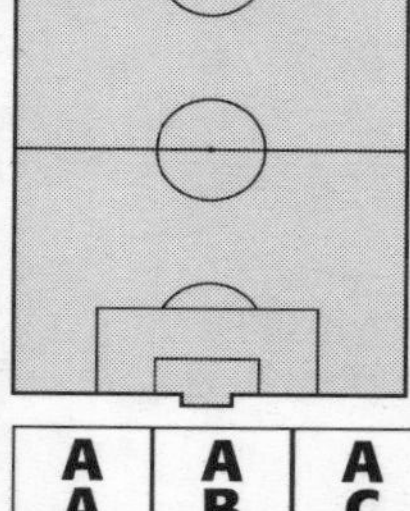

A A	A B	A C	A D	A E	A F	B A	B B	B C	B D	B E	B F
61	61	193	181	206	148	154	84	36	36	206	36

C A	C B	C C	C D	C E	C F	D A	D B	D C	D D	D E	D F
43	43	148	43	43	148	61	218	206	50	206	50

E A	E B	E C	E D	E E	E F	F A	F B	F C	F D	F E	F F
154	154	37	37	154	37	215	168	215	206	206	215

194 Matthew Scadding

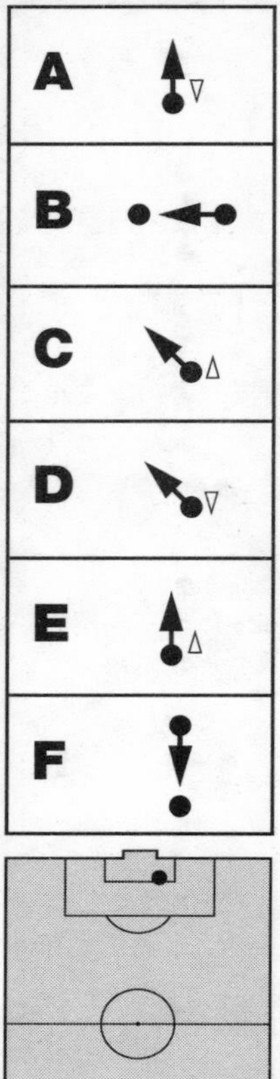

A

B

C

D

E

F

A A	A B	A C	A D	A E	A F	B A	B B	B C	B D	B E	B F
208	148	135	148	135	68	148	43	43	148	43	61

C A	C B	C C	C D	C E	C F	D A	D B	D C	D D	D E	D F
180	148	135	135	148	135	148	135	135	148	135	177

E A	E B	E C	E D	E E	E F	F A	F B	F C	F D	F E	F F
135	148	227	135	148	135	74	74	74	27	74	202

A A	A B	A C	A D	A E	A F	B A	B B	B C	B D	B E	B F
95	48	23	23	95	23	14	18	26	6	14	6

C A	C B	C C	C D	C E	C F	D A	D B	D C	D D	D E	D F
96	148	96	96	218	96	8	49	8	64	35	8

E A	E B	E C	E D	E E	E F	F A	F B	F C	F D	F E	F F
124	84	6	124	134	124	33	33	33	118	33	25

196 Aaron Hall / Free Kick

A A	A B	A C	A D	A E	A F	B A	B B	B C	B D	B E	B F
4	125	109	109	4	109	24	149	86	32	24	32

C A	C B	C C	C D	C E	C F	D A	D B	D C	D D	D E	D F
203	143	203	203	88	203	115	9	115	40	28	115

E A	E B	E C	E D	E E	E F	F A	F B	F C	F D	F E	F F
76	172	32	76	7	76	164	164	164	145	164	123

Ross Hewitt 197

A A	A B	A C	A D	A E	A F	B A	B B	B C	B D	B E	B F
197	212	58	89	192	212	192	183	221	221	9	28

C A	C B	C C	C D	C E	C F	D A	D B	D C	D D	D E	D F
184	212	197	184	144	30	92	92	92	92	30	213

E A	E B	E C	E D	E E	E F	F A	F B	F C	F D	F E	F F
228	228	228	228	228	88	203	173	203	192	88	7

198 Terry Hiner

A

B

C

D

E

F

A A	A B	A C	A D	A E	A F	B A	B B	B C	B D	B E	B F
153	107	107	107	182	107	177	177	49	141	177	177

C A	C B	C C	C D	C E	C F	D A	D B	D C	D D	D E	D F
136	153	189	189	217	210	141	222	217	75	217	75

E A	E B	E C	E D	E E	E F	F A	F B	F C	F D	F E	F F
232	166	217	56	232	56	34	34	34	35	34	34

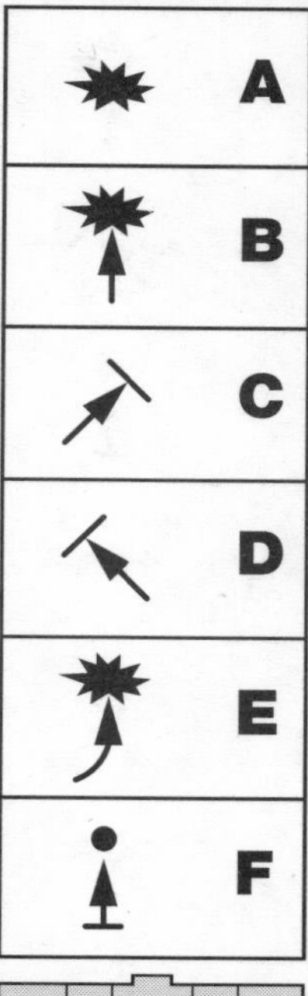

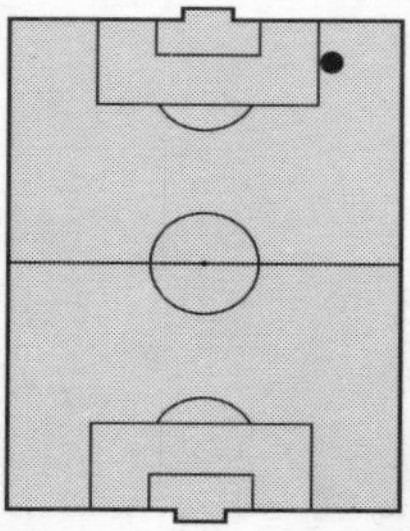

A A	A B	A C	A D	A E	A F	B A	B B	B C	B D	B E	B F
169	177	231	222	227	222	177	169	199	141	169	177

C A	C B	C C	C D	C E	C F	D A	D B	D C	D D	D E	D F
177	169	202	177	236	177	169	177	220	220	227	220

E A	E B	E C	E D	E E	E F	F A	F B	F C	F D	F E	F F
169	34	49	49	169	177	118	118	118	118	118	199

200 Fabien Deschamps

A A	A B	A C	A D	A E	A F	B A	B B	B C	B D	B E	B F
183	79	79	183	79	100	191	191	162	99	162	212

C A	C B	C C	C D	C E	C F	D A	D B	D C	D D	D E	D F
184	192	184	184	184	184	103	113	132	103	200	175

E A	E B	E C	E D	E E	E F	F A	F B	F C	F D	F E	F F
212	58	89	183	89	221	197	30	197	197	197	197

Brett Green 201

A A	A B	A C	A D	A E	A F	B A	B B	B C	B D	B E	B F
76	76	7	76	173	172	203	203	92	172	203	173

C A	C B	C C	C D	C E	C F	D A	D B	D C	D D	D E	D F
88	184	173	31	173	184	60	60	203	172	60	173

E A	E B	E C	E D	E E	E F	F A	F B	F C	F D	F E	F F
57	172	29	57	57	173	112	112	7	112	173	172

202 Laurencio

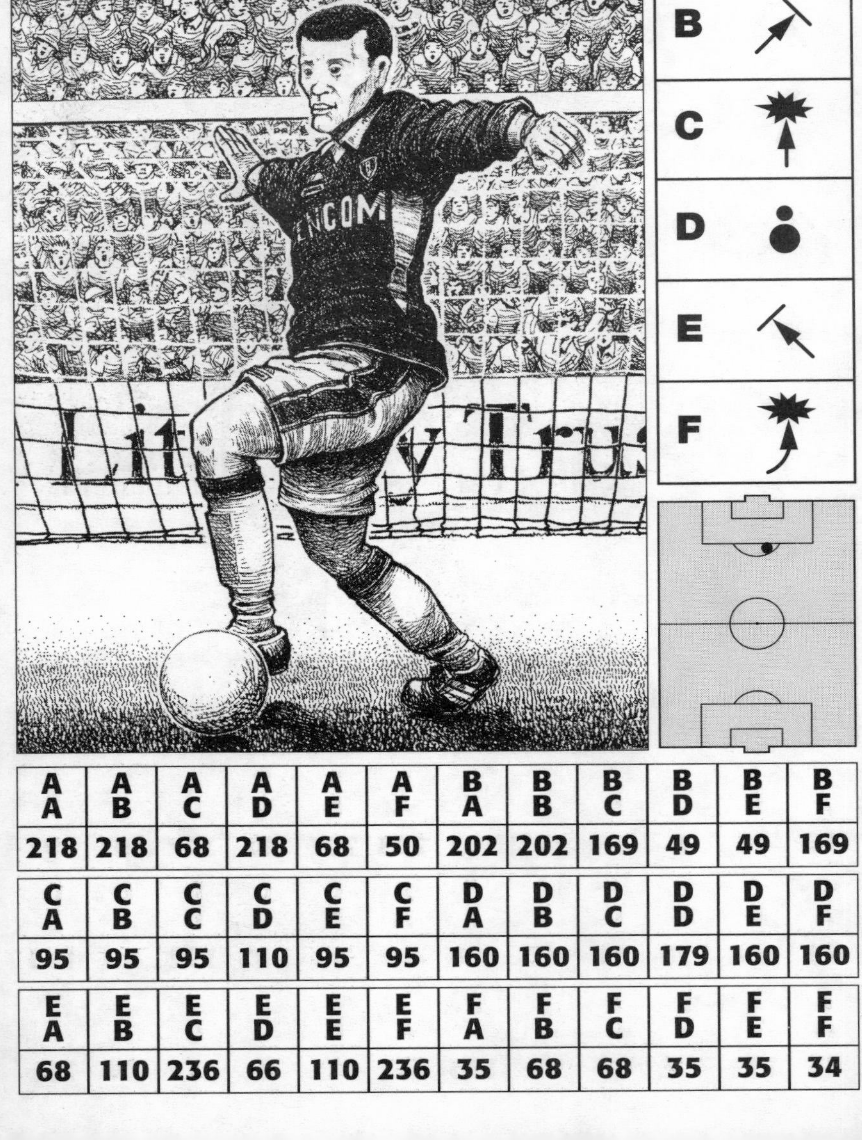

A A	A B	A C	A D	A E	A F	B A	B B	B C	B D	B E	B F
218	218	68	218	68	50	202	202	169	49	49	169

C A	C B	C C	C D	C E	C F	D A	D B	D C	D D	D E	D F
95	95	95	110	95	95	160	160	160	179	160	160

E A	E B	E C	E D	E E	E F	F A	F B	F C	F D	F E	F F
68	110	236	66	110	236	35	68	68	35	35	34

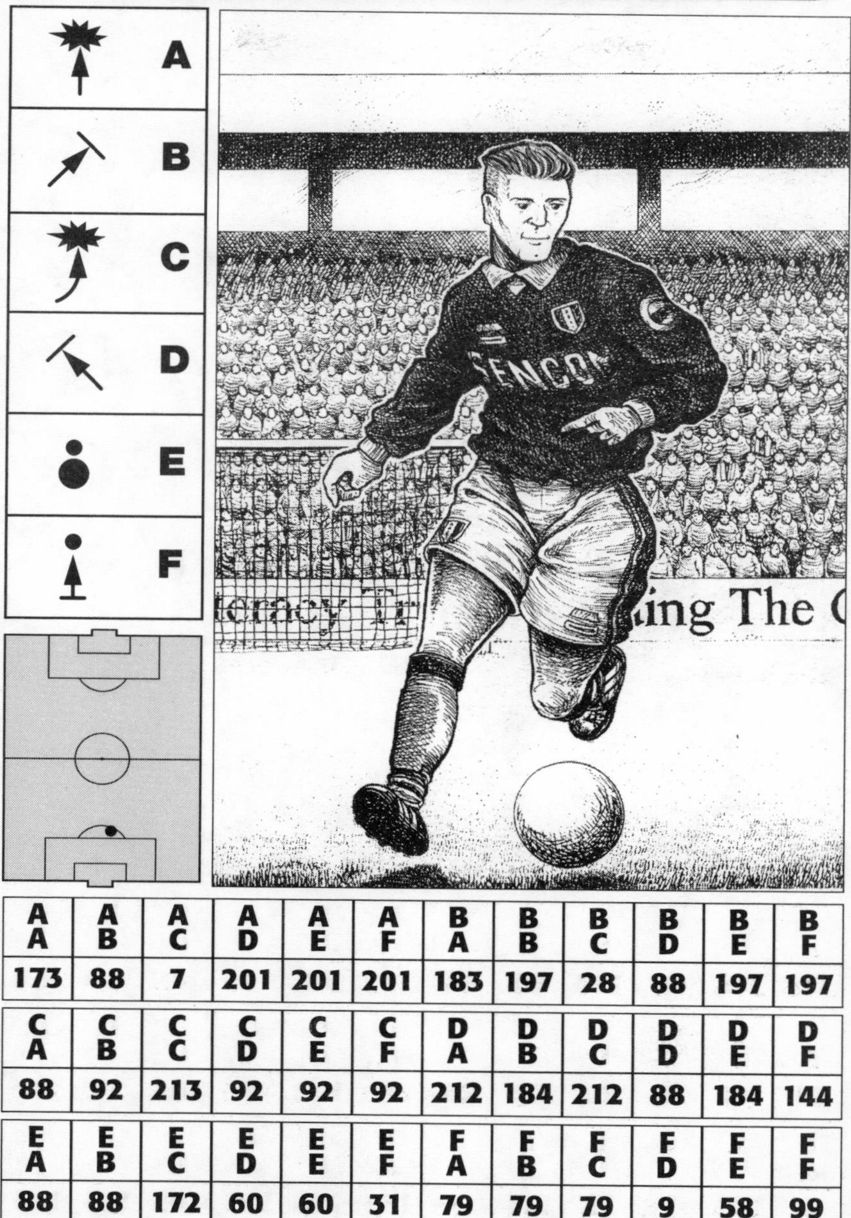

A A	A B	A C	A D	A E	A F	B A	B B	B C	B D	B E	B F
173	88	7	201	201	201	183	197	28	88	197	197

C A	C B	C C	C D	C E	C F	D A	D B	D C	D D	D E	D F
88	92	213	92	92	92	212	184	212	88	184	144

E A	E B	E C	E D	E E	E F	F A	F B	F C	F D	F E	F F
88	88	172	60	60	31	79	79	79	9	58	99

204 Fabien Deschamps / Goal Kick

A A	A B	A C	A D	A E	A F	B A	B B	B C	B D	B E	B F
46	46	46	112	46	46	4	30	4	4	109	92

C A	C B	C C	C D	C E	C F	D A	D B	D C	D D	D E	D F
20	146	20	20	125	20	7	172	7	201	76	92

E A	E B	E C	E D	E E	E F	F A	F B	F C	F D	F E	F F
3	101	3	76	111	3	163	163	163	185	163	163

A A	A B	A C	A D	A E	A F	B A	B B	B C	B D	B E	B F
206	208	180	208	208	208	84	193	218	193	193	193

C A	C B	C C	C D	C E	C F	D A	D B	D C	D D	D E	D F
72	180	215	72	147	180	207	71	207	178	207	229

E A	E B	E C	E D	E E	E F	F A	F B	F C	F D	F E	F F
127	216	134	216	216	216	134	37	110	37	37	37

206 Dave Chell

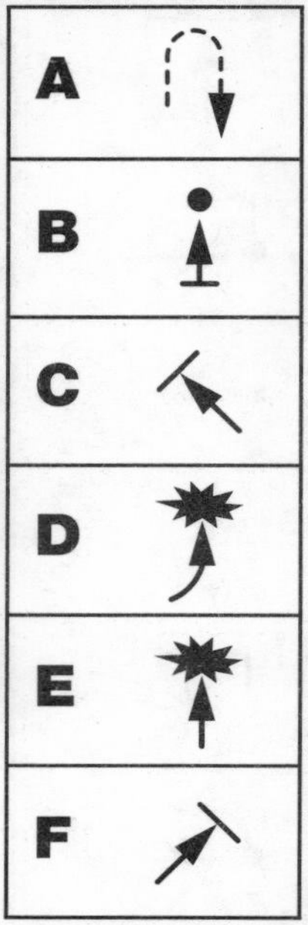

A 

B

C 

D 

E 

F 

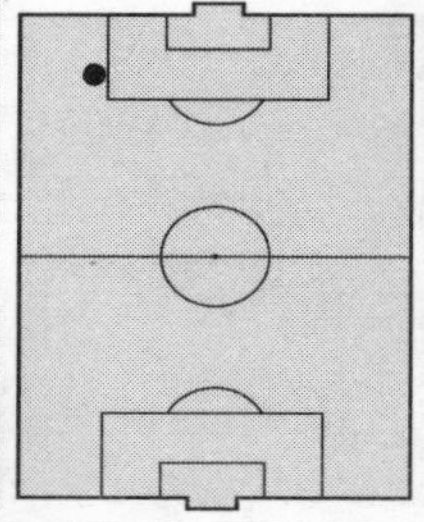

A A	A B	A C	A D	A E	A F	B A	B B	B C	B D	B E	B F
147	206	193	180	147	147	37	193	84	233	193	84

C A	C B	C C	C D	C E	C F	D A	D B	D C	D D	D E	D F
216	193	233	233	193	224	73	73	73	233	233	73

E A	E B	E C	E D	E E	E F	F A	F B	F C	F D	F E	F F
127	127	224	127	127	127	179	179	179	179	179	37

Ross Hewitt 207

A A	A B	A C	A D	A E	A F	B A	B B	B C	B D	B E	B F
168	216	224	67	216	216	168	205	205	71	205	205

C A	C B	C C	C D	C E	C F	D A	D B	D C	D D	D E	D F
215	215	147	37	215	215	168	225	225	178	225	225

E A	E B	E C	E D	E E	E F	F A	F B	F C	F D	F E	F F
208	202	206	208	208	147	193	84	224	193	193	206

208 Matthew Scadding

A A	A B	A C	A D	A E	A F	B A	B B	B C	B D	B E	B F
135	227	135	135	180	148	180	135	180	148	135	135

C A	C B	C C	C D	C E	C F	D A	D B	D C	D D	D E	D F
72	148	227	180	135	227	135	135	148	180	227	135

E A	E B	E C	E D	E E	E F	F A	F B	F C	F D	F E	F F
135	135	227	227	148	227	148	180	135	135	135	135

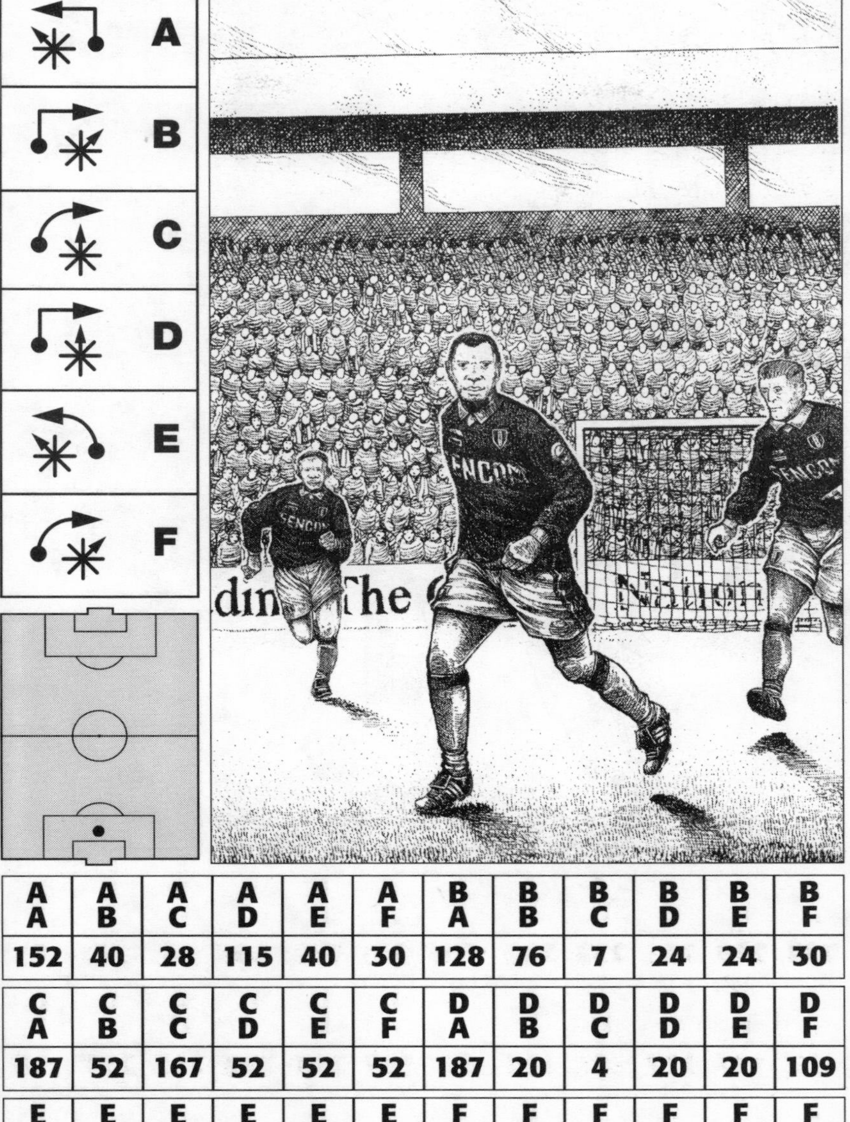

A A	A B	A C	A D	A E	A F	B A	B B	B C	B D	B E	B F
152	40	28	115	40	30	128	76	7	24	24	30

C A	C B	C C	C D	C E	C F	D A	D B	D C	D D	D E	D F
187	52	167	52	52	52	187	20	4	20	20	109

E A	E B	E C	E D	E E	E F	F A	F B	F C	F D	F E	F F
187	145	129	104	145	145	195	32	118	133	133	133

210 Brett Green

A A	A B	A C	A D	A E	A F	B A	B B	B C	B D	B E	B F
227	210	231	222	227	75	35	75	35	34	35	8

C A	C B	C C	C D	C E	C F	D A	D B	D C	D D	D E	D F
117	117	117	8	117	63	189	217	227	217	231	198

E A	E B	E C	E D	E E	E F	F A	F B	F C	F D	F E	F F
105	231	105	65	105	65	160	231	160	15	160	15

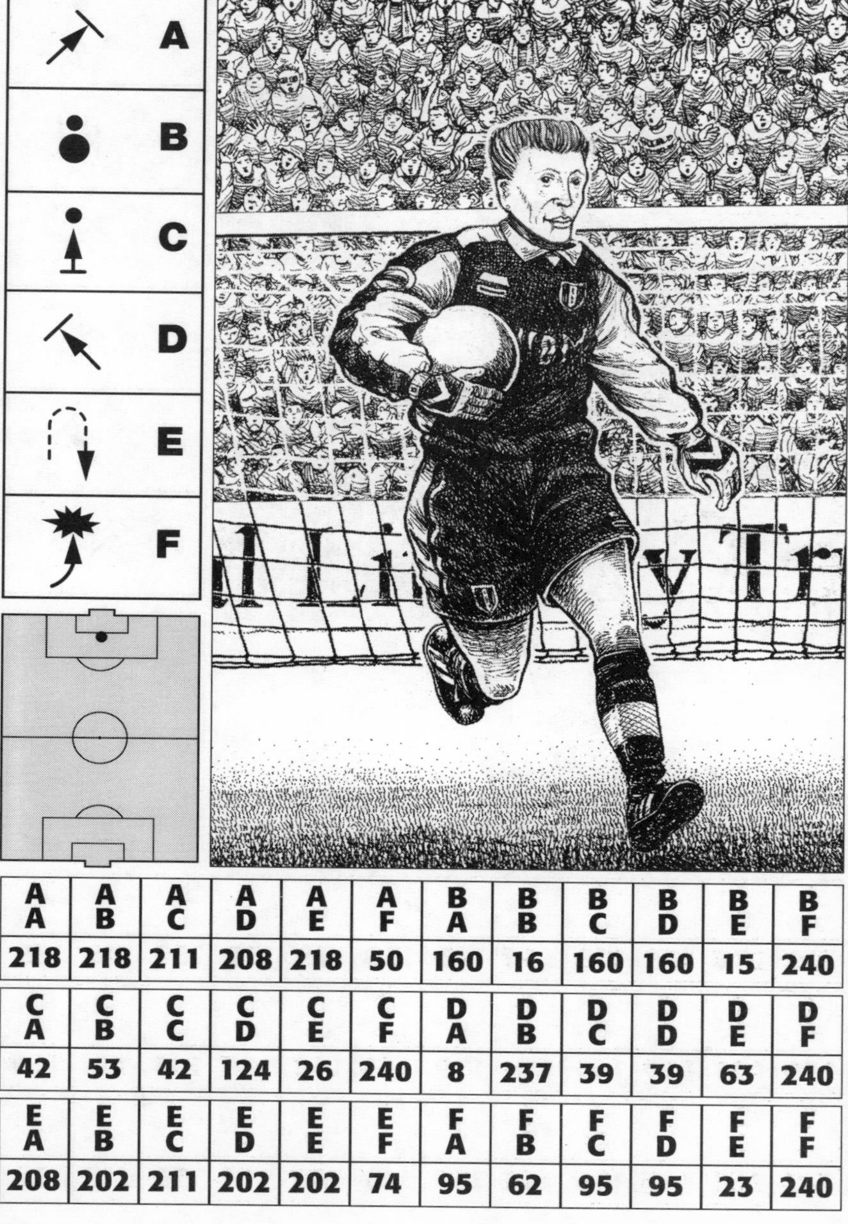

A A	A B	A C	A D	A E	A F	B A	B B	B C	B D	B E	B F
218	218	211	208	218	50	160	16	160	160	15	240

C A	C B	C C	C D	C E	C F	D A	D B	D C	D D	D E	D F
42	53	42	124	26	240	8	237	39	39	63	240

E A	E B	E C	E D	E E	E F	F A	F B	F C	F D	F E	F F
208	202	211	202	202	74	95	62	95	95	23	240

212 Henri Le Clerc / Penalty

A A	A B	A C	A D	A E	A F	B A	B B	B C	B D	B E	B F
119	175	175	119	175	143	130	119	119	130	119	119

C A	C B	C C	C D	C E	C F	D A	D B	D C	D D	D E	D F
119	130	119	143	119	119	143	119	170	184	60	119

E A	E B	E C	E D	E E	E F	F A	F B	F C	F D	F E	F F
175	119	143	119	119	175	119	143	119	119	119	130

Free Kick / Helmut Bremen

213

A A	A B	A C	A D	A E	A F	B A	B B	B C	B D	B E	B F
221	221	221	221	221	221	119	130	143	119	130	130

C A	C B	C C	C D	C E	C F	D A	D B	D C	D D	D E	D F
184	184	184	184	143	184	143	119	119	175	175	119

E A	E B	E C	E D	E E	E F	F A	F B	F C	F D	F E	F F
175	119	130	119	143	119	203	203	203	203	203	203

214 Brett Green / Free Kick

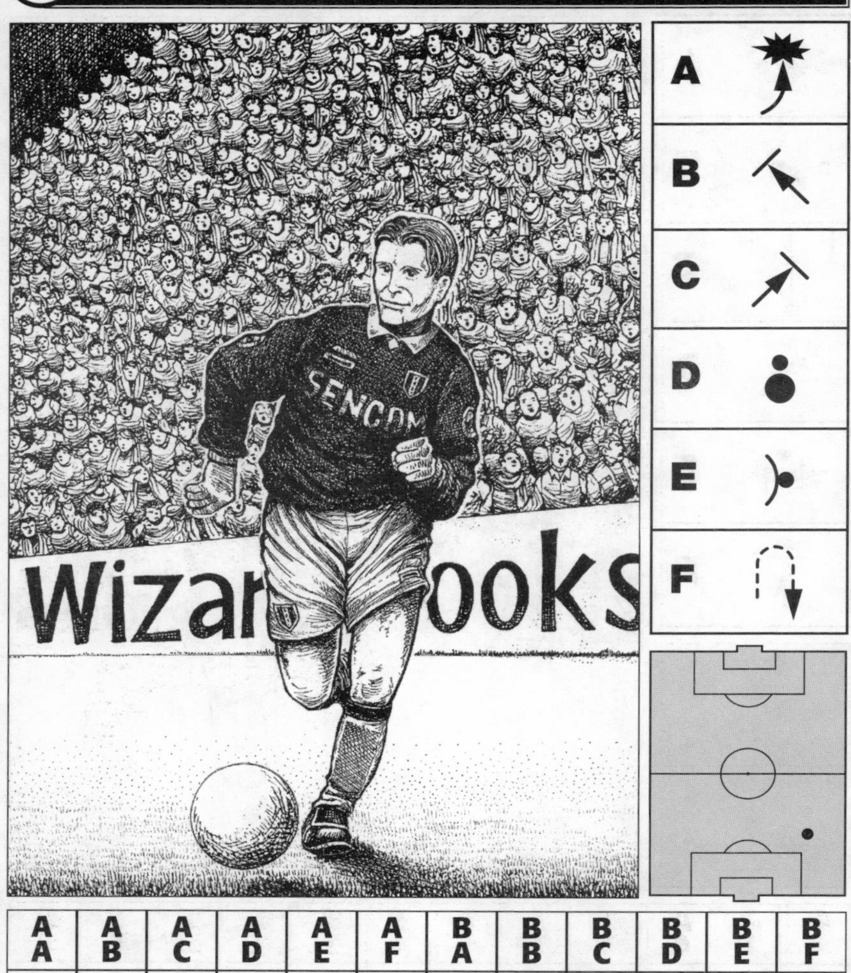

A A	A B	A C	A D	A E	A F	B A	B B	B C	B D	B E	B F
109	7	76	76	76	7	190	101	69	101	101	101

C A	C B	C C	C D	C E	C F	D A	D B	D C	D D	D E	D F
102	156	10	156	156	10	92	76	92	30	7	92

E A	E B	E C	E D	E E	E F	F A	F B	F C	F D	F E	F F
184	76	184	144	7	184	3	111	111	111	111	3

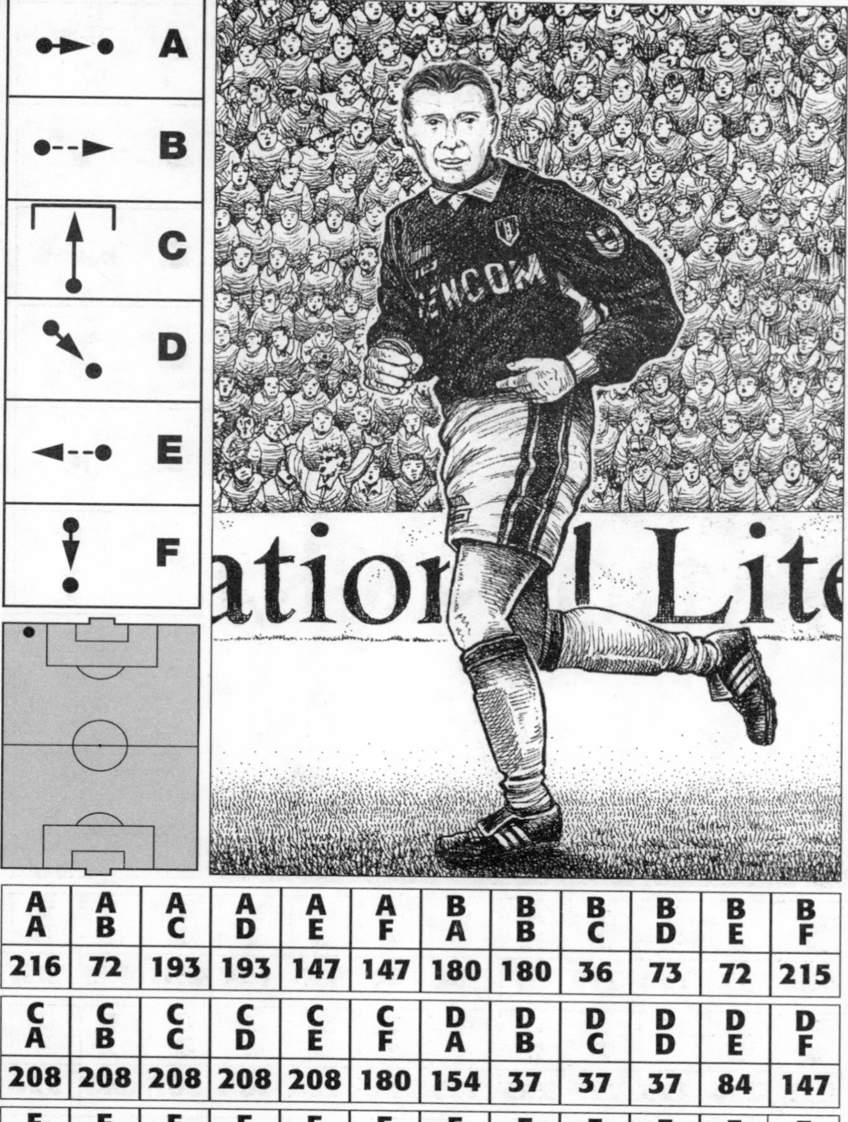

A A	A B	A C	A D	A E	A F	B A	B B	B C	B D	B E	B F
216	72	193	193	147	147	180	180	36	73	72	215

C A	C B	C C	C D	C E	C F	D A	D B	D C	D D	D E	D F
208	208	208	208	208	180	154	37	37	37	84	147

E A	E B	E C	E D	E E	E F	F A	F B	F C	F D	F E	F F
72	180	147	229	180	205	127	216	216	216	224	216

216 Dave Chell

A A	A B	A C	A D	A E	A F	B A	B B	B C	B D	B E	B F
154	37	154	216	37	154	84	193	154	224	193	224

C A	C B	C C	C D	C E	C F	D A	D B	D C	D D	D E	D F
178	224	225	225	225	225	71	224	168	207	207	224

E A	E B	E C	E D	E E	E F	F A	F B	F C	F D	F E	F F
96	96	96	110	84	96	127	215	72	215	215	224

A	A	A	A	A	A	B	B	B	B	B	B
A	B	C	D	E	F	A	B	C	D	E	F
141	198	141	56	217	227	222	198	222	75	217	231

C	C	C	C	C	C	D	D	D	D	D	D
A	B	C	D	E	F	A	B	C	D	E	F
198	136	136	198	107	182	179	8	34	179	179	179

E	E	E	E	E	E	F	F	F	F	F	F
A	B	C	D	E	F	A	B	C	D	E	F
35	56	75	35	35	35	210	210	210	153	210	189

218 Dave Chell

A A	A B	A C	A D	A E	A F	B A	B B	B C	B D	B E	B F
233	84	218	218	233	233	96	96	202	202	236	74

C A	C B	C C	C D	C E	C F	D A	D B	D C	D D	D E	D F
129	129	129	6	129	129	96	134	124	96	233	37

E A	E B	E C	E D	E E	E F	F A	F B	F C	F D	F E	F F
96	110	62	110	236	211	35	35	35	35	35	35

A A	A B	A C	A D	A E	A F	B A	B B	B C	B D	B E	B F
116	57	29	101	57	57	116	230	230	102	230	230

C A	C B	C C	C D	C E	C F	D A	D B	D C	D D	D E	D F
171	171	45	201	171	171	116	156	156	70	156	156

E A	E B	E C	E D	E E	E F	F A	F B	F C	F D	F E	F F
184	192	46	184	184	45	112	172	29	112	112	46

Laurencio

A	
B	
C	
D	
E	
F	

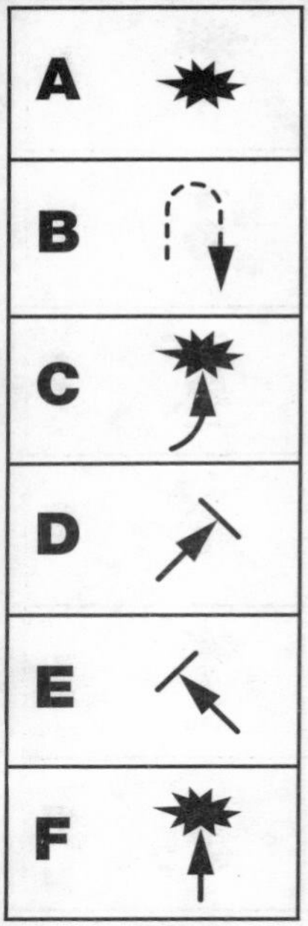

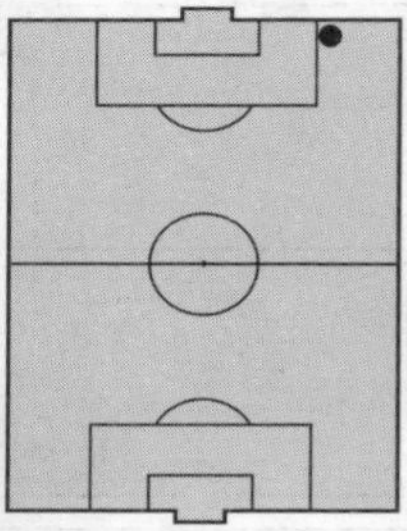

A A	A B	A C	A D	A E	A F	B A	B B	B C	B D	B E	B F
231	222	231	140	222	231	35	8	35	35	35	35

C A	C B	C C	C D	C E	C F	D A	D B	D C	D D	D E	D F
105	65	105	105	105	105	169	199	227	199	199	227

E A	E B	E C	E D	E E	E F	F A	F B	F C	F D	F E	F F
136	107	136	182	136	136	95	23	95	95	62	95

A A	A B	A C	A D	A E	A F	B A	B B	B C	B D	B E	B F
9	79	99	79	28	79	197	197	197	9	92	197

C A	C B	C C	C D	C E	C F	D A	D B	D C	D D	D E	D F
183	92	30	92	213	92	184	184	184	192	184	144

E A	E B	E C	E D	E E	E F	F A	F B	F C	F D	F E	F F
183	221	78	100	183	100	183	115	115	115	28	115

222 Brett Green

A A	A B	A C	A D	A E	A F	B A	B B	B C	B D	B E	B F
199	199	75	169	199	227	35	169	34	35	35	35

C A	C B	C C	C D	C E	C F	D A	D B	D C	D D	D E	D F
64	64	8	64	64	64	75	217	217	182	217	182

E A	E B	E C	E D	E E	E F	F A	F B	F C	F D	F E	F F
75	75	136	153	107	182	141	75	141	222	56	231

A A	A B	A C	A D	A E	A F	B A	B B	B C	B D	B E	B F
34	34	34	34	34	34	135	180	148	135	180	180

C A	C B	C C	C D	C E	C F	D A	D B	D C	D D	D E	D F
208	208	208	208	148	208	148	135	135	227	227	135

E A	E B	E C	E D	E E	E F	F A	F B	F C	F D	F E	F F
227	135	180	135	148	135	96	96	96	96	96	96

224 Dave Chell

A A	A B	A C	A D	A E	A F	B A	B B	B C	B D	B E	B F
234	165	234	216	178	234	216	216	127	127	224	127

C A	C B	C C	C D	C E	C F	D A	D B	D C	D D	D E	D F
179	179	124	179	165	23	224	165	216	134	37	134

E A	E B	E C	E D	E E	E F	F A	F B	F C	F D	F E	F F
147	165	147	147	215	147	216	37	224	84	165	84

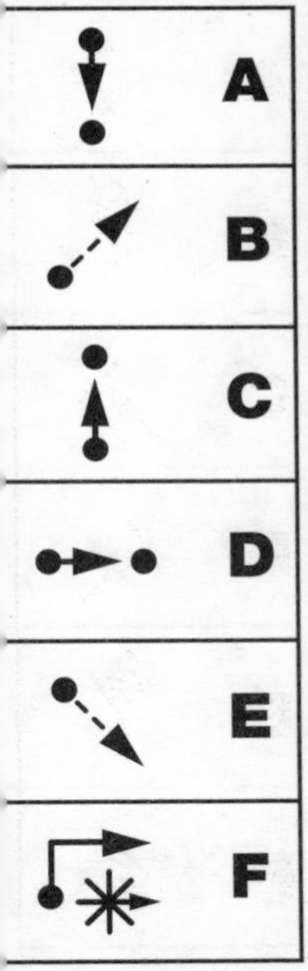

A

B

C

D

E

F

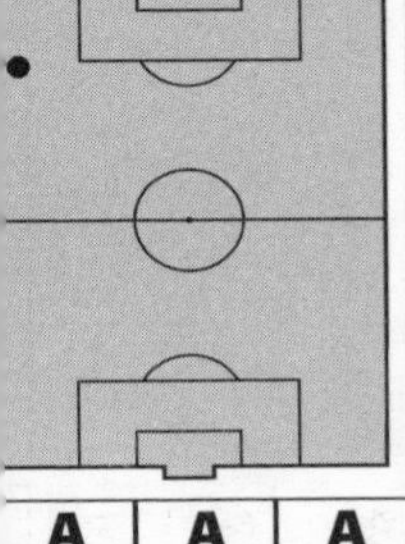

A A	A B	A C	A D	A E	A F	B A	B B	B C	B D	B E	B F
67	67	67	67	67	71	215	215	147	225	215	178

C A	C B	C C	C D	C E	C F	D A	D B	D C	D D	D E	D F
207	207	225	207	168	234	216	216	216	234	216	234

E A	E B	E C	E D	E E	E F	F A	F B	F C	F D	F E	F F
22	22	127	127	22	38	224	134	37	127	37	37

226 Helmut Bremen

A A	A B	A C	A D	A E	A F	B A	B B	B C	B D	B E	B F
160	160	235	160	235	160	104	12	59	104	12	18

C A	C B	C C	C D	C E	C F	D A	D B	D C	D D	D E	D F
161	161	235	226	235	161	167	19	16	18	19	167

E A	E B	E C	E D	E E	E F	F A	F B	F C	F D	F E	F F
129	129	26	129	123	18	145	145	18	164	18	164

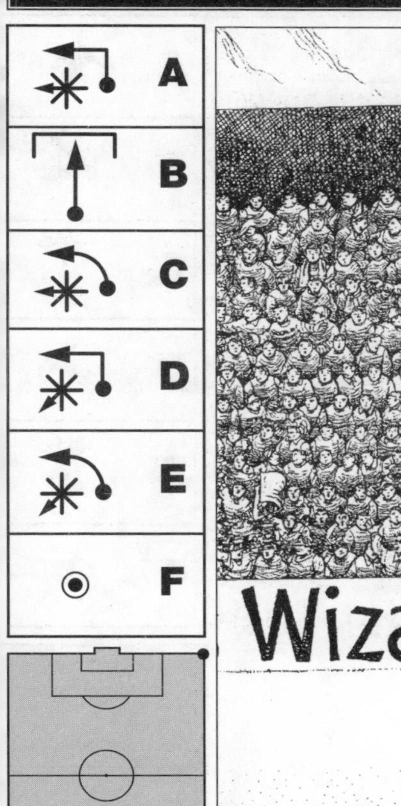

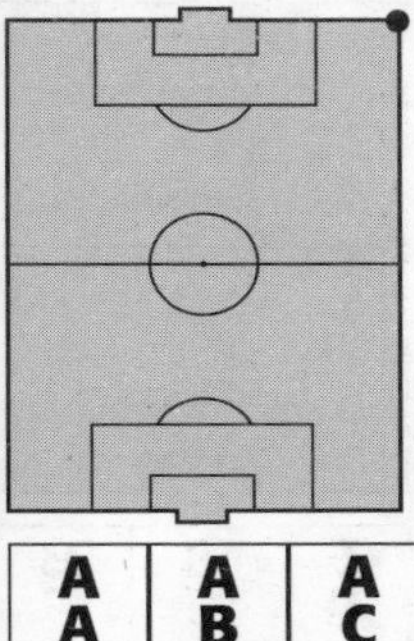

A A	A B	A C	A D	A E	A F	B A	B B	B C	B D	B E	B F
177	177	177	177	177	177	148	148	208	148	240	208

C A	C B	C C	C D	C E	C F	D A	D B	D C	D D	D E	D F
43	148	208	148	240	43	56	56	56	56	56	56

E A	E B	E C	E D	E E	E F	F A	F B	F C	F D	F E	F F
34	34	34	34	34	34	68	68	68	68	68	68

228 Henri Le Clerc

A	A	A	A	A	A	B	B	B	B	B	B
A	B	C	D	E	F	A	B	C	D	E	F
119	143	175	119	172	143	170	170	143	170	170	170

C	C	C	C	C	C	D	D	D	D	D	D
A	B	C	D	E	F	A	B	C	D	E	F
60	184	119	130	143	119	143	143	130	119	175	130

E	E	E	E	E	E	F	F	F	F	F	F
A	B	C	D	E	F	A	B	C	D	E	F
119	119	143	119	162	143	60	60	60	60	60	60

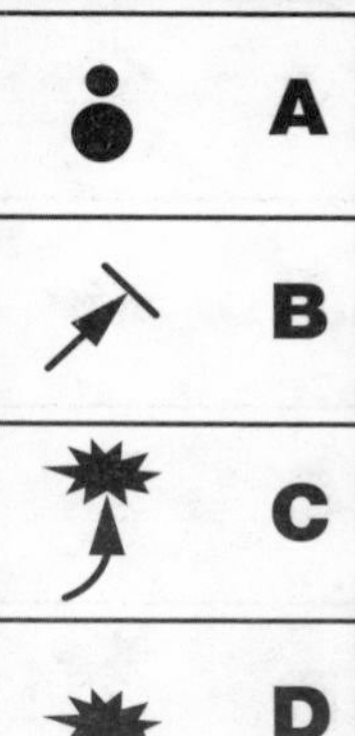

A

B

C

D

E

F

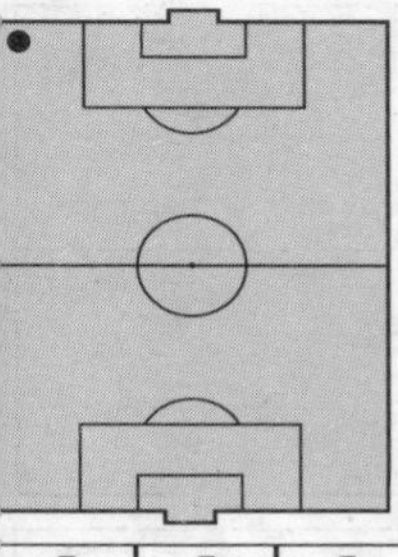

AA	AB	AC	AD	AE	AF	BA	BB	BC	BD	BE	BF
14	216	127	127	127	22	95	84	134	134	134	124

CA	CB	CC	CD	CE	CF	DA	DB	DC	DD	DE	DF
147	229	180	180	72	205	178	234	234	234	234	225

EA	EB	EC	ED	EE	EF	FA	FB	FC	FD	FE	FF
168	168	72	71	205	207	123	14	129	129	129	123

230 Aaron Hall

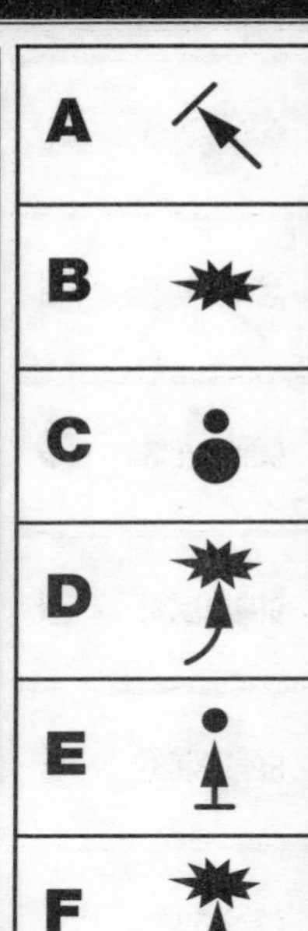

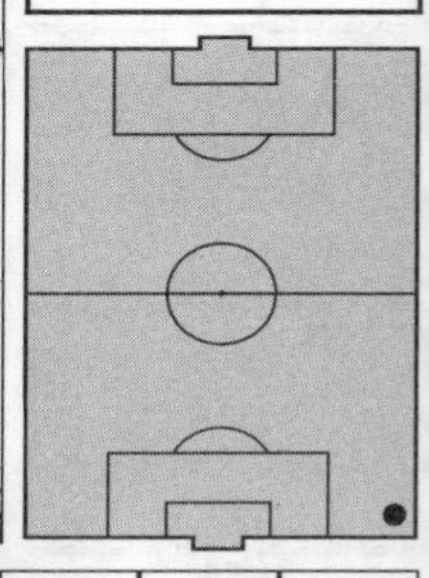

A A	A B	A C	A D	A E	A F	B A	B B	B C	B D	B E	B F
46	184	130	184	184	184	172	112	88	112	112	112

C A	C B	C C	C D	C E	C F	D A	D B	D C	D D	D E	D F
77	130	171	77	45	130	219	102	219	70	219	98

E A	E B	E C	E D	E E	E F	F A	F B	F C	F D	F E	F F
3	57	7	57	57	57	7	201	30	201	201	201

GOAL KICK!	A
GOAL KICK!	B
GOAL KICK!	C
GOAL KICK!	D
GOAL KICK!	E
GOAL KICK!	F

A A	A B	A C	A D	A E	A F	B A	B B	B C	B D	B E	B F
126	126	126	126	126	126	126	126	126	126	126	126

C A	C B	C C	C D	C E	C F	D A	D B	D C	D D	D E	D F
126	126	126	126	126	126	126	126	126	126	126	126

E A	E B	E C	E D	E E	E F	F A	F B	F C	F D	F E	F F
126	126	126	126	126	126	126	126	126	126	126	126

232 Matthew Scadding / Free Kick

A A	A B	A C	A D	A E	A F	B A	B B	B C	B D	B E	B F
148	135	135	227	135	240	177	177	177	177	177	177

C A	C B	C C	C D	C E	C F	D A	D B	D C	D D	D E	D F
68	68	68	68	68	68	135	148	135	148	135	61

E A	E B	E C	E D	E E	E F	F A	F B	F C	F D	F E	F F
74	74	74	148	61	240	148	148	208	208	218	240

A A	A B	A C	A D	A E	A F	B A	B B	B C	B D	B E	B F
134	14	14	14	6	14	16	179	160	160	15	15

C A	C B	C C	C D	C E	C F	D A	D B	D C	D D	D E	D F
20	93	146	146	52	52	40	164	164	164	164	145

E A	E B	E C	E D	E E	E F	F A	F B	F C	F D	F E	F F
53	42	42	22	26	26	83	97	97	67	97	59

234 Ross Hewitt

A A	A B	A C	A D	A E	A F	B A	B B	B C	B D	B E	B F
225	234	127	165	178	159	165	168	168	168	168	165

C A	C B	C C	C D	C E	C F	D A	D B	D C	D D	D E	D F
216	127	225	127	127	225	147	224	225	224	224	165

E A	E B	E C	E D	E E	E F	F A	F B	F C	F D	F E	F F
42	42	22	165	225	42	14	14	127	165	224	14

A A	A B	A C	A D	A E	A F	B A	B B	B C	B D	B E	B F
109	109	109	4	30	109	164	18	164	145	167	18

C A	C B	C C	C D	C E	C F	D A	D B	D C	D D	D E	D F
115	40	115	28	9	115	25	25	33	11	118	11

E A	E B	E C	E D	E E	E F	F A	F B	F C	F D	F E	F F
76	76	24	7	172	76	146	146	146	52	93	52

236 Dave Chell / Free Kick

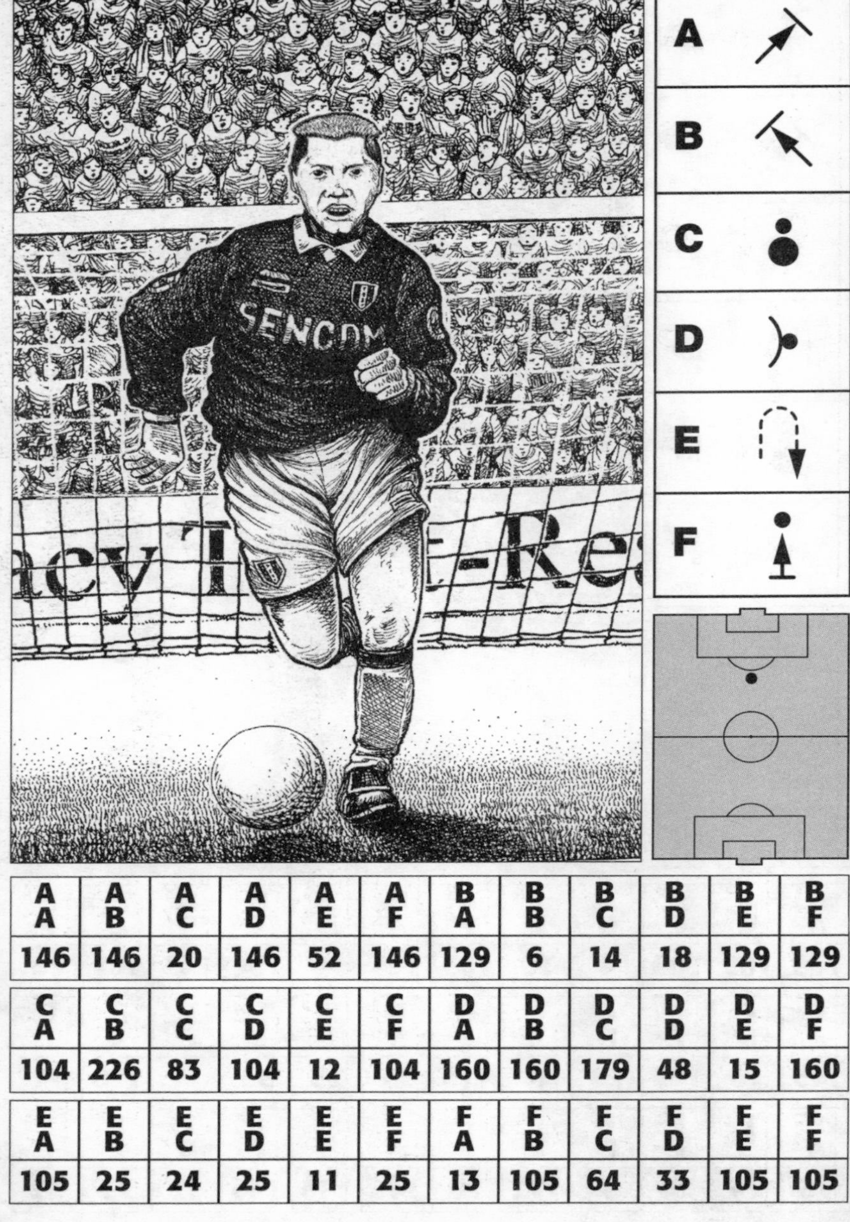

A A	A B	A C	A D	A E	A F	B A	B B	B C	B D	B E	B F
146	146	20	146	52	146	129	6	14	18	129	129

C A	C B	C C	C D	C E	C F	D A	D B	D C	D D	D E	D F
104	226	83	104	12	104	160	160	179	48	15	160

E A	E B	E C	E D	E E	E F	F A	F B	F C	F D	F E	F F
105	25	24	25	11	25	13	105	64	33	105	105

Aaron Hall 237

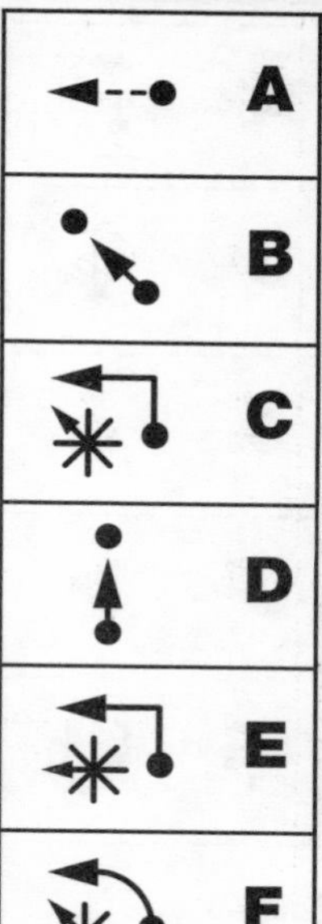

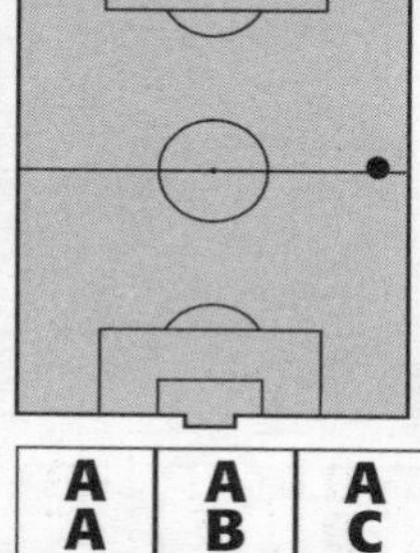

A A	A B	A C	A D	A E	A F	B A	B B	B C	B D	B E	B F
17	17	237	51	241	241	5	5	242	105	242	5

C A	C B	C C	C D	C E	C F	D A	D B	D C	D D	D E	D F
65	64	105	13	13	13	80	80	80	55	242	80

E A	E B	E C	E D	E E	E F	F A	F B	F C	F D	F E	F F
17	105	241	65	65	65	49	8	13	8	8	8

238 Brett Green / Free Kick

A A	A B	A C	A D	A E	A F	B A	B B	B C	B D	B E	B F
160	15	160	161	13	160	146	52	146	125	33	146

C A	C B	C C	C D	C E	C F	D A	D B	D C	D D	D E	D F
241	17	5	65	241	241	86	51	86	3	86	86

E A	E B	E C	E D	E E	E F	F A	F B	F C	F D	F E	F F
5	39	39	39	39	39	80	94	94	94	94	142

A A	A B	A C	A D	A E	A F	B A	B B	B C	B D	B E	B F
59	123	129	145	129	129	127	22	127	6	127	127

C A	C B	C C	C D	C E	C F	D A	D B	D C	D D	D E	D F
159	159	159	42	159	67	224	224	225	234	224	67

E A	E B	E C	E D	E E	E F	F A	F B	F C	F D	F E	F F
134	124	22	23	134	134	53	42	42	159	42	67

Matthew Scadding / Goal Kick

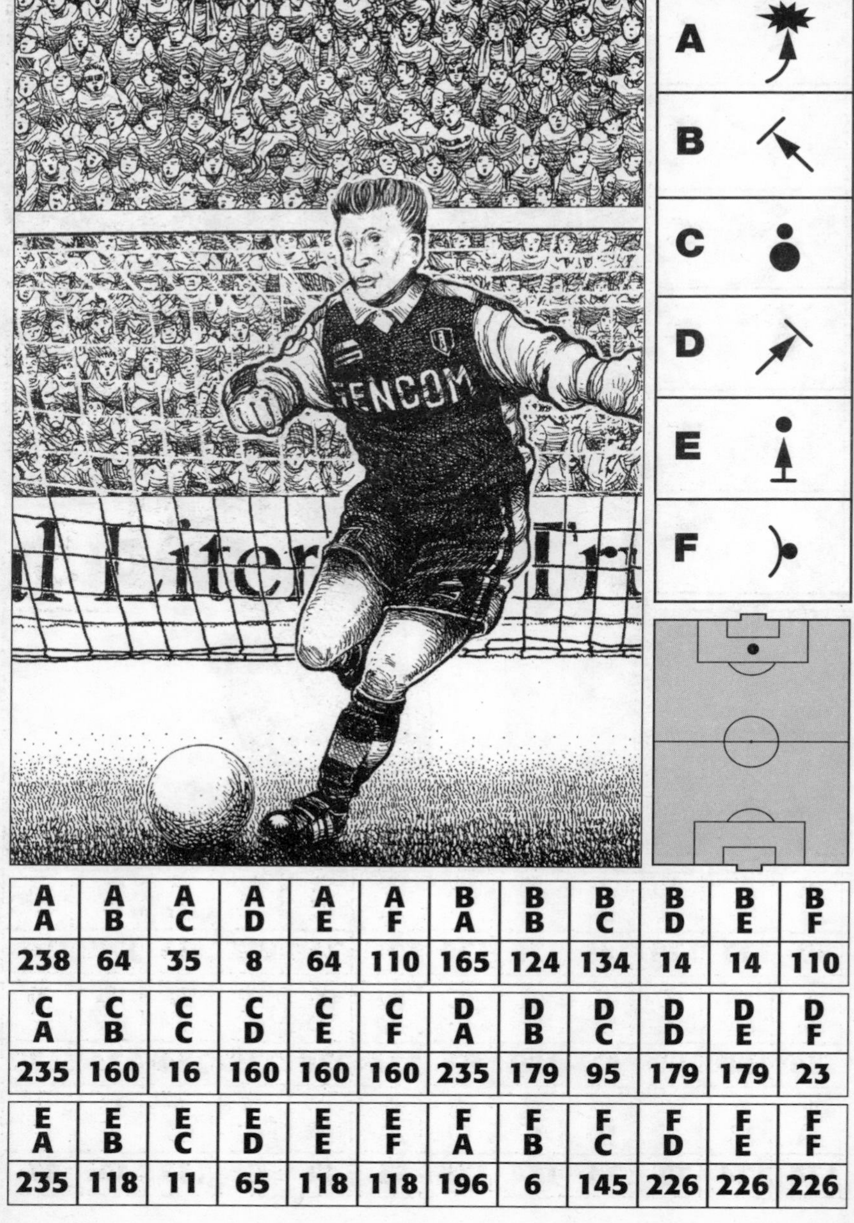

A A	A B	A C	A D	A E	A F	B A	B B	B C	B D	B E	B F
238	64	35	8	64	110	165	124	134	14	14	110

C A	C B	C C	C D	C E	C F	D A	D B	D C	D D	D E	D F
235	160	16	160	160	160	235	179	95	179	179	23

E A	E B	E C	E D	E E	E F	F A	F B	F C	F D	F E	F F
235	118	11	65	118	118	196	6	145	226	226	226

A A	A B	A C	A D	A E	A F	B A	B B	B C	B D	B E	B F
65	17	25	11	25	25	142	242	237	55	242	241

C A	C B	C C	C D	C E	C F	D A	D B	D C	D D	D E	D F
190	101	101	69	101	17	109	20	109	109	4	109

E A	E B	E C	E D	E E	E F	F A	F B	F C	F D	F E	F F
76	24	76	76	7	76	5	86	51	17	86	86

242 Aaron Hall

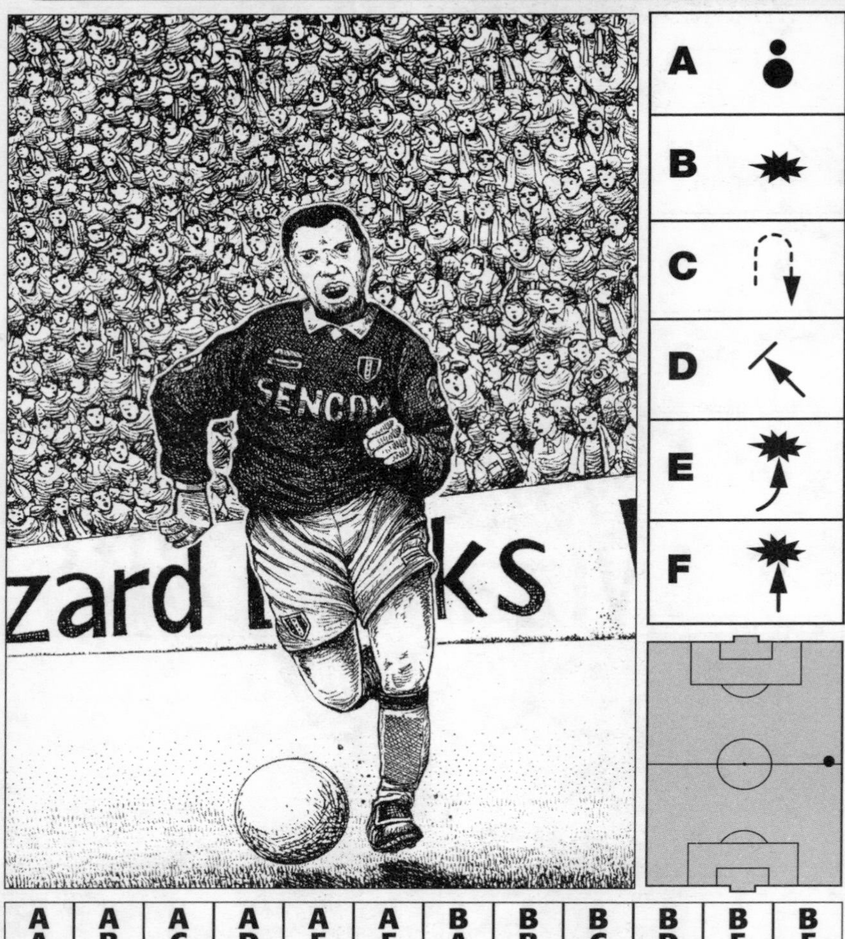

A A	A B	A C	A D	A E	A F	B A	B B	B C	B D	B E	B F
241	17	241	242	142	237	101	190	69	101	80	237

C A	C B	C C	C D	C E	C F	D A	D B	D C	D D	D E	D F
17	32	32	11	32	32	86	237	51	237	17	237

E A	E B	E C	E D	E E	E F	F A	F B	F C	F D	F E	F F
94	55	94	94	55	55	51	109	109	133	109	109

MOVES AND SYMBOLS

ATTACKING MOVES WHEN YOU HAVE THE BALL

SYMBOL	MOVE	NOTES
	Run Forward	Player retains possession and runs forward
	Run Right Horizontal	Player retains possession and runs to the right without advancing
	Run Right Diagonal	Player retains possession and runs to the right diagonally
	Run Left Horizontal	Player retains possession and runs to the left without advancing
	Run Left Diagonal	Player retains possession and runs to the left diagonally
	Short Pass Forward	Player passes to another player directly ahead
	Short Pass Right Horizontal	Player passes to another player directly to his right
	Short Pass Right Diagonal	Player passes to another player to his right and ahead of him
	Short Pass Left Horizontal	Player passes to another player directly to his left
	Short Pass Left Diagonal	Player passes to another player to his left and ahead of him

SYMBOL	MOVE	NOTES
△ or ▽	**Shot Forward**	A shot at goal. Use HI (△) and LOW (▽) when applicable and marked on the page
△ or ▽	**Shot Right**	A shot at goal. Use HI (△) and LOW (▽) when applicable and marked on the page
△ or ▽	**Shot Left**	A shot at goal. Use HI (△) and LOW (▽) when applicable and marked on the page
	Back Pass	A back pass to another player directly behind
	Back Pass Diagonal Left	A back pass to another player behind to the left
	Back Pass Diagonal Right	A back pass to another player behind to the right
or	**Centre**	A ball into the centre of the pitch. An arrow shows the intended direction of the ball
	Run Back	Player retains ball and retreats into space to the rear
	Run Back Left	Player retains ball and runs back to the left
	Run Back Right	Player retains ball and runs back to the right

SYMBOL	MOVE	NOTES
	**Long Pass**	A weighted ball aimed at another player some distance away. The direction of the pass depends on where the player is on the pitch
	**Medium Pass**	A weighted ball to another player in an area quite close to the player. The direction of the pass depends on where the player is on the pitch
	**Pass Into The Box**	A carefully aimed pass into the opponent's penalty box
	**Throw-in Short**	A throw-in aimed at a player close by. The direction of the throw depends on where the player is on the pitch
	**Throw-In Long**	A throw in aimed at a player at long distance. The direction of the throw depends on where the player is on the pitch

DEFENDING MOVES WHEN YOU DON'T HAVE THE BALL

SYMBOL	MOVE	NOTES
	**Block Left**	Defender blocks the ball/attacker left
	**Block Right**	Defender blocks the ball/attacker right
	**Tackle**	Defender attempts to tackle player in possession of the ball
	Bodycheck	Defender plays the attacker and not the ball!
	**Sliding Tackle**	Defender performs a sliding tackle to make contact with the ball
	Chest	Defender anticipates a high ball from the attacker and attempts to get his body in the way
	**Track Back**	Keeping up with advancing opponent; useful to deal with forward passes
	Header	Intercept high balls by knocking them down
	Close Down	Get in close to opponent and prevent him from running forward, left or right

GOALKEEPER MOVES

SYMBOL	MOVE	NOTES
	**Jump**	Goalie jumps to collect a high ball or a high shot
	**Dive Right**	Goalie dives to his right
	**Dive Left**	Goalie dives to his left
	**Block**	Goalie stays rooted to the spot and attempts to stop the ball from a shot forward
	**Block right**	Goalie blocks to his right
	**Block left**	Goalie blocks to his left
	Rush Out	Goalie runs out straight to close down attacker and close the angles
	**Rush Out Right**	As above but runs out to his right
	**Rush Out Left**	As above but runs out to his left

TYNE ATHLETIC 1ST TEAM

OUTFIELD PLAYERS

All players are allowed to use any of the 6 throw-in moves.

MOVES WHEN YOU HAVE THE BALL

PLAYER										
GREEN	●	●	●	●	●	●	●	●	●	●
LAURENCIO	●	●	●	●	●	●	●	●	●	●
CHELL	●	●	●	●	●	●	●	●	●	●
PASQUALLE	●	●	●	●	●	●	●	●	●	●
BREMEN	●	●	●	●	●	●	●	●	●	●
HINER	●	●	●	●	●	●	●	●	●	●
HEWITT	●	●	●	●	●	●	●	●	●	●
HALL	●	●	●	●	●	●	●	●	●	●
DESCHAMPS	●	●	●	●	●	●	●	●	●	●
LE CLERC	●	●	●	●	●	●	●	●	●	●

● **Dot indicates that a player can perform this move**

TYNE ATHLETIC 1ST TEAM

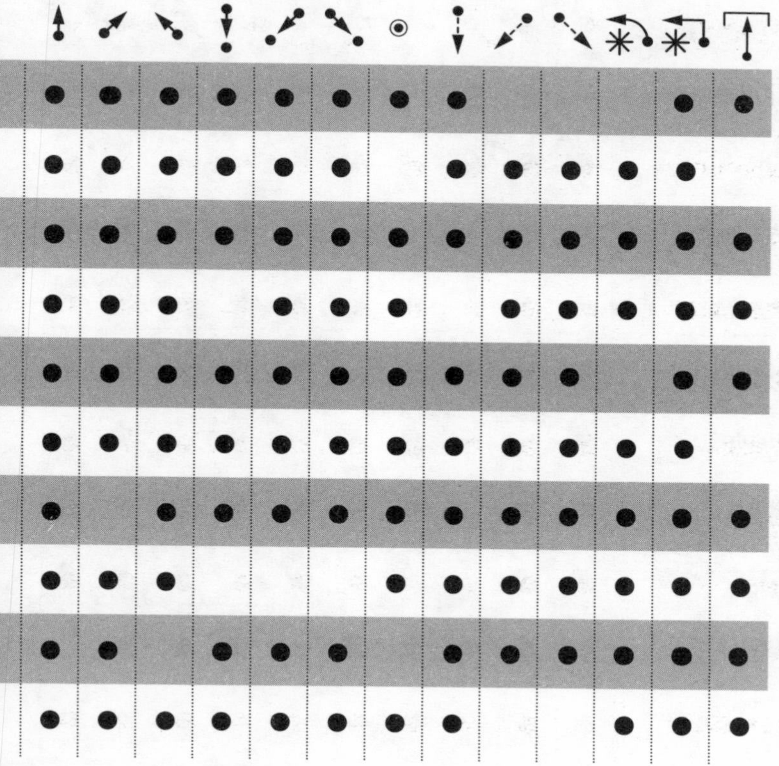

TYNE ATHLETIC 1ST TEAM

MOVES WHEN YOUR OPPONENT HAS THE BALL

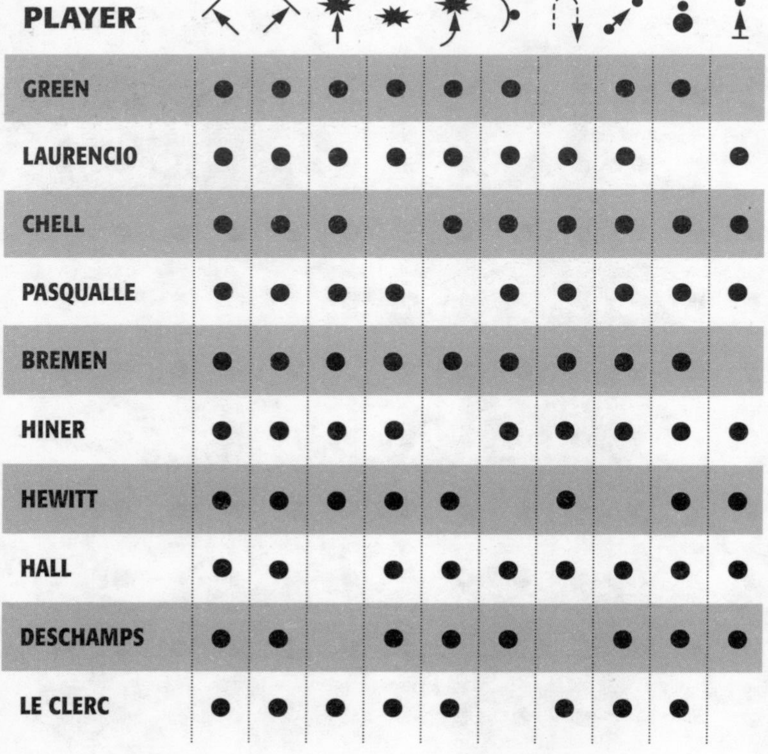

PLAYER										
GREEN	●	●	●	●	●	●		●	●	
LAURENCIO	●	●	●	●	●	●	●	●		●
CHELL	●	●	●		●	●	●	●	●	●
PASQUALLE	●	●	●	●		●	●	●	●	●
BREMEN	●	●	●	●	●	●	●	●	●	
HINER	●	●	●	●		●	●	●	●	●
HEWITT	●	●	●	●	●		●		●	●
HALL	●	●		●	●	●	●	●	●	●
DESCHAMPS	●	●		●	●	●		●	●	●
LE CLERC	●	●	●	●	●		●	●	●	

● **Dot indicates that a player can perform this move**

TYNE ATHLETIC 1ST TEAM

GOALKEEPERS

Goalkeepers can make any short, medium or long pass.

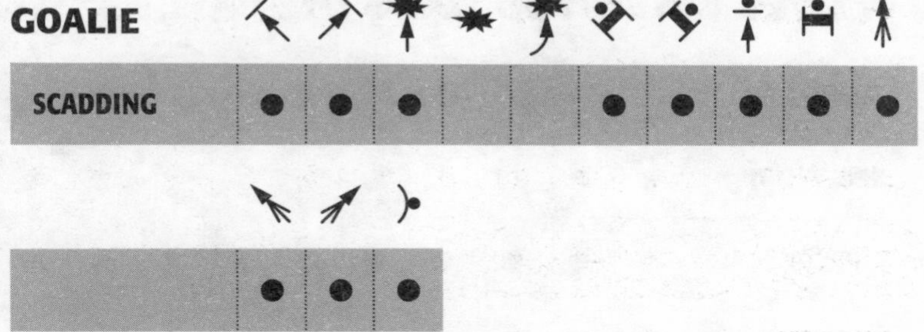

TYNE ATHLETIC RESERVE TEAM

OUTFIELD PLAYERS

All players are allowed to use any of the 6 throw-in moves.

MOVES WHEN YOU HAVE THE BALL

PLAYER	↑	→	↗	←	↖	↑	→	↗	←	↖
BROWNING	●	●		●	●	●			●	●
FARATTA	●	●	●	●	●	●	●	●	●	●
REDHILL	●	●	●	●	●	●	●	●	●	●
ECONICOFF	●	●	●	●	●	●	●	●	●	●
SMITH	●			●	●	●			●	●
ROBERTOS	●	●	●	●	●	●	●	●	●	●
HARRISON	●	●	●			●	●	●		
SYMONS						●	●	●	●	●
BLINKHORST	●	●	●	●	●	●	●	●	●	●
FORAN	●	●	●	●	●	●	●	●	●	●

● **Dot indicates that a player can perform this move**

TYNE ATHLETIC RESERVE TEAM

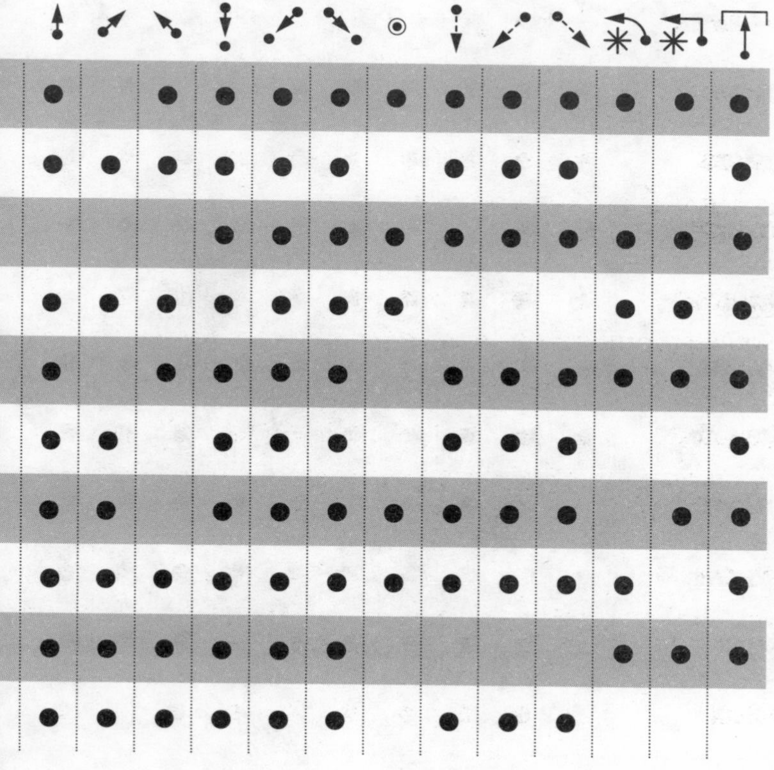

TYNE ATHLETIC RESERVE TEAM

MOVES WHEN YOUR OPPONENT HAS THE BALL

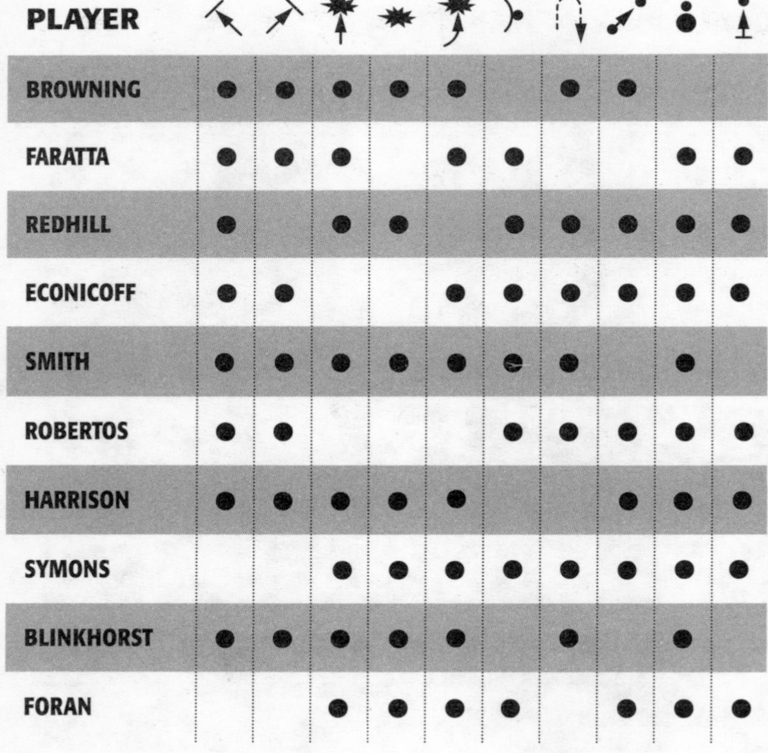

PLAYER										
BROWNING	●	●	●	●	●		●	●		
FARATTA	●	●	●		●	●			●	●
REDHILL	●		●	●		●	●	●	●	●
ECONICOFF	●	●			●	●	●	●	●	●
SMITH	●	●	●	●	●	●	●		●	
ROBERTOS	●	●				●	●	●	●	●
HARRISON	●	●	●	●	●			●	●	●
SYMONS			●	●	●	●	●	●	●	●
BLINKHORST	●	●	●	●	●		●		●	
FORAN			●	●	●	●		●	●	●

● **Dot indicates that a player can perform this move**

TYNE ATHLETIC RESERVE TEAM

GOALKEEPERS

Goalkeepers can make any short, medium or long pass.

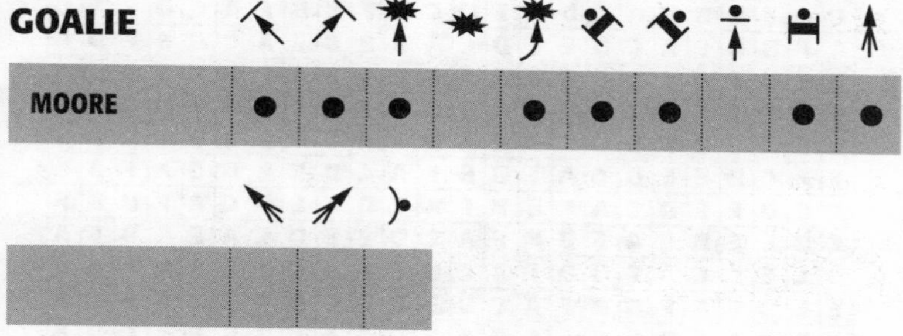

RANDOM LETTER GENERATOR

B	F	A	C	D	E	E	D	C	A	F	B	B	F	A	C	D	E	E	D	C	A	F	B
F	A	C	D	E	E	D	C	A	F	B	B	F	A	C	D	E	E	D	C	A	F	B	B
A	C	D	E	E	D	C	A	F	B	B	F	A	C	D	E	E	D	C	A	F	B	B	F
C	D	E	E	D	C	A	F	B	B	F	A	C	D	E	E	D	C	A	F	B	B	F	A
D	E	E	D	C	A	F	B	B	F	A	C	D	E	E	D	C	A	F	B	B	F	A	C
E	E	D	C	A	F	B	B	F	A	C	D	E	E	D	C	A	F	B	B	F	A	C	D
E	D	C	A	F	B	B	F	A	C	D	E	E	D	C	A	F	B	B	F	A	C	D	E
D	C	A	F	B	B	F	A	C	D	E	E	D	C	A	F	B	B	F	A	C	D	E	E
C	A	F	B	B	F	A	C	D	E	E	D	C	A	F	B	B	F	A	C	D	E	E	D
A	F	B	B	F	A	C	D	E	E	D	C	A	F	B	B	F	A	C	D	E	E	D	C
F	B	B	F	A	C	D	E	E	D	C	A	F	B	B	F	A	C	D	E	E	D	C	A
B	B	F	A	C	D	E	E	D	C	A	F	B	B	F	A	C	D	E	E	D	C	A	F
B	F	A	C	D	E	E	D	C	A	F	B	B	F	A	C	D	E	E	D	C	A	F	B
F	A	C	D	E	E	D	C	A	F	B	B	F	A	C	D	E	E	D	C	A	F	B	B
A	C	D	E	E	D	C	A	F	B	B	F	A	C	D	E	E	D	C	A	F	B	B	F
C	D	E	E	D	C	A	F	B	B	F	A	C	D	E	E	D	C	A	F	B	B	F	A
D	E	E	D	C	A	F	B	B	F	A	C	D	E	E	D	C	A	F	B	B	F	A	C
E	E	D	C	A	F	B	B	F	A	C	D	E	E	D	C	A	F	B	B	F	A	C	D
E	D	C	A	F	B	B	F	A	C	D	E	E	D	C	A	F	B	B	F	A	C	D	E
D	C	A	F	B	B	F	A	C	D	E	E	D	C	A	F	B	B	F	A	C	D	E	E
C	A	F	B	B	F	A	C	D	E	E	D	C	A	F	B	B	F	A	C	D	E	E	D
A	F	B	B	F	A	C	D	E	E	D	C	A	F	B	B	F	A	C	D	E	E	D	C
F	B	B	F	A	C	D	E	E	D	C	A	F	B	B	F	A	C	D	E	E	D	C	A
B	B	F	A	C	D	E	E	D	C	A	F	B	B	F	A	C	D	E	E	D	C	A	F